NAPOLEON
AND
MADEMOISELLE
GEORGE

NAPOLEON
AND
MADEMOISELLE
GEORGE

Edith Saunders

NEW YORK

E. P. DUTTON & CO., INC.

1959

First published in the U.S.A., 1959
By E. P. Dutton & Co., Inc.

FIRST EDITION

Library of Congress Catalog Card Number: 59-5780

PREFACE

AMONG Napoleon's many interests was a love of the theatre, and particularly of French classical tragedy. 'If Corneille were living I would make him a prince,' he once said. From the tragedies of Corneille he could recite many scenes by heart, and *Cinna* was his favourite play. One of his pleasures as ruler of France was that of directing the fortunes of the Comédie Française. That unique theatre, constituted by Louis XIV in 1680, had been through many vicissitudes during the revolution; on becoming First Consul Napoleon proved himself a most generous patron, not only providing it with an annual subsidy of 100,000 livres but regularly attending its performances. Both as Consul and Emperor he called on the company to perform frequently at his principal residences, as well as to accompany him on his diplomatic journeys abroad.

Talma, moreover, the leading actor of the Comédie Française, was one of his personal friends, a man whom he received regularly and always found time to talk to, even at the height of his power. In these circumstances, it would perhaps have been surprising if Napoleon had not found at least one actress of the Comédie Française in whom to interest himself. And, indeed, not long after the company had recovered its fortunes under the Consulate, Mlle George made her début and caught his attention. So beautiful that people said on seeing her that such must Helen of Troy have been, Mlle George was singularly fitted to appear on the stage in classical roles. It was the autumn of 1802, the Peace of Amiens was not yet broken and the First Consul had a comparatively undisturbed mind. Seeing her with his friend Talma in his favourite plays, in *Cinna*, *Phèdre* and *Iphigénie en Aulide*, he felt the inevitable attraction.

v

He lost little time in making the acquaintance of Mlle George, by whom he was greatly charmed. His connection with her lasted for some years; like Talma, she was loyal to him after his downfall, and in exile he remembered them both gratefully.

The First Consul's interest in the young actress went beyond mere friendship to an attachment which, coming as it did at a time when he was living on the best of terms with his wife, Joséphine, occasioned much gossip. The episode is spoken of in the memoirs of Lucien Bonaparte, and also in those of Mme de Rémusat. But the most interesting details are given by the actress herself. Mlle George, who lived to the age of eighty, began writing her memoirs in 1857. On the death of her nephew in 1902 they were sold among his possessions and were published later by their purchaser, P. A. Cheramy. Though they do not form a coherent narrative, they are full of interesting details about the stage and society in Napoleonic times and have supplied a large part of the material for the earlier chapters of this book. Unfortunately they go no further than 1808. For the later part of her life, however, we have much information from Alexandre Dumas, Victor Hugo and other writers and critics of the times of King Louis Philippe. For Mlle George was not only re-nowned as the star of the Consulate and mistress of Napoleon, but as the divinity of French romanticism. Though she fell with the Empire whose spoilt child she had been, she enjoyed a splendid revival, becoming in her forceful middle years the lead-ing actress of romantic drama and exponent of the cult of Bonapartism.

In addition to P. A. Cheramy's edition of Mlle George's memoirs, I have been very much assisted by the interesting studies of her life by A. Augustin-Thierry and H. Fleischmann. The dialogue I have used is taken from Mlle George's memoirs, or from other contemporary sources. In the former case it is sometimes translated as it stands in the original and given as a quotation, and in others, where the original has been too long and involved to be used in full, or where I have needed to intersperse the passage with my own comments or with informa-tion found elsewhere, it is adapted, put in the third person and incorporated into the main text of the book. But I have always adhered closely to the sense of the original. A list of sources is given at the end of the book.

E. S.

ILLUSTRATIONS

1

NAPOLEON, who looms so large in history, is one of those heroic figures that shed lustre even on the least of those with whom they are associated. Napoleon's valet, Constant, Napoleon's coachman, César—though we may look in vain for anything admirable about them—have their special status and nothing can reduce them to the commonplace. They stand in a splendid light, where scholars scrutinize them and endlessly reflect upon the things they may have seen.

It is this light that shines upon Mlle George, the actress of the Comédie Française who became Napoleon's mistress during the Consulate and was his devotee throughout her life. The gifts of an actress are lost to posterity, and, celebrated though she was in her day, she is chiefly remembered now for having been loved by the First Consul, then in full triumph as the victor of Marengo, the author of the Peace of Amiens. Through this she has her part in the undercurrents affecting the course of great events, and so claims her small place in history.

She was born at Bayeux on 23 February 1787, and was christened Marguerite-Joséphine. Her father, George Weymer, was a German from the Rhineland who had abandoned his trade as a tailor to form a company of strolling players in France. He had married the principal actress of his troupe, Mlle Marie Verteuil, and they already had a son, Charles, aged four. A few months after the birth of their second child they settled down in Amiens where George Weymer had been offered the post of director of the theatre. Here they led a happy, busy life and made many friends. It was not easy running a theatre in those times. France was in a ferment, the revolution was brewing and there was a feeling of insecurity everywhere and much poverty.

However, the Weymers were hard-working and ingenious, and they managed remarkably well. George Weymer was by turn conductor of the orchestra, operatic baritone and leading actor, and his wife, still known in public as Mlle Verteuil, was the perpetually youthful and innocent heroine of every play. Yet this was but a small part of the day's work, and they were ready at other times to turn their hands to such things as carpentry, accounts, sewing and entertaining—in fact to all that went with organizing a theatre and a home.

The children were taught music, dancing and arithmetic at an early age, so that they might take their part as soon as possible in the hard task of amusing the public. Happily they both showed a precocious disposition in this respect. Charles took his place in the orchestra before he was ten, and at five his little sister, known to her family as Mimi, made her first appearance on the stage. By now the country was at war with Austria and Prussia, and the monarchy was overthrown. Life was becoming increasingly difficult, and people were not inclined to spend their money on entertainment. At a time when his theatre was particularly ill-attended, George Weymer had amused himself by teaching his small daughter to play the part of a milkmaid in a one-act opera called *La Petite Victoire*; she responded delightedly, and her performance was so excellent that he decided to let her appear in public as a special attraction.

There was no difficulty about this. The family lived in rooms attached to the theatre and the stage was Mimi's playroom. She was accustomed to being there, and was too young to be worried by the presence of an audience. She was a lovely, solid, rosy child, merry and smiling, and in the special costume made by her mother she looked delightful. An exceptionally tall man was chosen to play the part of her lover and, as she entered into the performance with an obvious relish, the effect was irresistible. People laughed, applauded, told their friends, and the theatre was crowded each night for several weeks.

Mimi, always adored by her parents and made much of by their friends, received still more praise and attention at this time and fully realized that she was a wonderful little person. The applause

2

she won on the stage was very much to her taste, and it left her with a craving for more. But her parents told her she was much too young for the theatre and must attend to her lessons. Mimi, however, did not forget her triumphs; and when the stage was not in use she was often found there, rehearsing those parts her mother played, Dorine or Lisette, with all the appropriate gestures.

She began to show an aptitude for music, too, and from time to time was allowed to reinforce the orchestra, where she strummed confidently on an old spinet. But, hidden from the brilliant stage, unseen by the audience, it was really not much fun performing among the musicians. It was far more interesting sitting in the box office and helping to sell tickets, a task which also fell to her on occasion.

The months passed, and Mimi watched rehearsals and learnt much by imitation. Her father soon found that she knew many roles by heart, and he realized she had a true vocation for the stage. And eventually he allowed her to appear again; she played a minor role with great success, and from now onwards acted regularly.

Such an attraction was a blessing in these revolutionary times, for it was not attended by any political danger. The theatre, so capable of influencing public opinion, was closely watched. The first symptoms of the French revolution, indeed, had manifested themselves on the stage of the Comédie Française in the spring of 1784 when Beaumarchais's *Mariage de Figaro* was performed, a play which poured ridicule on aristocratic privilege. Later, as the revolution broke out, the actors of the great company had been divided into two factions who could not live together. The Republicans had departed to act in the theatre of the Palais-Royal, while the Royalists remained at the theatre of the Faubourg St Germain (later known as the Odéon), which was regarded as a centre of counter-revolution. News had come in the autumn of 1793 that all the royalist actors had been arrested and imprisoned. They had been destined for the guillotine or deportation, and had only been saved by the audacity of a former colleague, a young actor who had obtained a clerical post with the Comité du Salut Publique and had calmly thrown the dossiers prepared against the offending actors into the river. Delay and confusion had resulted, and before this was overcome the downfall of Robespierre had put an end to the Reign of Terror and the actors had been set free. Such dangers as this were enough to make all theatrical managers cautious.

By the time she was twelve Mimi was able to take the leading part in all the popular plays of the repertory, plays such as *Paul et Virginie* and *Le Jugement de Paris*. Her acting, learnt from observation, was not of a brilliant school; but it was efficient and she was much admired by local audiences. It was a pleasure to look at her, for she was a child of unusual beauty. She had never lost the solid, contented look of her earliest years, but was growing up in statuesque fashion, showing a graceful perfection of form at every stage and more resembling the fabled Rhinemaidens of her father's home than the girls of France.

Acting was her passion, but her general education was not neglected and she continued to have lessons from the best available teachers. The theatre made but a precarious living for the family, and George Weymer had to look for means of adding to his income in order to pay for the education of his children. Helped by friends in Amiens, he usually had additional work of one kind or another, and many a night, after briskly performing as *jeune premier* on the stage, he would sit up till the sun rose, copying music.

To Mimi, time, slow-moving, seemed as limitless as life seemed wonderful. Sheltered by the kindest of parents from fears of the outside world, she heard no more than faint echoes of the political storms that raged. Close at hand was her family, her theatre, her home which was so cheerfully harmonious, and she had no conception whatsoever that anything else could touch her.

All her life she was to remember vividly her happy childhood. Writing her memoirs in her old age she says: 'We were all hard at work. How often I have looked back with longing to the joyous time of my childhood. We were not well off, but we were all so happy. With so much to do we could never be dull. And then, my parents were very much liked in the town. There was

4

not a party or fête to which the children of Mme George were not invited. It was a delightful existence, and to dream of any other would have saddened our hearts.'

From the stories of her early life at Amiens, which are told with a direct but colourful simplicity in her memoirs, we can sense the atmosphere of that vanished age, whose customs are so remote from us while human feelings are so close. Her recollections are always self-revealing, too, showing her faults as well as her virtues. They show her as an amiable, lively girl, quick and intelligent, though not thoughtful, full of affection for her family and friends, and well disposed towards the world in general. They also show that she possessed from the beginning the features that shaped the course of her life, features so fundamental that she was never conscious of them and never away from their influence. These were self-indulgence and an inability to keep her money in her pocket. All later experience came from this.

One day, my father said to me—I suppose I was about ten years old—'My child, my dear Mimi, will you take charge of the box office for about an hour? Your mother has to act in the first play. Take her muff with you to keep your hands warm.'

'Yes, Papa.'

And there I was, installed in the box office. What for? Certainly not to receive money. It was a frightful night, snow was falling, and in the provinces, where carriages were more than rare in those times, no one came to the theatre in such weather.

However, a few people gradually arrived, and soon I had several sols in my muff. I was bored, I felt hungry. And presently I gave the money to a certain Fanchonette who had been told to sit with me and sent her to buy half a dozen hot apple turnovers from the pastrycook down the road. With these delightful turnovers I regaled everyone within reach. But now, there being no public, my father arrives on the scene and says—Oh Heaven!—'My dear Mimi, there will be no performance, and we are returning the money.'

'Ah, *mon Dieu!*' I cried. 'You mustn't do that, Papa, it would never do. Take my advice.'

But while we were arguing, quite a crowd of people turned up. The weather had improved, the play would be performed. Thus innocence is protected! The lesson went home, however, and I told my father what I had done, adding, 'I know I was wrong. But I have my own purse, Papa, and I would have paid you back.'

On another occasion, Mimi decided to spend her savings on ribbon and artificial flowers for her mother to wear at some special performance at the theatre. She went to a small draper's shop where she was well known, chose what she wanted and promised to pay later on.

Once the performance was over I said, 'Oh, let them wait!' And from day to day I delved into my money box in order to buy macaroons and turnovers.

'Well, Mimi, and when are you coming to pay that bill?'

'Tomorrow, Madame, tomorrow.'

And tomorrow never arrived.

Having emptied her money box, Mimi scarcely dared leave the house. But one morning her father said to her:

'Have you finished your lessons?'

'Yes, Papa.'

'Well, child, just take this letter to the post for me, will you?'

The post was beyond the shops, and I made the most incredible detours to get to it. And in the end I had to confess the truth to my father.

'Don't say anything to Mama,' I said. 'Here is my lovely little copper chain. Sell it, Papa, and pay for me. . . .' My good, kind father—I was always his idol!

Such was Mimi's disposition. She was an actress through and through, she loved luxury, she craved admiration. And with such an early capacity for living on credit, it remained only for Providence to step in and place her in the select company of the Comédie Française which she was so fitted to adorn.

Providence, indeed, duly performed this task one October day of 1801 through the agency of Mlle Raucourt, the leading tragic actress of France. From time to time, some great actor from Paris would honour the citizens of Amiens with a visit to their theatre, and Mlle Raucourt had come to perform in *Dido*. She was one of those who had been imprisoned and destined for the guillotine. For some years after her liberation her life had been difficult and uncertain, for it was not until 1799 that both factions of the

6

Comédie Française made their peace and reunited into one company. Shortly after their reconciliation the Consulate was formed, and Napoleon had taken steps to restore their fortunes. She now enjoyed a splendid position; but being turned forty she wished to train a young actress who would eventually take her own place as the leading tragedienne of the company. She had obtained a grant from the Government for this purpose, and for some time had been looking for a suitable pupil. She found her in George Weymer's daughter, Mimi, who was now fourteen years old.

'Alas, Mlle Raucourt,' says Mimi in her memoirs, 'my happy, childish life, which I had believed was eternal, was to come to an end. And its place was to be taken by a new existence, brilliant, ambitious and uneasy! An artist in Paris, at the greatest theatre in the world! A wonderful life, and sad enough at times! Good-bye, Amiens; good-bye to my delightful expeditions on the river, my merry parties with other girls of the town. . . . But I will come back. You will see me arrive at the theatre in my own carriage; you will crowd in to gaze at your little Mimi. Well, dear friends, you may be certain Mimi will never forget her plain cotton dresses and her best blue stockings.'

The grant which the actress Raucourt offered Mimi was 1,000 francs for her expenses during the year of her training. It was a large sum in the eyes of George Weymer, and yet he hesitated at first to accept the offer. Mimi herself was perfectly happy at Amiens, and he did not want to part with her, nor with his wife, who would be obliged to go and live with her in Paris. Nor did he much like the idea of his child coming under the influence of the great Raucourt, whose reputation, if above reproach as an artist, was the worst possible in other respects. But Mme Weymer who had struggled through a hard youth as a poor, strolling player, was enthralled at the thought of such opportunities and George Weymer allowed his misgivings to subside. After all, his wife had come unscathed through a career which is full of temptations, and his daughter would surely follow her example. There had been more than one virtuous woman among the great actresses of France, even if it was not at all easy to think of one of them on the spur of the moment.

7

The Weymer family watched the impressive departure of Raucourt, who drove off to Paris in her private carriage, a heavy carosse drawn by three horses and painted with garlands of flowers. There were very few in these hard times who travelled in this princely fashion, which was ruinously expensive since one was swindled at every inn. Now that all men were equal, those who wanted deference had to pay heavily for it in gold. As the dignified equipage disappeared in vast clouds of dust, the hard-working family marvelled.

Raucourt had taken her leave graciously but without familiarity and had indicated that Mimi was to follow her to Paris immediately. George Weymer hurried off to book five seats in the public diligence. A third child had been born in 1793, a little girl called Bébelle. She was to be taken to Paris with her mother and sister. The nursemaid, Marianne, was to go to look after her, and George Weymer himself must accompany them all and see them safely installed. There was just time for a farewell performance for Mimi. *Adèle, ou la Chaumière* was given, and the young actress received the applause of a crowded and enthusiastic audience who cheered her, rejoiced with her and cast before her not only flowers and boxes of sweets, but pieces of jewellery.

Three days later the triumphant Mimi, favoured child of a ruined country where deprivation and uncertainty were the general lot, embarked on her journey to Paris and a brilliant career. The roads had fallen into disrepair and the journey took two days. But now the diligence rolled heavily along the cobbled streets of the capital and into a sombre, noisy courtyard, its terminus. A hotel was found, and the next morning Mimi was escorted by her parents to the home of Mlle Raucourt.

They went on foot, having no money to spare for a hired conveyance. The walk seemed interminable, for Raucourt lived well outside the city in the Allée des Veuves. This was in the vicinity of the present Avenue Montaigne, off the Champs Elysées. It was then a semi-rural district where the actress chose to live in order to have a large garden round her; for she was as fond of flowers as her friend Joséphine Bonaparte, and often exchanged rare and curious plants with her.

8

Arriving at last at Raucourt's home, *La Chaumière*, the Weymers found her in her most friendly mood. She had with her a friend whom she had met during her imprisonment, Mme de Ponty, a young aristocrat who had lost everything during the revolution and to whom she now gave a home. Both of them talked amiably and held out glowing promises of a splendid career for Mimi. When the visit was over, George Weymer and his wife returned to the centre of Paris filled with gratitude and satisfaction. While they talked, Mimi walked along in silence, glancing from time to time at a copy of Corneille's *Cinna*, which Raucourt had given her with instructions to learn the part of Emilie.

That afternoon George Weymer set about seeking a home for his family, and eventually he found an inexpensive room with a small ante-room in the Hôtel de Perou. Mme Weymer and Mimi would share the main room, and the servant would occupy the ante-room with the younger sister. The Hôtel de Perou was in the narrow rue Neuve des Petits Champs, and from their windows, says Mimi, there was a 'fine view of Parisian gutters'. But leading out of the street was the fascinating Palais Royal with its arcades and gardens and the most fashionable shops in the world, and beyond that the National Theatre for which Mimi was to be trained.

The rest of the day was spent in moving, and early the next morning the poor, hard-working father had to hurry off to his theatre at Amiens without having allowed himself a moment for those simple enjoyments for which Paris was so noted. And as he drove off in the diligence, Mme Weymer and her daughter walked up the Champs Elysées for the first dramatic lesson.

2

THREE times a week Mme Weymer took her daughter to *La Chaumière* for lessons. The world of aristocratic privilege had been overthrown, but no one had yet had the good idea of introducing omnibuses; so they had to go on foot, and Mme Weymer found the walks wearying and detestable. There were no footpaths in the narrow streets of Paris; cabriolets and phaetons dashed along aggressively, and pedestrians had to await their passing close to the walls and submit to being showered with mud or slush. And outside the city, in the Champs Elysées, one was exposed to the wind and rain. But Mme Weymer drove herself to the effort throughout the winter; a girl of fourteen could not be allowed out alone.

Raucourt, whose dissipations in the days of the old monarchy had scandalized all Paris, was still noted for a certain eccentricity of manner and would often receive them jauntily dressed in masculine clothing. Mme Weymer, as an actress, thought little of this, but she was rather surprised to find that a small child of Mme de Ponty's habitually addressed the great actress as *papa*. Well, it was a joke, of course, but not in the best of taste. Fortunately the distinction of *La Chaumière*, and still more of the actress's friends, gave one confidence.

La Chaumière was a typical fantasy of the period, inspired by Jean-Jacques Rousseau. It was a comic-opera thatched cottage, its outer walls painted to represent cracked and faded bricks. It was surrounded by flowering plants in perfect order, and stood in an English garden, or what the French imagined to be such, a garden of winding paths and streams, rustic bridges, grottos and fabricated ruins. Indoors, the would-be cottage contained ample accommodation for servants and masters, a splendid salon, and everything needed for social life. *La Chaumière*, indeed, was a miniature palace disguised to represent a wealthy artist's opium dream of the poor countryman's hovel. Raucourt had purchased the pleasing retreat from Mme Tallien, and it was still frequented by artists and ambitious men.

Mme Tallien had befriended Napoleon Bonaparte in the days when he was poor and unknown, and it was here, in her salon, that he had become acquainted with Joséphine de Beauharnais, now his wife. Here, too, he came to know intimately the great tragic actor Talma, a man with whom he shared many interests.

Raucourt, having known Joséphine Bonaparte long before that lady was anyone in particular, was now very much the friend of Caesar and most of the leaders of Consular society were at home in her salon. As she was instructing her pupil, the Prince d'Hénin or Talleyrand would stroll in and sit watching while Mimi went through her lines as Atalide or Cleopatra; Mme Elisa Bacciochi, Napoleon's eldest sister, often called and was most kind and friendly to the great actress's protégée. Napoleon was not the only Bonaparte who loved the theatre; it was the passion of the whole family, his mother included.

Mimi was introduced to the actress's friends as 'George'. Raucourt, in her brief dealings with the Weymer family, had not become aware of any other name, and 'George' Mimi had to be from now on, whether she liked it or not, for the critics and the public had already been notified that 'Mademoiselle George' was shortly to make her début. Raucourt was fully persuaded that this was in fact her pupil's name, and it was useless to mention any other to her. Fortunately, Mimi had a placid nature and did not take offence over such trifles. George or Marguerite, what did it matter? And so today, on her tomb in the cemetery of Père Lachaise is the simple word *George*, carved in immense letters as though she had been a king of England.

She was at first uneasy in the presence of Raucourt's friends; but all of them treated her with great courtesy, and she gradually became more confident. When she recited well they applauded her, and she began to find their presence a stimulus. Sometimes Talma would call and instruct her. He was the greatest actor of all time, in the opinion of many. His father lived in England, where he enjoyed the distinction of being dentist to his Majesty King George III. Talma himself had been trained as a dentist, but had renounced this profession for the stage. Partly brought up in England, he was a great admirer of Shakespeare, from whose works he would often recite for the pleasure of his friends. An admiration for English institutions had given him liberal views, and it was he who had led those Republican actors who had broken away from the main body of the Comédie Française at the height of the revolution.

Talma had no greater admirer than General Bonaparte. The two men had become acquainted, it is usually thought, in 1795, when Napoleon was twenty-six years old, an unknown officer without employment. Talma, six years older, was already well known and was married to a rich woman; he is said to have lent money to the young officer in difficult times. Napoleon had followed his career with an eager interest, never missing an opportunity of seeing him on the stage. And, after watching the heroes of antiquity interpreted by Talma, he enjoyed discussing them with the learned actor who, like himself, was a great reader of Plutarch. An ambitious young soldier, who dreamed of strutting to good effect on the stage of politics, he had had much to learn from the actor who could so ably express all that was heroic in the human character. And rising quickly to fame, Napoleon had had in Talma a most useful model. The noble simplicity which Talma could so well assume, the air of magnanimity, the display of inflexible will, the deliberate exhibitions of fearful rage, the stern gaze—all these, the stock-in-trade of the fine tragic actor, were adopted by Napoleon and were to become associated with him.

It was Talma's former house in the rue Chantereine that became Napoleon's home when he married Joséphine de Beauharnais in 1796; and in this house three years later, after the Italian and Egyptian campaigns had made him the hero of France, the *coup d'état* of 18 brumaire was planned.

General Bonaparte, as First Consul, was now too great to be seen in the salons of Parisians; but his brother Lucien took to calling at *La Chaumière* in the early weeks of 1802. He was just back from an ambassadorial mission in Spain, where he had enriched himself enormously and acquired a fine collection of works of art. Like his sister, Elisa, he showed a great interest in Mlle George. The beautiful girl, over-developed for her age and appearing to be not less than seventeen or eighteen, was a type to appeal strongly to him, and he not only encouraged her to talk to him but offered her instruction. His teaching was not without its value, since he possessed much knowledge of the art of acting.

Thus Mimi was brought into a new world where not only the greatest actors of France were about her but the leaders of political events. By his friendship with Talma and his personal love of the stage, the First Consul was intimately connected with the actors of the Comédie Française and was always in mind as their benefactor. The name Bonaparte was revered by all Paris at this time. Hohenlinden and Marengo were still being discussed with rapture. Mimi soon caught the prevailing mood and began to worship the First Consul as a hero, almost a divinity.

Soon after their arrival in Paris, Mme Weymer and her daughter had been given seats in the balcony of the Théâtre Français, and they attended the performances nightly. These evenings were enthralling; nothing more unlike the performances at Amiens could have been imagined. Not only were the boxes and stalls occupied by a brilliant company—generals in their smart uniforms and jewelled ladies scantily attired in silk and muslin—but a critical and independent populace crowded in each night to cheer and roar, whistle, denounce and applaud. And the acting was remarkably brilliant in its own way. The natural school did not exist. The audiences of that time did not go to the theatre merely to see men and women behaving as they themselves did at home; they wanted resounding elocution and superhuman emotions, and this is what they were given.

The artificial form of acting, with its heroic gestures, appeared magnificent to Raucourt's pupil, and she absorbed its methods with the whole of her being. As a small child she had imitated the mincing gait of Mlle Verteuil, and she now imitated the whole range of histrionic technique set before her.

How great an impression the actor Talma made upon her when she first saw him playing the part of Orestes: 'There was tragedy if you like!' she writes in her memoirs. 'What a gift that was, that could make the spectator's blood run cold! What terror he inspired! He could shed tears, melancholy, heart-rending tears; he could turn pale at will, even livid. Where did he learn to create these terrible effects? Only genius can explain it. Talma was sublime. All passion, all poetic and human emotion found expression in this man. Ah, Talma! If you could emerge from your shroud, men would come to hear you from the ends of the earth! I left the theatre feeling really ill after this unforgettable performance.'

Mimi watched her own teacher, too, Raucourt, who could electrify the audience by her imprecations and ardent gestures. Raucourt was supremely good in the roles of Semiramis, Cleopatra, Medea and Lady Macbeth. She had never been at home in those parts which required feminine charm; but, like Talma, she could be majestic, imperious, disdainful. She could fall into violent furies or transports of loud despair. Her voice had immense volume; and when her tempestuous cries rang through the theatre the Parisian felt he was getting value for his money. Mimi had many moments of discouragement when her teacher was acting; it was a genre she was unable to imitate successfully. Often, on hearing the great tragedienne roaring out some splendid line of Racine, she would feel she was quite unworthy to follow in her footsteps and would wonder why she had been chosen.

Then she would watch the successful younger actresses, such as Mlle Mars and Mlle Fleury, and would despair of ever joining them as a member of the theatre.

The audiences were as interesting as the performances; and from time to time she and her mother would catch a glimpse of General Bonaparte and his wife in the Consular box. These evenings were the most wonderful of all, and Mimi felt almost suffocated by an emotional adoration of the dimly discerned figure in uniform, an adoration which included Mme Bonaparte and any other member of the great family who happened to be present. Very often Mme Bonaparte's two children would be there, Eugène and Hortense de Beauharnais, and also one or other of the Consul's beautiful sisters. When the Consul had been present, Mimi would walk home along the rue de la Loi (as the rue de Richelieu was then called) in an exalted mood, listening incredulously to her mother's incessant complaints. Marie Verteuil tottered along in her best shoes, shivering, exasperated by the wind, the rain or the snow, while Mimi was warmed and upheld by devotional feelings. Though so close together, she and her mother walked in different worlds.

14

The winter of 1801–2 was brilliant. France seemed to have emerged from the shadows and to owe this to one man alone. General Bonaparte had brought order out of the revolutionary chaos. He had proved himself a great victor and a lover of peace, and he had restored internal harmony. Only a year ago, to travel in the provinces had been to risk robbery and murder. But today one could travel in perfect safety about the country. Moreover, the General had given the country a civil code which was largely his own work. That this leader of armies, this governor of conquered provinces, was a fine administrator was not surprising. But that he stood so high as a legislator was indeed remarkable, and it won all society over to him.

He was revered for having brought peace and order. He had recently achieved the Peace of Lunéville, and the preliminaries of peace with England had been signed. Peace had even been made between France and God by the diplomatic exertions of Bonaparte, and a Concordat signed last July. Everything which recalled the extremes of the revolution was disappearing, and yet the advantages gained were firmly held and were respected by all Europe. Europe now acknowledged the French Republic, and highly esteemed the man worthy to rule over it, General Bonaparte.

This could be seen by the enormous influx into Paris of foreigners of note, all of whom sought through their embassies to be presented to the First Consul at his severely elegant court.

It is difficult for us today, knowing the whole disastrous story of Napoleon's life, to enter into the feelings of his contemporaries in the year 1802. But it can reasonably be claimed that at this time he had done nothing but good in his country. The war in which he had won such notable victories was none of his fault, and he had hastened to bring it to an end. He had shown himself a peacemaker, and had not yet had time to feel the intoxicating effects of having gained the earth. He was only thirty-two years old.

Lucien Bonaparte, on his return from Italy, had purchased the Hôtel de Brienne in the rue Saint-Dominique, a mansion suitable to contain his splendid collection of paintings by the masters. His sister, Elisa Bacciochi, was living with him and, as a patron of the arts, she invited Raucourt and her pupil to call as soon as the house was ready for the reception of visitors. The first visit was followed by many others; the Hôtel de Brienne was a scene of luxurious refinement where Mimi, in her provincial dresses, the product of some unheard-of dressmaker from the back streets of Amiens, felt sadly out of place at first. But she was soon put at her ease by the kindness of her hosts, who paid special attention to her. The Bonapartes took to calling her Georgina, and others soon followed their example. At the theatre she was always to be known as George, but from now onwards she was usually called Georgina by her friends.

Often, when Raucourt and her pupil dined with Lucien Bonaparte, they would find the noble Laetitia Ramolino there, the incomparable mother of the First Consul and his six brothers and sisters. This Olympian Lady was very kind to Mimi, or Georgina, to give her her new name, and liked to hear her recite. To please his mother, Lucien would suggest after dinner that Raucourt, Georgina and himself should act scenes from one of the great tragedies, an entertainment which always delighted the elder Mme Bonaparte.

As the weeks passed and spring arrived, Lucien Bonaparte's interest in Georgina became more marked. He was not sorry, as he says in his memoirs, to divert the attention of gossips from his real preoccupations at this time. He was thinking of marrying a certain Mme Juberthon, whose husband, as de Bourrienne puts it, had been dispatched for greater convenience to a malaria-ridden region abroad; but this lady, although beautiful and intelligent, was not sufficiently well born to be an acceptable sister-in-law to the First Consul, and Lucien was keeping the affair dark. There was a condition attached to this projected marriage. Mme Juberthon, already Lucien's mistress, had become pregnant and she was to be raised to the status of his wife only if the child turned out to be a son. By his first wife, now dead, Lucien had had only daughters; his brother Joseph had likewise only daughters, and Napoleon had no children at all, although Joséphine had a grown-up son and daughter by her first marriage.

The large and powerful Bonaparte family was without sons, a matter of concern to them all now that Napoleon had reached a place where it was obvious that even the monarchy was not inaccessible to him. Joséphine herself had not yet lost hope of producing an heir, although to others the time seemed to be passed and her brothers and sisters-in-law were already urging her husband to divorce her. It was dread of divorce that had made Joséphine marry off her daughter, Hortense, at the beginning of this year to yet another Bonaparte brother, Louis. She hoped that if the two had a son, Napoleon would consent to adopt him and her own position would thus become secure. She had first offered the girl to Lucien, but Lucien was not attracted by her and refused. Nor was Louis attracted; but, less fortunate than his brother, he had to give way.

There was much gossip in Paris about this great wedding. Neither the handsome young bridegroom nor the eighteen-year-old Hortense had attempted to disguise the unutterable gloom they felt on being thus united for life; and now that they were married Louis did nothing but sulk and Hortense spent most of the day weeping. Hortense was in love with Duroc, an aide-de-camp of Napoleon's. Napoleon had been willing to let her marry him, but Duroc, who did not return her feelings, had refused the honour. Thus, although her position was enviable in the eyes of the world, Hortense was plunged in the deepest misery.

However, the distraught bride had to swallow her feelings from time to time while she received visitors in her splendid home in the rue des Victoires. And there Raucourt took her young pupil one afternoon. Georgina was curious to see Mme Louis, and she found her very attractive, though exceedingly pale and thin. Hortense had been educated in the school of the celebrated Mme Campan, all of whose pupils had the studied good manners of the *ancien régime*. She showed her visitors a charming courtesy, and asked Georgina to recite to her.

It was a chilly afternoon, and as her guests were leaving she took a beautiful cashmere shawl off her own shoulders and wrapped it round Georgina for extra warmth.

17

'I will send it back to you tomorrow, Madame,' said Raucourt as she thanked her.

'Please do not,' said Hortense. 'Mlle George must keep it; it will remind her of me.'

An Indian cashmere shawl was a most costly article of attire, available only to the rich. Georgina was overjoyed by the wonderful gift. Long after fine clothes and jewels had become commonplace in her life she kept the shawl given to her by the woman who was soon to become Queen of Holland. She had not much of a capacity for keeping anything, but this she had to the end of her life.

3

THE Peace of Amiens was signed at the end of March, and on Easter Sunday sixty cannon shots announced that a Te Deum was to be chanted in the Cathedral of Notre-Dame. The First Consul, in a scarlet velvet coat and black breeches, drove to the ceremony in a coach drawn by eight horses. Gold and crimson shone in the streets as it had not done since the days before the revolution; great bells broke a silence of ten years, and in the Cathedral two orchestras played under Cherubini and Méhul while Napoleon, the hero, the peacemaker, the defender of religion, took his place beneath a fine draped canopy surmounted with plumes to receive the oath of the French clergy in their traditional robes. Nearby was the entire Bonaparte family. And Mme Laetitia, the hero's mother, who had once scarcely known how to feed and clothe her children, might now feel that her task was completed. Mme Mère could see before her her five vigorous and handsome sons and all her beautiful married daughters, not yet crowned, but at least enriched and rewarded. As the *Journal des Débats* put it in all seriousness, she could on this solemn occasion 'feel that she was midway between her sons and Heaven which had given them to her'.

Sparta, as Victor Hugo was to say of this notable year 1802, was replaced by Rome. General Bonaparte was made Consul for life, and there were rumours that he would soon assume the title of Emperor: Bonaparte was about to become Napoleon. A grateful nation saw in him not only Julius Caesar, the great soldier, but Augustus Caesar who restored the public fortunes and made the Roman Empire peaceful and glorious.

The spring and summer were bright and happy. The English were coming over in thousands, all of them rich and ready to spend their money. A panorama of the City of London had been opened in the Chaussée d'Antan. The milliners, dressmakers and jewellers of the rue de la Loi surpassed themselves in the creation of costly follies; the boulevards were densely thronged, and the Palais Royal was more attractive and disreputable than ever.

General and Mme Bonaparte spent much of their time at Malmaison, their country house, and a small private theatre was inaugurated there in May with the Italian comedy *La Serva Padrona*, light-hearted and suited to the hour.

So exhilarating was social life at this time that Mlle Raucourt almost forgot her pupil in the interest of attending fêtes and receptions. Among other events was Talma's wedding to the actress Caroline Vanhove, whom he had loved for some time. He had divorced his first wife and now counted himself the happiest man in Paris and was lavish in his entertainments. A further distraction for Raucourt was the country house near Orléans which she had just bought. It was named *Mon Plaisir*, and she was continually going off to spend a few days there. Time after time Georgina and her mother walked out to *La Chaumière* along roads now thick with dust, only to be told that Raucourt was absent.

Mme Weymer was worried. No date had been arranged for her daughter's début, and there were rumours that another young actress had been found who was competent to fill the place assigned to Mlle George as Raucourt's successor. This actress, Mlle Duchesnois, was supported by the playwright Legouvé and General de Valence, and she was said to be magnificent in the role of Phèdre. If this unwanted upstart obtained a hearing first and managed to please the public, Georgina might be forced to take second place at the Comédie Française.

Although the summer days were so radiant and Paris was so animated and cheerful, the Weymer family found life very difficult. George Weymer had scarcely been able to pay his way at Amiens without the help of his wife and daughter, and now he was alone, for his son Charles had joined the family in Paris. Charles, who felt that at the age of nineteen he had as much right to the opportunities of the capital as his sister, had come to have violin lessons with the celebrated Kreutzer; and although he had found one or two pupils he earned very little.

The rooms in the rue Neuve des Petits Champs were stifling in the warm weather, and to pass away these inactive days Mme Weymer would take her daughters to the Gardens of the Tuileries while Marianne, the maid, went down to the river to do the washing before preparing the dinner. In the public gardens were soldiers, children with their nursemaids, and foreigners from all nations; and sometimes General Bonaparte might be seen walking across from the Palace of the Tuileries (the Palais du Gouvernement, as it had been re-named during the revolution); some business would have brought him into Paris for a day or two, and he would dine in public at a restaurant in a corner of the gardens. South of the palace and its gardens flowed the river, where footpaths were being replaced by quays, and on the north was the newly opened street, the civilized and dignified rue de Rivoli, which stands for ever to the Corsican tyrant's credit.

If it was very hot, the walk to the Tuileries would be too much for Mme Weymer and she would take the two girls to the closer Gardens of the Palais Royal, where the rushing of the fountains sounded so cool beneath the shady trees. Here one might sit for hours in 1802, enjoying a spectacle unparalleled. Every enticement that could persuade the rich foreigner to spend was offered. The Palais Royal was the centre of fashion, of gambling and of gastronomy. Here were famous restaurants, such as those of M. Chevet and M. Corcellet, and here were some of the smartest milliners and dressmakers. Formerly the great Parisian dressmakers sent forth their newest designs on fashion dolls; but since the revolution they had taken to dressing up a living doll—a model in the latest styles—and sending her to trip lightly round the galleries and paths of the Palais Royal, painted, smiling and alluring in the high-waisted transparent muslin dresses lovingly made by gifted couturières. Mme Weymer was enraptured by these mannequin parades; but Georgina looked more longingly at the premises of M. Berthellemot, the most expensive confectioner in Paris, who displayed incredibly rich sweets and chocolates in boxes devised by artists. It was hard to pass by such a shop on one's way home to dinner. Food was very dear in Paris, and once a week George Weymer sent a large basket of vegetables from Amiens, from which were composed the main dishes of the family.

In June Raucourt left Paris altogether; but a week or two later Georgina and her mother were invited to accompany Mme de Ponty by coach to Orléans so that lessons might be resumed.

Throughout the journey, Mme de Ponty complained about the horrors of life in the country, and Georgina and her mother, who knew nothing of rural life, arrived uneasily at their destination, little disposed to enjoy themselves, fearing the damp, the silence and one thing and another that they believed a town protected them from. *Mon Plaisir* was a fine mansion, built in the style of the Trianon of Versailles, and like that palace surrounded by elegant grounds populated by a considerable company of marble statues. Raucourt welcomed her guests, but appeared to have forgotten the stage; all day long she was in her rose garden and the conservatories, putting them in order with her gardeners. There was no talk of lessons; instead, Georgina was told to enjoy herself in the gardens or to join her hostess on a cross-country gallop. Since the ladies of the Consulate loved to resemble statues, Raucourt rode in a costume *à l'antique*, a white muslin dress reaching only to her knees.

Georgina, at a loss, wandered sadly among the rose bushes or sat about reading Corneille. She did her best to avoid the entertainments offered by Raucourt; but one morning she was led away on a rabbit hunt, having through misfortune run into her teacher just as she was setting off with a gun.

'Good morning, George,' cried Raucourt, catching sight of her pupil. 'I'm just off to shoot rabbits. Come with me. You've no idea how amusing it is.'

George, as she records in her memoirs, begged in vain to be excused. 'Please don't ask me to come, Madam,' she said. 'I should be terrified. I don't like hunting.'

'Well, what a coward you are!'

'Please leave me behind with Mama and Mme de Ponty. I will study. I should enjoy it much more.'

'Get along with you! You won't go very far if you're as timid as all that! How are you going to face a crowded audience in Paris if you dare not even hunt rabbits?'

'But, Madam, there will be no one in the audience with a gun. . . .'

But she was obliged to follow the determined Raucourt, and before long a rabbit was shot and she was told that it was her task to go and pick it up. 'Oh, no!' she cried in horror. 'Over this I really revolt and will not obey you. For one thing, I should never come back. You would wait in vain for your rabbit. I should be discovered dead at its side.' And after this, Raucourt, rather impatient with her, made no further attempts to interest her in sport.

There were excursions to the castles of the Loire valley that were far more enjoyable, and one of the young actors of the Comédie Française, Lafon, came on a visit, bringing with him the atmosphere and conversation of Paris. Life became more tolerable now, with visits to the theatre at Orléans and even recitations and lessons at home. But neither Georgina nor her mother had any feeling for the beauty of the country, and they were much relieved when their visit was over and they were back in their cramped and airless rooms in the rue Neuve des Petits Champs.

In Paris, the Weymers soon heard more about Mlle Duchesnois, the actress who was trying to step into the position for which Raucourt had destined Georgina. This Duchesnois was in reality named Catherine Joséphine Rafuin, a woman of the lowest class who had begun life as a servant. She was twenty-five years old, very plain, but intelligent and gifted. She had always had a passion for acting, and somehow she had contrived to join a group of amateur actors, and by good fortune the playwright Legouvé saw her perform and introduced her to the influential circle of Mme de Genlis. Her patrons found her sad and silent in society. Full of inward passion, she had been harshly treated by life and was afraid to speak. But on the stage she came to life, and her melodious voice and graceful figure made one forget her plain face.

Such news was unwelcome to the Weymer family, but they did not worry unduly, for Mlle Raucourt assured them there was no need to do so. The Minister responsible, she said, had promised her that Mlle George should be authorized to make her début at the Comédie Française before any other aspirant.

In all respects the outlook was growing brighter for the Weymers. Charles was admitted into the orchestra of the Théâtre Feydeau as second violinist, owing to the influence of his master, Kreutzer; and the youngest child, Bébelle, became a student of the school of ballet dancing at the Opera. Raucourt, moreover, suddenly woke up with regard to her pupil. Lessons were again given regularly, and definite plans were made for Georgina's début during the autumn. A round of visits was made, too, to people whose place in society made them desirable patrons.

One afternoon Raucourt and her pupil drove out to the Palace of St Cloud, where the First Consul and his wife were staying. They were admitted at once into the presence of Mme Bonaparte. At this time Joséphine was thirty-nine years old. Her beauty was decidedly faded, but she had all the time and opportunity in the world to disguise the fact, and she did so very successfully by her excellent taste in dress and the use of cosmetics. Attired in some fragile masterpiece from the workrooms of M. Leroy or Mme Germont, with her hair gracefully arranged and entwined with flowers and pearls, perfumed and smoothly powdered, Joséphine was always delightful to look at. Moreover, she wore a perpetual smile which was friendly and in no way forced. The opposite of her husband, her humour never varied. Though flighty and untruthful, she radiated tolerance and friendliness, and now she hurried towards her friend Fanny Raucourt with open arms, genuinely pleased to see her. Her voice was soft, her manner a little gushing but otherwise simple and unaffected. 'Mlle George' was presented to her and curtsied; Joséphine beamed upon her and thought her the sweetest child imaginable in her shocking clothes (an opinion she was soon to have to change). And Georgina, like most people, felt strangely attracted to her. She was aware, she says in her memoirs, of a mysterious influence, a charm infinitely suave, that emanated from Joséphine and magnetized her.

After a little conversation, Georgina was asked to recite. Joséphine listened attentively and, the passage chosen being pathetic, was soon shedding tears. And when the visit ended, she kissed the girl and told Raucourt to be sure to bring her again before long.

It was not long, indeed, before Raucourt and Georgina paid another visit to Joséphine at St Cloud. News came one day that the friends of Mlle Duchesnois had contrived to obtain a permit for their protégée's début at the Comédie Française, and that it would take place on the third of August. Great was the agitation of Raucourt, her friends and the Weymer family. The event was felt to be outrageous and Raucourt was urged not to tolerate such an insult. Everyone knew she had been given a grant to train an actress of her own choosing; that an outsider should be pushed in like this was an unheard of thing, and it had clearly been engineered by her enemies. So Raucourt ordered George to put on her best clothes for a visit to Joséphine, and George wore a newly washed and ironed dress of white muslin, cut *à la vierge*, a blue belt and a pair of grey gloves. And off they drove in Raucourt's càrosse to beg Mme Bonaparte to intervene. What Raucourt did not know was that it was Joséphine herself who had obtained the order for the début of Duchesnois. General de Valence, the son-in-law of Mme de Genlis, had told her the story of Duchesnois, and begged her to help the poor woman who, last winter, even in the coldest weather, had had no shawl or cloak to put over her one cotton dress. Joséphine, always sympathetic and anxious to assist those in need, had at once consented.

Joséphine, however, received her visitors with the same smooth smiles and words as before, and listened politely while Raucourt explained what had happened. Raucourt had lost her usual composure; the actors of the Comédie Française all had their enemies, and she had worked herself up into a state of great anger and resentment over the Duchesnois incident, which she took as a personal affront. She spoke bitterly and at length.

'Come now, my dear Fanny,' said Joséphine blandly when she was able to make herself heard. 'Try to be a little calmer. My God! You will be making yourself really ill if you get into such a state! Now, let us look at the matter reasonably. How can the début of Mlle Duchesnois possibly harm our dear, charming little Mlle George? Duchesnois is twenty-eight years old, they tell me. What comparison can there be between a woman of twenty-eight and a beautiful girl of fourteen? None whatever.'

And having out of politeness to her guests added three years to the age of Duchesnois and subtracted one from that of George (who by now was fifteen), the amiable Joséphine turned her smiling face to the latter and said, 'And you, my dear, what do you think about it? You're not really quite so upset as your teacher is, I'm sure!' And she put her arm round the girl and kissed her.

Georgina, however, who was greatly distressed by the news that Duchesnois was to appear before her, replied by bursting into tears.

'Ah, she's crying, the poor little soul,' said Joséphine, full of sympathy. 'Well,' she continued, turning to Raucourt, 'since she's so upset, and you want her at all costs to make her début before Duchesnois, I'll ask the First Consul to come in. We'll get him to decide the point.'

And Joséphine was about to send for her husband, and would, indeed, have persuaded him to give the desired order. For she could never refuse an appeal, and was quite equal to undoing the good she had done to one suppliant yesterday, by answering an opposite request today. But, happily for the poor Duchesnois, Georgina now lost her head.

'Oh, no, Madame,' she cried. 'I beg you, do not ask him to come. I like being here alone with you. You're so kind, so very kind that I'm not in the least frightened. Besides, I should spoil all my chances straight away if he came. I should behave like an idiot in front of him. And it doesn't really matter if I do have to make my début after Mlle Duchesnois. It will make me work all the harder.' She turned to Raucourt. 'Don't you agree, Madame?' she said. 'Can't we leave it at that, and not worry Mme Bonaparte any more?'

Joséphine laughed, took Georgina in her arms and kissed her. 'You see, Fanny,' she said, 'she is more sensible over it than we are. We must do as she says, and I'm sure it will bring her luck. And then when it is her turn we will all turn up to applaud our little protégée!'

There were more kisses and then the visitors left, Joséphine following them with her smiles, inwardly relieved, no doubt, that she had contrived for once to get out of a difficult situation without offending either side.

In the carriage, Georgina was severely lectured on the way back to Paris. 'You little goose!' said Raucourt. 'You've made a fine mess of everything. The Consul would have given the order for you to appear first; but Joséphine was too kind to insist when she saw how silly you were about meeting him. And, of course, I was obliged to give in. . . . Well, no more reproaches, they are useless. You must take your courage in both hands now and make the best of the situation.'

Georgina felt she had been a fool. But it was perhaps some instinct that foresaw her future glories that had preserved her from meeting Napoleon Bonaparte on this occasion. It was no doubt better that he should catch sight of her for the first time behind the footlights, in all her splendour as an actress of the Comédie Française. This afternoon, at St Cloud, standing between the illustrious Raucourt and the polished, bejewelled Joséphine, she was nothing but an insignificant little girl in a cotton dress. Had Napoleon seen her thus for the first time, he would always have had such a picture of her somewhere at the back of his mind.

4

THE début of an actor or actress at the Comédie Française had, in those times, a significance it has long since lost. The aspirant had to be judged by the public, who had a right to decide whether he was to be accepted by the theatre or rejected. The theatre then had its habitués, those who came regularly to every play in the repertory and understood the habits and traditions of the place. They were faithful to the theatre and its staff, but they greatly valued their own power over reputations and made their feelings felt in no uncertain way. The new actor had to undergo a series of tests. Much depended on the very first appearance; but if that was successful he still had to prove that he could please the public in numerous other roles. The public attended these initial performances eagerly and in their most critical frame of mind, and it was because of the importance of this testing time that Raucourt was so disturbed by the emergence of Duchesnois. She could judge from what she had heard that this protégée of Mme de Genlis and her friends had a gift above the ordinary, and the last thing she wanted was that the public should have some new high standard in mind just as Mlle George appeared.

Since the appeal to Joséphine had failed, the début of Duchesnois was now inevitable. And she duly appeared on the appointed day in Racine's *Phèdre*. The First Consul was present with his wife, and the performance was most brilliant. Such fine, inspired acting had not been seen for many years; it brought to mind the great performances of Dumesnil, and before her of Adrienne Lecouvreur; and it was not to be seen again until Rachel appeared much later in the century with a similar gift. The effect of Duchesnois's acting was positive and absolute, and it carried her audience away in a unison of unqualified admiration. An eminent place in the Comédie Française appeared to be hers by right.

Yet off the stage this great actress could never hold her own.

The actors of the Comédie Française were difficult people unless one approached them in the way they thought proper; they did not much care to have strangers thrust upon them from the unknown, particularly gifted strangers whose social manners were neither confident nor ingratiating. Duchesnois, instead of dominating the lesser men and women of the theatre who were now obliged to admit her into their midst, was exceedingly humble and awaited kindness from them. The result was a fury of envy, malice and contempt on their part, and all her days she was destined to be an unhappy outsider, miserably aware of an imagined inferiority which yet made her performances, since she plunged into them as into an escape from life, the more wonderful,

Her parents had kept a small village tavern and had given her scant care. Brought up to drudgery, she had escaped at the age of sixteen to a more refined slavery, that of a seamstress; then, half starved, she had tried to keep herself alive in Paris by prostitution, going from one bitter experience to another. Men had never been kind to her, and now that she had achieved success she still shrank away from them, fearful of contempt. It was this diffidence, no doubt, that encouraged her colleagues to persecute her. No one wastes time delivering slights where they will not be felt.

Raucourt had her share in the hostile attitude that was taken towards her. She was a proud woman, and felt that, if Duchesnois should now be established as the great tragic actress of France, her own efforts to fill that place with an actress of her own choice would be ridiculed. The idea that she, the great Raucourt, might be made to look foolish was intolerable; in a state of violent anger, she told her friends that she would destroy Duchesnois if it cost her all her fortune. Duchesnois, in fact, only found sympathy through the faults of her colleagues. There were some who were hostile to Raucourt, and these, as time went by, showed themselves friendly and helpful to the newcomer.

Georgina's coaching was intensified, and permission was obtained for her to make her first appearance at the end of November. She was formally introduced to the company of actors, and writes in her memoirs: 'I was given the kindliest welcome into the Comédie Française and was treated as the child

28

of the house.' It was decided that she should play the role of Clytemnestra in *Iphigénie en Aulide*, with Talma in the role of Achilles and his wife, Caroline Vanhove, in that of Iphigénie.

Raucourt, who possessed great strength of purpose, was now to be seen everywhere where persons of influence could be drawn into an intrigue against Duchesnois or a campaign of publicity on behalf of George. And her power was such that Duchesnois was kept almost entirely from the roles she played best and was seen very little during the autumn. An intensive propaganda was circulated regarding Mlle George, whose beauty and superior talent, it was said, would put Duchesnois completely in the shade. To all this the public attended with its usual trust.

It may be imagined that the Weymer family were prejudiced against Duchesnois, and that they listened readily to those who spoke of her mediocrity, her common origin and her age. Georgina, good-hearted though she was, felt an aversion for her before she had even seen her. Thus, at the outset of her career, she was provided with one of those implacable hatreds which were as much a part of the life of a fashionable actress as were the love affairs with men of note and the display of luxury. Just such a hatred existed between Talma and Lafon; Lafon, indeed, had such a horror of Talma that he could not even be induced to mention his name, but always spoke of him as 'that other'.

Georgina now had to spend much time with the theatrical costume designer and she was dazzled by the fine dresses prepared for her use in the various plays of the repertory. Raucourt's friends, too, sent her gifts after the manner of the time. The Prince d'Hénin gave her a splendid tiger-skin for wear in the role of Dido; Mme Laetitia, the First Consul's mother, gave her an immense stuffed bird of paradise made into a head-dress. Such objects, whether entirely suitable or not, must always be worn when the generous patron was present in the theatre.

Another courteous habit of the time was that the débutante had to visit the great actresses of the past who were in retirement. One afternoon Raucourt took Georgina to call on her own teacher, the celebrated Mlle Clairon, once beautiful, spoilt and adored and now eighty years old and unable to forgive society for no longer worshipping her. 'Mlle Clairon received us very coldly,' say the memoirs of Mlle George. 'A little woman of frigid manners, bordering upon impertinence. Disdainful. Mlle Raucourt kissed her hand, which she scarcely raised. Her air was self-important and devoid of kindliness. She was composed of pride, that woman! Posed in a great armchair *à la Voltaire*, not even making a pretence to rise, she acknowledged our arrival with a slight inclination of the head. She made the air cold around her, and I wished myself far away.'

'My dear Mme Clairon,' said Raucourt, 'will you allow me to present my pupil to you?'

'Aha! You have a pupil. And what is she going to do?'

'First she will play the roles of princesses, later on of queens.'

'I hope,' said Mlle Clairon acidly, 'that you will find more to praise in her than I ever found in you.'

After a little more conversation on these lines, the great Clairon turned to Georgina and said:

'Well, child, let us see what you can do. Recite one of your roles to me.'

'Another time, dear Madame,' Raucourt hastened to say, seeing the consternation on her pupil's face. 'George has a cold in the head and would not do herself justice today.'

Clairon made no reply, and Raucourt rose to bring the visit to an end.

'What do you think of her, George?' Raucourt said as they drove away. 'Amiable, isn't she!'

'I think,' said George, 'that icicles fall on your shoulders directly you enter her house.'

Mme d'Abrantès gives a similar account of this actress who had once received homage from Louis XV, Voltaire, Diderot and David Garrick and was now forgotten.

From the home of Mlle Clairon, Raucourt drove with her pupil to a convent where the Government kept rooms for impoverished artists. Here they visited Mlle Dumesnil, twelve years older than Clairon and formerly her greatest rival. An elderly servant led the visitors into the old actress's bedroom, and Georgina, who in her lifetime was to act before some who survived to see the first World War, had before her eyes a woman born in the reign of Louis XIV. Dumesnil had been bedridden for some years, and she was propped up against her pillows wrapped in a blue dressing-gown, her frilled nightcap surmounted by a large silk bow. She was a shrivelled and seemingly lifeless figure, but she responded graciously to the respectful salutations of Raucourt.

'My dear Fanny,' she said, 'I am delighted to see you. And this beautiful child is your pupil? When is she to make her début?'

'Very soon, dear Dumesnil.'

'And what role is she playing?'

'Clytemnestra.'

'At her age? You've got some courage, Fanny!'

'Not really, my dear friend. The little rogue can express maternal feelings extremely well.'

'Well, so much the better for her; she will please the women as well as the men. May I recite the first scene to her? Would you mind, Fanny?'

'Would I mind, Dumesnil! What an idea! I only hope and pray she is able to note and remember every syllable she hears!'

Now, calmly and easily, the old actress went through the lines of Clytemnestra. Her voice, which had been so tired and feeble in conversation, became clear and melodious and was perfectly controlled; the bedroom seemed to Georgina to fade away and the eloquence of the experienced, finely-trained voice to invoke the whole setting and atmosphere of Racine's work. The dying actress was splendidly alive, and they were on the stage.

When the recitation was over, Georgina was asked to act a few scenes and was given valuable advice regarding many of the roles she would have to play. 'If I'm still alive, Fanny,' Dumesnil said when the visit came to an end, 'come and tell me all about Mlle George's début. Good-bye, my dear children. I am really rather tired. Here I am, trying to end my days in peace, but when I talk of the stage it shakes me up again in spite of myself. Let me kiss you both and wish you good luck.'

November was nearly over. The rehearsals proceeded

31

smoothly, with Talma, who was normally a somewhat moody character, in the best possible form, still in the throes of a passionate love for his wife, and happy to be acting with her. He was interested in Mlle George, too, who was so beautiful and so respectfully attentive to all he said, and he took great trouble in training her, supplementing the coaching of Raucourt with his own excellent teaching. Everyone was anxious to see the girl succeed. Mme Joséphine sent encouraging messages and promised to attend the first performance with her husband; and most of the Bonapartes and other notable people in Paris were to be present.

The only misfortune to arise was that Duchesnois was permitted to appear in her great role of Phèdre on November the 18th. Joséphine, or some other highly-placed person perhaps, had asked to see her, and there had been no alternative but to acquiesce. She gave a brilliant performance, and the audience seemed delirious with enthusiasm. She was called for at the end, bouquets were cast on the stage, and among them was a beautiful little crown of flowers. The audience cheered and shouted that the crown was meant to be placed on her head. Duchesnois bowed modestly and left it where it was. Nor did her colleagues, bowing and smiling behind her, take any notice of it until the audience had voiced their wishes so loudly and emphatically that it was impossible to ignore them any longer. Then one of the actors, Naudet, outwardly pleased and gracious but inwardly cursing, lifted the crown from the boards and respectfully placed it on Duchesnois's head. It was the height of success. Behind the scenes, gossip and slander prospered and the offending actress was still more coldly treated.

Georgina listened to the malicious gossip but took no part in it, though she was anxious to wrest the laurels from her rival. The corrupt society which was forming her character had not yet warped her happy nature, and she was still childish and high-spirited. She ran home in the early hours from the last rehearsal, alone, rejoicing in her freedom and the chilly air, pulling the bell-ropes at all the front doors as she passed them. Windows opened behind her, and laughing to herself she flew away from the angry shouts of citizens roused from their sleep and little suspecting that the young vagabond was Clytemnestra from the Comédie Française.

5

At midday on November the 28th, a long queue was already waiting outside the Théâtre Français. And when the actors began to arrive, at half-past four or so, excited crowds surged round them, struggling to catch sight of Mlle George, of whom such extraordinary rumours had been spread. The police had to be brought to clear a passage, and Raucourt sprained an ankle in the jostling crowd.

Long before six o'clock, when the performance was due to begin, every seat was taken. Raucourt, leaving nothing to chance, had had four hundred tickets distributed to friends and hired applauders. There was little place in the stalls and boxes for the friends of Duchesnois; the theatre was made into an impregnable fortress on behalf of George. All the Weymer family were present. George Weymer had come specially from Amiens; Charles was sitting with his master, the great Kreutzer. The critics had arrived; the Prince d'Hénin, Lucien Bonaparte, Chaptal, Joseph Fouché and scores of other men of renown were to be seen. And among the women, the wonderfully dressed women in the fantasies devised by artists after long day-dreaming in the Louvre, among the visions in high-waisted, flimsy dresses, were the two celebrated beauties, Mme Tallien and Mme Récamier. Only the Consular box with its scarlet drapery and gold tassels remained empty.

Shortly after six, silence fell. The First Consul had just arrived with his wife and other members of his family. For a moment he stood at the front of his box, severely regarding the brilliant audience. He wore a richly embroidered blue coat with white revers over black satin knee-breeches, and at his side there hung the Egyptian scimitar he had conquered from Mourad-bey. Now he turned and sat next to Joséphine—Joséphine in pink muslin, pearls and diamonds, her face made smooth as a flower-petal with suave cosmetics. Joséphine smiled at the faces raised towards her from the auditorium; her sisters-in-law, in their pale high-waisted dresses and their costly jewels, took their places beside her, and the curtain immediately rose.

Mlle Raucourt, unable to walk after her accident outside the theatre, had been carried into a small stage box. The play began, and Georgina waited in a state of terror, for Clytemnestra does not enter until the second act. 'I was never brave,' she writes. 'How many times, before entering the scene, I have been paralysed with fright and have prayed to God for some accident that would prevent my having to appear! Accident . . . but in fact it was simply to die that I wanted. . . .' However, the dreaded moment arrived, Caroline Vanhove was finishing a lengthy speech and Georgina stepped forward. In desperation she rose above her fears, and then she heard herself with a kind of inward surprise declaiming confidently. This confidence increased as a murmur of admiration rose from the audience.

'How beautiful she is!' people were whispering to their neighbours. 'Did you ever see anything like her? She is perfect. A Greek statue come to life, a goddess carved by Phidias or Praxiteles.' The society of the Consulate, so passionately devoted to the world of Greece and Rome, was quick to compare her with classical models. 'She is the sister of Apollo,' said the critic Geoffroy. And that evening she was given the name she kept throughout Napoleon's reign: 'the Venus of Paris'.

Her performance, though it was remarkable enough that a girl of fifteen could act in verse on such a stage, was not on the level of her beauty, and was far beneath that of Duchesnois. There was a certain monotony in her recitation, and a too obvious imitation of the manner of Raucourt. But her beauty went a long way and, moreover, the audience was largely composed of the friends of her teacher. In the cheaper seats, however, the ordinary citizens of Paris were represented, and most of them were admirers of Duchesnois. The second act went smoothly, while everyone was under the first effect of her appearance; but during the third act critical voices began to be heard and sometimes, after a particularly long and difficult passage to which she had been unable to give life, there was a whistle. Admirers of Lafon were present, too, who knew his hatred for Talma and accordingly hissed the noble Achilles when he made his impressive entrées. As the play moved on, these critics warmed to the attack and there were many disorderly scenes. George herself was hissed, her friends lost their tempers and shouted at her critics, the excitement grew, canes were raised and blows given. On the stage, the actors whispered words of encouragement to the débutante. As she heaped violent reproaches on his head in the fourth act, Agamemnon managed to whisper to her, 'Very good, my child, very good. They want to intimidate you, but don't give way.' And Raucourt called out from the stage box as Clytemnestra faltered half-way through her long tirade, 'Courage, George!' And thus emboldened, George put new force into her voice, such ringing force that the hostile cries subsided and she ended by bringing silence to the crowd before her.

Throughout the final act the audience was quiet and respectful, and when the last curtain fell the applause was loud and unanimous. George was cheered and called for; she had won the day, and she was acclaimed vociferously as she bowed smiling and unruffled, far less tired now than before the performance began. There were calls for Raucourt, too; but an actor came on to explain that she was unable to stand, and so could only send her thanks. There were cries of sympathy and more cheers, and then everyone who had the slightest claim to do so surged behind the scenes to invade the actors' dressing-rooms.

It was an evening never to be forgotten. 'Such memories cannot fade,' Mlle George wrote in her old age. 'The great crowd of people of fashion, the artists struggling along the corridors to the room that could only hold a few of them at a time . . . oh, it was most wonderful and impressive. Mme Dugazon, St Aubin, all the artists of the Grand Opera, all of them had come to give their support to Raucourt's pupil.'

It was an evening such as very few people live through, particularly at the age of fifteen. And because it came to her when she was so young, Georgina was able to enjoy it with the fullest rapture and in perfect seriousness. Napoleon and Joséphine sent messages of congratulation to Raucourt, with kind enquiries about her injury; Lucien Bonaparte sent a friend to pay his compliments to Georgina. Kreutzer, his coat torn, struggled to Raucourt's dressing-room with Charles Weymer, excited and enthusiastic. Everyone was talking, and no one listened to a word except Georgina, who heard herself exalted by all. People were breathless and incoherent. Hats were lost, canes broken, and coats and dresses rendered unfit for further wear. Such was the theatre in those times. Only Napoleon and Joséphine and their attendants retired immaculate and dignified to their carriages.

A supper party was held in honour of the débutante, a brilliant affair from which Georgina arrived home in the morning hardly more exhausted than she was exalted. She was not a little intoxicated, and her parents told her firmly that from now onwards she was to come straight home after every performance. She had to work. She had made a wonderful beginning, but the public would grow more critical as time went on, and her reputation had to be established.

6

GEORGINA was now given a small salary, and during the next few weeks she played the leading feminine roles of classical drama one by one. Raucourt and Talma continued to coach her, and her performance improved, her confidence grew. Yet it was soon clear that she had no need to exert herself unduly, for the critic Geoffroy had decided in her favour. Proud of his power to make or destroy reputations, Geoffroy poured his most eloquent praise upon her. He was a man who was not easily pleased and had a way of looking exclusively for faults. He would not even admit the merits of Talma, who was without doubt one of the great actors of all time, but enjoyed heaping venomous sarcasms upon him even after his finest performances. Therefore the unqualified admiration of Mlle George carried great weight and her name was made. As Dido, Semiramis, Hermione and Arsinoë she won column upon column of adulation in the *Journal des Débats*.

Geoffroy had praised Duchesnois, too, at the time of her début. But since her appearance in the middle of November this actress had been seen very little, and then only in minor roles. She was eclipsed for the time being, and Geoffroy took pride in raising her rival to the heights. Suddenly Georgina found herself the most conspicuous figure in Paris, and crowds assembled to stare at her as she arrived at the theatre. She was the great George, the genius beyond compare, who had little to do but appear. In the highest society she became the object of a cult; she was more than the Venus of Paris, she was one of the glories of France.

With her brilliant abilities and her superb beauty, Georgina could not have failed as an actress, even had she been without patronage and publicity. Had she been allowed to appear quietly and normally, the theatre-going public would have supported her, though it would have been critical and she would have had to work strenuously before winning its fullest approval. Raucourt and the vain Geoffroy did her no true service in promoting her with such determined zeal, for they deprived her of the incentive to make those supreme efforts that are essential for perfection in art.

That curious French institution known as the *claque* was already in being; in fact it had existed in the days of Mlle Clairon. It consisted of a band of special applauders, commissioned to excite public enthusiasm by clapping, weeping, laughing and otherwise reacting in the manner hoped for by both author and actor. As well as the organized, regular *claque*, there were amateurs: young men fond of the theatre but short of money and glad to obtain a seat either free or at a reduced price in return for a few cheers and some vigorous clapping. This deplorable habit, we are told by Arthur Pougin in his interesting *Dictionnaire du Théâtre*, originates with no less a person than Nero, who made use of it when entertaining the Romans with his flute. Mlle Raucourt, it is needless to say, profited by it to the full throughout the period of her pupil's début. Night after night, practically all the seats in the stalls were occupied by friends and applauders, and wonderful ovations were given.

The Weymer family were rapidly losing their heads, although poor Marie Verteuil did her best to keep her authority over her daughter and constantly urged her to work. George Weymer, now that Georgina was safely launched, returned to Amiens, which he had abandoned for two or three exciting weeks. There he spent all his spare time in reminding people that he was the father of Mlle George, and in preparing for the press a work with the following title: *The Opinions and the Eulogies of the Paris Journals on the Début of my Daughter, George Weymer.*

Before he left Paris, he found a suitable home for his daughter, a small flat in the rue Ste Anne, conveniently near the theatre and well within her means. It was on the first floor of a corner house. Beneath it were the stables of a public coach company, and upstairs were the apartments of the celebrated Mme Germont, *couturière* to Mme Napoleon Bonaparte. Opposite were the premises of a blacksmith; from these there emerged a great deal of cheerful song to accompany the metallic clamour of his trade. Georgina was charmed with her flat. The salon, which was Mme Weymer's bedroom at night, was furnished with a sofa and chairs upholstered with black horsehair. An adjoining room, the dining-room by day, served as Georgina's bedroom, and a small room leading from it was used as her boudoir. Another small room was the bedroom of Marianne and Bébelle. The lively sounds of horses and stable-boys mingled with the laughter of young seamstresses running up and down the stairs to the workrooms of Mme Germont, or chattering as they put fine sewing into those white muslin and organdie dresses which Napoleon's tastes had made so popular with the ladies of court society. Georgina quickly made friends with the seamstresses, several of whom were about her own age; and on her free evenings, when the workrooms upstairs closed, she would rush outside with them to play 'Puss in the corner'. But this happy state of affairs did not last for very long. One evening Mme Weymer found out what was going on and promptly forbade her daughter ever to play in the streets again. What would people think? she asked. And Mlle George records that she had from now onwards to conduct herself 'like a successful actress and be bored to death in the evenings'.

However, her mother engaged a *femme de chambre* for her round about this time, a lively girl named Clémentine. This was a source of great pleasure to Georgina, for the *soubrette* was true to tradition, a devoted little chatterbox and a loyal friend.

Already the guileless Georgina was being pursued by admirers, and Mme Weymer was bent on keeping them at bay. The first to attempt to break through the defences was Lucien Bonaparte, who sent splendid presents to the young actress. He was still attempting to hide the extent of his attachment to Mme Juberthon from his powerful brother, and, fabulously rich as he was, there was no reason why he should not permit himself the luxury of a mistress from the Comédie Française. He is said to have approached Raucourt on the matter, who acted as his intermediary. A fine house was offered to the young actress, with the assurance that Lucien Bonaparte wished to relieve her of all material cares; he would pay for the upkeep of her establishment and for any coaching she desired.

Such conduct was not unusual in those times. All through the eighteenth century it had been a common thing for actresses to be provided for by men of wealth, and the habit had certainly started because of the inadequacy of theatrical salaries. An actress who was successful and was taken up by society found it impossible to live in fitting style on what she honestly earned, yet her livelihood, and even that of her theatre, depended much on her social successes; the wealthy lover had therefore become a part of her career, and such men were regarded as being in some respects patrons of the arts. The Weymer family, however, were honest and scrupulous, and they did not care for the conditions of Lucien's offer. If Georgina accepted the house she was to live in it alone. No member of her family was to be allowed to share it with her. The offer was therefore declined.

Lucien had been foiled; other men began to call with gifts and flattery, were received politely by the actress's mother and then went their way. Mme Weymer had her method of accepting the flowers, and even the jewels and the money presented to her daughter. 'If you are offering this gift to the artist, Sir,' she would say, 'my daughter will accept it as an artist.' After this the gallant donor could only disclaim any personal feelings in the matter, and the presents would be received and enjoyed. Such a state of affairs might have continued long enough, had Mme Weymer had her way. She hoped her daughter would eventually make a good marriage and until that time devote herself exclusively to her work. But her hopes and precautions were shortly to be brought to nothing by the arrival of her sister, Mme Munier, an artful woman who was determined to exploit the situation.

Georgina's Aunt Munier was a widow who had long been living peaceably in Amiens, where the time had passed by happily enough in housekeeping and gossip. But now there came the great event of her niece's rise to fame; and after listening to George Weymer's enraptured descriptions of the successes of his Mimi, from which outbursts of eloquence he would turn to his book, leaving her to look on speechless while his quill pen flashed across the pages of praise he was copying from the newspapers —after all this, Mme Munier lost her taste for the tranquillity of Amiens and hastened to leave it for the capital.

She joined the family in the rue St Anne, bringing with her a servant, Joseph. Somehow or other, space was made for them both in the small flat, and Georgina, pleased by everything at this time, was delighted to have the society of her lively, talkative aunt. *Très coquette et assez légère* is the opinion of Mlle George in her old age as she looks back to these times. Mme Munier designed to do well for herself out of her niece's good fortune, and she made herself as agreeable as possible to the girl. Soon she was putting Mme Weymer in the shade as she talked graciously to visitors; it was very much to her taste to receive a certain homage as the great actress's aunt, and every night she was at the theatre, displaying herself, smiling, and missing nothing of what was going on, except on the stage. And afterwards she would pour flattery on her niece.

'My dear child,' she would say, 'you were superb tonight. You should have heard the things being said about you! You are the greatest actress the French stage has seen for more than a century! The most beautiful it has *ever* seen! Oh, it is all wonderful to hear. . . .'

Mme Weymer, on the other hand, tried to help her daughter by repeating the criticisms she heard. 'I heard several people criticizing your exits this evening,' she would say, 'and, really, Mimi, they were not good. Now you must think about this and remember you still have a lot to learn.' But Georgina felt that her fine training had placed her on a level far above her mother's, and she was beginning to resent such advice.

> My mother [she says in her memoirs] made a thousand criticisms each time I acted. She was right, but I did not like it at all. Perfidious flattery ruins us, yet it always gives us pleasure, and so we reject good to enjoy evil. That which should have made me very grateful to my mother made me turn away from her; and the very thing which should have alienated me from my aunt drew me to her. By her exaggerated praise Aunt Munier won my confidence and I grew very fond of her. To her I could easily say things I would never have dared to say to my mother. She was always so full of flattery, and decidedly one loves to be flattered! Oh, if we could only understand while we are young the nature of good and evil, and follow the one, avoiding the other!

Looking back, the old actress Mlle George saw her faults and mistakes clearly enough. Yet it would have been difficult indeed for a girl of sixteen to resist the temptations of her position. Her aunt laughed at her scruples and her simplicity; she hinted that Mme Weymer was old-fashioned and inclined to stand in her daughter's way. Georgina, she said, being famous now in all Europe, must be free to live her own life. She even attempted to make the girl feel sorry for herself. How was it, she asked, that she had no carriage and had to live in such cramped conditions? With all her brilliance, she was entitled to live as elegantly and comfortably as anyone in society. Georgina only laughed. She thought her new home delightful, and she enjoyed running home from the theatre at night with Clémentine. Mme Munier, however, was not at all fond of walking but, on the contrary, very much felt the need of a carriage to drive about in. And she soon told everyone of note with whom she could get into conversation of the deprivations to which her niece was subjected.

Opportunities for such chatter occurred frequently enough, particularly at the theatre in the evenings. These evenings were very enjoyable to Mme Munier; she and Mme Weymer would watch the spectacle from Georgina's box, and would receive visits from distinguished members of the audience, who treated them with deference. In the foyer, the corridors behind the scenes and the actors' rooms, all the elegance of Consular Paris assembled during the intervals, and not many nights had passed before Mme Munier was on friendly terms with a number of elderly men whose polished gallantry was a pleasant change from the provincial simplicities she was accustomed to. Among these men was a certain Chevalier de Veuil, with whom she rapidly came to an understanding regarding her niece's position.

Parisian society was now even more corrupt than it had been in the *ancien régime*. The reaction against the revolution had thrown democratic and rational ideals into the background, and people were as avid for gaiety and pleasure as they had been under the Bourbon kings. The urbanity of the eighteenth century had returned, though the former coherence of society was lost and adventurers abounded. There was a feeling about that all was permitted so long as the outward amenities of life were not disturbed. The Chevalier de Veuil was one of those men, of whom there were so many, whom no one knew anything about, but who was received everywhere because his manners were those of the nobility. He had his carriage, he dressed elegantly and wore the ribbon of some unknown order in his buttonhole. Mlle George tells how he would visit her box at the theatre, usually accompanied by some distinguished foreigner whom he appeared to be entertaining.

The chevalier, indeed, lived by his wits. When rich men came to Paris from abroad he made himself known to them and was soon showing them round, taking them to the fashionable salons of Paris and presenting them to persons of renown. Yet, beginning always with introductions to people of fashion, he contrived ultimately to lead his wealthy dupes into a notorious gambling circle. And he further acted as agent between rich men and the pretty, accessible women of Paris whom he offered them as mistresses. He was a *grand-seigneur-procureur*, a phenomenon of the time. An actress was fair game, and he was quick to seize upon Mlle George's Aunt Munier. It was not long before he called at the flat in the rue Ste Anne.

He was graciously received by Georgina, her aunt and her unsuspecting mother, and he made himself exceedingly agreeable. But, accustomed to the homes of the wealthy, he was ill at ease in the small and plainly furnished salon where Mme Weymer slept at night. Despite the rigours of the recent revolution, it appeared he had never before realized that such hardship existed. Was it possible, he asked, that a woman of talent was living in misery when there were so many distinguished men who would count it an honour to come to her aid?

'I'm perfectly happy here, Monsieur,' said Georgina, truthfully. And now the blacksmith over the road began hammering and singing cheerfully.

'Ah, *miséricorde!*' exclaimed the chevalier, jumping. 'What a ghastly noise. You can't hear yourselves speaking here!'

'Don't let it worry you,' said Georgina as her visitor threw up his slender white hands in dismay. 'It's only my neighbour, the blacksmith, who has a lot of customers today.'

'But you can't possibly remain here.'

'Why not? I won't leave my blacksmith, I like him very much.'

'Dear lady, one needs to be as young as you are to endure such an infernal pandemonium.'

'But I really quite enjoy it, you know.'

'Well, I came to enquire whether you would be kind enough to receive the Prince Sapiéha, a distinguished man who adores artists and seeks their society. He never misses one of your performances, and he would be most happy if he might call on you.'

'Why not, if my mother will allow it? We receive a great many visitors, as my neighbour the blacksmith could tell you; therefore I can very well receive the Prince Sapiéha.'[1]

The Prince Sapiéha had come from Poland and was a man of immeasurable wealth. Mme Weymer showed some hesitation over receiving him, but her scruples were overruled by Mme Munier. The Prince duly called and Mme Weymer was reassured by his courtesy and correct behaviour. His visit was brief, his manner quiet and simple, and he limited himself to a conversation on the arts. He was therefore permitted and even encouraged to call again.

Georgina liked the Prince, who was tall and handsome; and the Prince was dazzled by the young actress's beauty and the reputation she enjoyed in Paris. Soon the Chevalier de Veuil was successful in his enterprise. The deal was concluded, and the foreigner was made to pay fabulously for the Parisian pleasure offered him. Aunt Munier was authorized to look for apartments, and she joyfully set out on her search. Shortly after, Georgina was taken to see the beautiful flat chosen for her. It was in the rue St Honoré, a fine set of rooms on the first floor with a large balcony; beneath were stables and a coach house, and the rent was 2,400 francs a year.

Georgina, although alarmed, could not hide her delight. She told her aunt, she says in her memoirs, that she would love to possess such a home; but how could they furnish such large rooms? What was the use of a stable and coach house to her?

'Don't worry about anything,' said Aunt Munier. 'I have been asked to see to everything for you.'

'But who by?'

'By the Prince Sapiéha.'

'Oh, the Prince Sapiéha! But I shouldn't want to accept anything from him——'

'My dear child, you need have no scruples. To him it is a mere

[1] P. A. Cheramy, *Mémoires Inédits de Mademoiselle George* (1908), pp. 61–2.

nothing, and all he wants is to see you, as an artist of Paris, living as you deserve to live.'

Both Alexandre Dumas and Eugène de Mirecourt, contemporaries of Mlle George, touch upon this episode in the light in which it was presented to them by the actress, each telling it in his own way. De Mirecourt describes the manner in which the Prince Sapiéha offered the new home to Mlle George:

'Mademoiselle,' he said to her, 'I am exceedingly rich, and I have the greatest difficulty in disposing of my revenues. It would be a true service if you would help me a little.'

Seeing how surprised the girl was, and reading suspicion in her glance, he hastened to add:

'Please don't be suspicious. Think of me as a father. You are living very uncomfortably here, Mademoiselle, and I have taken it upon myself to provide better apartments for you. And here is the address with the key.'

'But I can't accept it, it's impossible, Monsieur,' cried George.

'Impossible? Why? Furniture costing some fifty thousand francs, diamonds, a few cashmere shawls—a mere pittance. It's easy to accept a trifle of that kind from a man embarrassed by an income of two millions, and who asks no more, Mademoiselle, than to be your friend. Shake my hand at the theatre next time you play Clytemnestra, and I shall be repaid a hundredfold . . . I am your humble servant!'

With that, the Prince gave a profound bow, took his cane and his hat, and left. Never was homage to a woman's talents shown with more disinterestedness, originality and sincerity.

No doubt Mme Munier told some such story as this to the Weymer parents, for they were placated in some way and the whole family moved into the beautiful flat to enjoy that luxurious ease and elegance which the very rich allowed themselves during the Consulate. There was a carriage in the coach house, there were horses in the stables. Georgina's bedroom was hung with tapestry and embroidered muslin; the salon was decorated in red silk and black velvet, and the dining-room was entirely hung with white; the furniture was in the latest fashion, Greek in inspiration, chaste and severe. In the midst of such furniture one had to hold oneself well; one sat upright and did not recline.

Prince Sapiéha was less exacting than Lucien Bonaparte had been, and did not insist upon having his protégée to himself. Round the dinner table there always sat Mme Weymer, Mme Munier, Bébelle and Charles. Charles, indeed, was independent and lived alone, for he had obtained the position of first violinist at the Théâtre Feydau. But he always dined with his mother and sister; and the father, George Weymer, paid frequent visits to his daughter's home in Paris. The Prince, who so obligingly provided for them all in the name of art, appears to have been most discreet and tactful, and Georgina was able to keep up the pretence that her admirer was merely a patron; in view of the habits of thought of the time and the artificiality of social manners, this was not difficult; it was one of those polite fictions people were very ready to accept.

A change now came over Georgina; she ceased to be a little girl and saw herself very much as Mlle George, the goddess of the Consulate. The Polish prince was a model of deferential courtesy and gave her all she could desire in the way of jewels and beautiful clothes; for the first time she became aware of her own beauty, for she had spacious rooms to move about in and great mirrors reflected her on all sides. She saw how well she adorned both her surroundings and the fashions of the day. With her hair piled up on top of her head *à la Titus*, and her high-waisted dresses revealing much of her figure, she looked delightful where so many women of the time looked merely grotesque in their attempt to dress while remaining undressed. 'Our tunics of India muslin were really seductive,' she writes. 'With the arms and shoulders bare, one certainly looked very well. But for thin women it was a sad fashion. It was necessary to be statuesque to show the dress to advantage.'

At no time of her life had Mlle George any feelings either of modesty or immodesty regarding her own figure; she was proud of its perfection, but saw it with the detached eye of an artist, having nothing but contempt for those who, later in the century, came to regard nudity as indecency. She was ideally in her place in the society of the Consulate; and as the interpreter of classical roles she felt it fitting that she should be draped gracefully rather than covered. In her new home, of which she was the undisputed mistress, with a prince as her admirer and humble servant, surrounded by magnificent examples of gleaming, polished furniture and costly ornaments, waited on by flunkeys, she assumed easily the dignity and confidence imposed by her surroundings. Only one thing was needed now to persuade Mlle George that she was the most wonderful woman on earth, and that was the love of the greatest man on earth, the First Consul. This too was to be accorded to her by the Fates—those inscrutable Fates who lash the majority with privations and hardship. For one fine day, not many weeks after Mlle George's brilliant début, the Consul's valet, Constant, called and, bowing obsequiously, said that his master begged to have the honour of complimenting her in person upon her fine acting, and that he would send a carriage the following evening to convey her to the Palace of St Cloud.[1]

7

NAPOLEON and Joséphine were spending the winter months at St Cloud, and they were both following Mlle George's career with interest. From time to time they would drive into Paris in the evening to watch her perform, and afterwards would send her a small present or a note of thanks. They talked freely about her, and Napoleon had given no indication that he felt personally attracted.

At this time the domestic life of the First Consul and his wife was happy and even appeared to be ideal. It was a union, however, of its nature stormy although it had produced much love

[1] Mlle George does not give the date of this event, but according to the accounts of both Mme de Rémusat and Lucien Bonaparte it must have been in the early weeks of 1803.

of a remarkably intensive quality. They had been married in 1796, Joséphine, the older by six years, being then a widow of thirty-three with manners acquired at the court of Marie Antoinette. Napoleon was a lonely young man whose life had been spent mainly in a military school and barracks. He was unaccustomed to women, but yet exceedingly romantic, having fallen under the sway of Goethe's much-read novel, *Werther*. Joséphine knew how to put him at his ease and he quickly fell in love with her, depositing at her feet all the devotion of which he was capable. And his capacities in this as in all other directions were well above the normal.

Joséphine, swept off her feet by the intensity of his passion, and being in financial difficulties at the time, agreed to marry him. He projected on to her all his aspirations after perfection, and wanted only to be faithful to her throughout his life. His vivid, enthusiastic mind saw all things in ideal terms, and he had an unqualified respect for the institution of marriage. Joséphine, on the contrary, had no such conception in her mind, but was a typical pleasure-seeking lady of the Directory, ready to pander to men of all kinds if by so doing she could obtain luxuries for herself in difficult times. She had been imprisoned during the Reign of Terror, and her first husband had been one of the victims of the guillotine. Narrowly escaping with her own life, on regaining freedom she had joined in the unrestrained pleasures of a disorganized society, passing, in the wake of her friend Mme Tallien, from one lover to another. She was a strange wife for a severe young man with an innate sense of social order.

Only ten days after the marriage, Napoleon had to leave her to take command of the army in Italy. He spent his spare moments in writing letters such as the following:

> By what art is it that you have been able to captivate all my faculties, and to concentrate in yourself my moral existence? It is a magic, my sweet love, which will finish only with my life. . . . What lands, what countries separate us! What a time before you read these weak expressions of a troubled soul in which you reign! Ah, my adored wife, I know not what fate awaits me, but if it keeps me much longer from you it will be insupportable. I stop, my sweet

48

love; my soul is sad—my body is fatigued—my head is giddy—
men disgust me—I ought to hate them—they separate me from my
beloved.

Joséphine, though she passively enjoyed the homage of this
love, was not responsive, and Napoleon soon began to feel that
she was cold and insensible. The truth was that he was still
unknown to the world in those days, and her elegant friends let
her see that they were not impressed by the marriage, in which
they saw the desperate step of a woman who wanted a secure
position while there was still time. Napoleon's physique was
unimpressive; he had been poor and underfed in his youth and
was consequently thin, spindly and mediocre in appearance.
When he was absent on his campaigns, devoted to her and trusting absolutely in her love, Joséphine, far from missing him, was
flirting with a certain M. Charles, a man of fine appearance and
manners with whom she was not sorry to be seen by her critical
friends.

Napoleon's brothers and sisters soon informed him of his
wife's infidelity. Incredulous at first, he was distracted with grief
when he realized the charge was true, and decided to separate
from Joséphine. But by now he had risen into sudden and
brilliant fame, and his immense prestige far outweighed the
embroidered coats and powdered wigs of M. Charles. Joséphine
experienced a change of feeling and now fell into a state of
infatuation for her husband; when he spoke of divorce she wept
bitterly; and since he loved her as much as ever he forgave her,
and they settled down in Paris together.

Joséphine had come to love Napoleon as much as he could
wish; but all her immoral past had gradually been revealed to him
and he felt he had been betrayed and that there was no longer any
reason why he himself should trouble to remain faithful. From
now on, Joséphine had eyes for no other man; no one else had
equal attraction for her, and certainly no one else could provide
for her so adequately. But Napoleon was to allow himself a series
of mistresses in the course of ten years or so, a habit he only
dropped when he married the respectable Marie Louise. There

had been Pauline Fourès in Egypt, the Italian singer, Grassini, and Mme Branchu of the Paris Opera House. And there were other women, more obscure, who passed in and out of his private apartments, unobserved, distracting him for a few hours or a few nights.

So far the number of these women had been small and Joséphine had nothing to worry about in this respect. But she tended to be jealous and suspicious and was quickly upset if her husband appeared to be interested in another woman. She knew that her friends now envied her, and that every fashionable woman in Paris thought the First Consul infinitely attractive and fascinating. How was it, she might well wonder, that she and they had but a short time ago thought him insignificant and undignified?

The answer was that Napoleon had changed completely. A great ambitious spirit, formerly cramped and repressed, was now free from its chains and shackles and shone triumphantly through the mortal frame. He was no longer the socially diffident man of 1796, his public triumphs were too great for that. Nor was he any longer emaciated and hollow-eyed, for he had outgrown the effects of his famished youth. His loose, flowing hair, emblem of the romantic sentiments of his early twenties, of the cult for Werther, was neatly clipped, and he had come to look remarkably like the splendid reliefs on the medals so often struck in his honour. Moreover, the consciousness not only of great power but of having served his country well, of having done good in a disinterested spirit, illumined his expression and lent ease and confidence to his manner. At his best he was probably a man of unusual charm during his Consular period.

In his youth his family had been poor, harassed, even persecuted and driven out of Corsica. Now that the family was re-established in security and made eminent, no sense of humiliation damped ancestral pride. The Bonapartes, indeed, were an ancient Italian family which had produced senators and prelates in the Middle Ages and was allied to the Medici and other great houses. Napoleon grew increasingly conscious of the splendours of his race, and could not help feeling aware of connections with even earlier times. When he looked in a mirror he saw a head which seemed to relate him unmistakably to Julius Caesar; he had come to feel the nearness of the old order in Europe, the Roman Empire in which his ancestors no doubt held high places. With the megalomania which was now taking hold of him, though it was as yet harmless and little in evidence, he felt inwardly associated by right of birth and divine will with every resounding name in history, and therefore capable of all grandeur and heroism. All this might now be seen in his proud bearing.

This growing megalomania intensified his love for classical drama, which gave him such fine models to contemplate; since he could scarcely hope to meet his own equals in life, he never tired of gazing at Caesar, Orestes and Agamemnon on the stage. It perhaps encouraged him, too, to seek on occasion a mistress from among the actresses of tragedy. While he did not like actresses as such, and there is no record of his ever having dallied with an actress of modern comedy or a ballet dancer, he would from time to time invite an actress of the Comédie Française to call on him at night.

It seems that it was the imaginary character of the play that had really attracted his passions for a moment, for as likely as not the actress would arrive only to find he had lost interest. At the best of times there was a certain lack of sentiment about these encounters; Napoleon would have woken up to the fact that it was not, after all, the real Dido or Cleopatra who was present, and there would be no beating about the bush; according to Stendhal, his personal attendant Roustan was often kept present behind a screen throughout the interview, and the actress would be sent packing within a very short time and promptly forgotten.

Sometimes political affairs would overtake him and he had not even time to look up from his papers when the actress was announced. Such was Duchesnois's fate, for he felt a fleeting fancy in the theatre one night to make love to her, no doubt before the appearance of Mlle George.

It may seem surprising that a woman of Duchesnois's merit should accept such an invitation, but it must be remembered that women were of such inferior status at the time that they had no outlet for worldly ambitions except through the patronage of highly placed men. It is understandable that Duchesnois, meeting with such hostility at the Comédie Française, had visions of powerful support in her career when asked to visit the Consul.

When she arrived the Consul was busy working. Constant knocked at his door and he called out, 'Tell her to wait!'

Duchesnois waited an hour, and then another hour; and Constant now ventured to enter his master's study and remind him she was there.

'Tell her to get undressed,' said the Consul, drily.

Duchesnois did as she was told and waited shivering another hour, thinking, no doubt, of the many actresses before her time for whom such an evening was the door to success.

Eventually Constant went a third time to his master's study to see what he was doing. The Consul was entirely engrossed in his work.

'Tell her to go home,' he snapped.

Another actress, Thérèse Bourgoin, was treated in much the same fashion. 'Unfamiliar with courteous phrases,' says Frédéric Masson, who tells this story in *Napoléon et les Femmes*, 'and not hiding sufficiently the contempt he felt for women who came to him on the message of a valet . . . he could speak brutally and his manner would have been cynicism in any other. Yet, in fact, no one was less cynical than he was.'

Such affairs seem to have arisen from his sense of power and freedom and not from any sense of need, for despite the shattering of his illusions regarding Joséphine, he had found much pleasure in his married life. Now that her children were grown up, Joséphine was entirely engrossed by her devotion to Napoleon, and however out of humour he might be she never answered him with a sharp word but was invariably sweet and conciliatory. At all times she was tactful, knowing when to be silent and when to amuse him with a flow of lively gossip. He turned to her gladly in his leisure moments, finding repose in her company and pleasure in her appearance. For she took infinite trouble to please his eye.

The painter Isabey, speaking of this period, remarks: 'Joséphine was completely submissive to her husband's ascendency. I noticed with concern that her affection for him seemed to increase, while the General's love for her was diminishing as time went on.' Yet during recent months, during the happy summer and autumn of 1802, Joséphine was under the impression that Napoleon was as much in love with her as ever, and that his brief affairs with other women were always trifles of no importance, and that in any case they were a thing of the past. He was friendly and affectionate, and always shared her room at night. In the morning it was his habit to rise at eight o'clock, beginning the day's work immediately, giving orders and dictating letters while his valets dressed him and while he drank his coffee. He had his lunch in his own apartments, often receiving the visits of actors and artists at this time. Afterwards, without lingering over the meal, he would work until six in the evening, and he would then see Joséphine for the first time in the day and would probably go out for a drive with her. He would then dine quietly with her and the ladies and gentlemen of the household, and would afterwards spend a little time in the salon, talking. Then he would return to his study to continue working, while Joséphine finished the evening playing cards. She would wait until a servant came to tell her that Napoleon had retired to bed—it was usually between ten and eleven o'clock—and she would then dismiss her ladies and go at once to join him.

Such was the normal day's routine at St Cloud that Mlle George was now about to interrupt.

8

THE invitation brought by Constant filled the young actress with an elation tempered by anxiety. How envious her colleagues would be! But how would she maintain her composure in the presence of the ruler of France? Triumphant feelings prevailed, however, and she admits in her memoirs that she was carried away by vanity. Constant suggested calling for her at her home, but she told him he would find her at the theatre. Thus her departure to St Cloud would not pass unnoticed.

The carriage was to come for her at eight in the evening, and she passed a restless day. Throughout the morning she chattered about the coming visit with her maid, Clémentine; in the afternoon she drove up to the Bois de Boulogne and then visited her perfume-maker and her dressmaker. At six o'clock Clémentine dressed her in white muslin, put a lace veil over her shining dark curls and a pale cashmere shawl round her shoulders; and thus attired she drove to the Théâtre Français and sat in her box to watch the opening scenes of the night's performance with one or two of her friends. Punctually at eight o'clock Clémentine came to the box to say that a carriage was waiting for her mistress.

Sitting on the coachman's seat was César. Napoleon liked to indulge his servants, to allow them their little idiosyncrasies and failings, and this César was rather fond of his bottle of wine and under its influence would drive at a reckless pace. The other servant, the valet Constant, was a handsome, idle young man with plenty of curiosity and an impertinent tongue. It is true that Georgina encouraged familiarity.

'Dear me, I'm nearly frightened to death!' she began. 'I wish you would drive me home and tell the First Consul I'm not feeling well. I promise you I'll come some other time.'

'Take you home! A fine reception I should get from my master if I did!'

'But when I tell you I'm so terrified I shall be quite speechless! I shall just be frozen with fear, and your First Consul will think me the silliest creature he's ever seen. Don't you see it will be really dreadful for me?'

Constant, lounging in his master's fine coach, leaned back and roared with laughter. Such situations as this greatly relieved the tedium of service and he was enjoying himself. 'Don't worry,' he said. 'You'll see how kind the Consul is. He'll soon put you at your ease. I can tell you this, he's waiting for you very impatiently.'

Right up the Champs Elysées the carriage swayed behind galloping horses, the rugged César cursing and cracking his whip on the coachman's box, and Mlle George playing her innocent role within before the appreciative eyes of the valet Constant. Through the dark Bois de Boulogne they drove, the actress chattering the whole way, so that it seemed only a moment after leaving the theatre that they arrived at St Cloud.

'Well, here we are, Mademoiselle,' Constant said. 'Come now, everything will be all right! But go on looking frightened, because he'll like it.'

He led her on to a terrace, where another interested valet awaited her arrival; this was Roustan, the celebrated black servant from Egypt, a handsome, powerful man who was devoted to his master, remaining close to him at all times with the dramatic air of one who awaited assassins and was ready to lay down his life. Through the vast windows, Georgina saw a brilliantly lighted bedroom, the size of a ballroom. Into this she was now led. The outer door was closed and she was left alone.

'Here I was,' she writes, 'alone in this great room; an enormous bed at one end, with heavy curtains of green silk.' She looked about her curiously. There was a divan near the fireplace, but that was almost as unwieldy as the bed itself. There were huge lighted candles in massive candelabra all round the room, and a splendid lustre suspended above. Everything the room contained was large, and she looked in vain for some such shadowy corner as seemed suitable for the kind of interview she supposed was to take place. But no such corner existed. Bonaparte, indeed, was hardly the man to seek shadowy corners for sentimental or other occasions, and all was aglare. Mlle George took a seat between the massive bed and the no less massive fireplace where a brisk fire burned, and drew her veil down over her face.

'Now I can hear a slight movement,' she writes. 'Oh, how my heart beats! It is he! The Consul enters by the door nearest the fireplace, the one leading into the library.'

The Consul, she tells us, was wearing white silk stockings,

white satin knee-breeches, a green military jacket with red collar and embroideries; and under his arm he carried the three-cornered hat so often seen in his portraits.

I stood up and he came towards me, looking at me with that enchanting smile which had its equal in no one else. He took me by the hand and made me sit beside him on the enormous divan; then he took off my veil and threw it carelessly on to the floor. My beautiful veil! That's a fine thing to do! Suppose he walks on it and tears it for me! I don't like this at all.

'Your hand is trembling. You're not afraid of me? Do I appear so terrifying? I thought you so beautiful last night, Madame, that I wanted to compliment you on your performance. You see, I'm really much more polite and amiable than you are.'

'You, monsieur? In what way?'

'In what way? Didn't I send you 3,000 francs after hearing you as Emilie, to show you how much pleasure you had given me? I hoped you would ask permission to come and thank me in person. But the beautiful, proud Emilie said nothing.'

I stammered, I hardly knew what to say. 'But I didn't know . . . I dared not take such a liberty.'

'That's just a lame excuse! Were you really afraid of me?'

'Yes.'

'But you're not afraid now?'

'Oh, more than ever!'

The Consul laughed heartily.

'Tell me what your name is.'

'Joséphine Marguerite.'

'I am very fond of the name Joséphine. But I shall call you Georgina, if you'll allow me.'

The Consul found it difficult to persuade Georgina to talk, and eventually she told him the lights worried her. He called out to Roustan and told him to extinguish the candles in the lustre.

'Is that enough?' he asked.

' No,' she replied, 'I should like half those large candles put out.'

'Very well. Put them out, Roustan.'

56

Roustan went round the room extinguishing the lights, and then retired discreetly from view.

'Come, Georgina,' said the Consul, 'tell me all about yourself. Be good and sincere, and just tell me everything.'

He was so kind and unassuming [the actress writes] that all my fear left me. I told him the story of my unimportant little existence, how I came to Paris, and all my early misfortunes.

'Dear child, you must have been very poor. But how are you getting on now? Who gave you that fine cashmere shawl? That lace veil?'

Georgina told him about the Prince Sapiéha, representing him, as usual, as a patron; she soon realized, from his remarks, that the Consul was fully informed about the Prince, although he seemed pleased by her replies to his questions.

'Good!' he said. 'You haven't lied to me. You will come to me here from time to time, will you not? But I must ask you to be very discreet. Promise me that.'

Napoleon, immensely attracted by the young actress, was 'happy', as she puts it, 'to meet with a timid resistance'.

Mon Dieu! I am not saying that he was in love with me, but I certainly pleased him. I could not doubt that, at least. Would he otherwise have put up with all my childish caprices? Would he have passed a whole night in trying to persuade me? He was very agitated, very anxious to please me; and he gave in to my prayer, always begging him for more time.

'Not today. Wait. I will come back, I promise you.' He gave way: this man before whom all gave way. It was this, perhaps, that charmed him. We continued together in this way until five in the morning, and then it was time to go.

'You must be tired, dear Georgina. Until tomorrow. You will come, won't you?'

'Oh, yes, with great happiness. You are too good and kind not to be loved, and I do love you with all my heart!'

Napoleon put on her shawl, arranged her lace veil over her head, and then took her in his arms and kissed her on the forehead. And at this Georgina giggled and said, 'Oh, you're kissing Prince Sapiéha's veil!'

57

The observation showed a certain silliness; but the First Consul was in love and in a mood to enjoy the transports of jealousy. In a flash the lace veil was snatched off Georgina's head, the cashmere shawl off her shoulders. The veil was torn into fragments, the shawl trampled underfoot. Not only this, a modest cornelian necklace was snapped in pieces and flung aside, and an innocent ring containing a lock of Raucourt's hair was pulled from Georgina's finger and ground beneath the Consular heel.

'Dearest Georgina,' Napoleon said. 'You must have nothing except what I give you. Now don't be cross with me, or I shall not think much of your sentiments.'

One could not be annoyed for long with such a man. There was such charm and attraction in his voice that one was obliged to say: 'Really, he has done right.' (I swear on my life that all this is true.)

'You are quite right,' I said. 'No, I'm not cross, though I'm going to be rather cold going home.'

Napoleon rang for Constant and told him to fetch a white cashmere shawl and a large veil of English lace. And Constant was able to produce these objects in a moment, no doubt from Joséphine's ample store rooms.

The Consul escorted Georgina to the waiting carriage, saying, 'I will see you tomorrow, Georgina.'

'And there,' says Mlle George, 'is literally my first meeting with this immense man.'

Constant, who had had to wait up in an ante-room all night, was very tired and dozed all the way to Paris; but he roused up when they reached the house in the rue St Honoré and said, 'I will come for you again tonight, Madame, at eight o'clock.'

'No, I am not at all sure,' said Georgina, assailed by doubts in the chill of dawn. 'Come during the afternoon and I'll let you know. Tell the Consul I am very tired but will do my best to keep my promise.'

Her next and very typical sentence gives us the information that Talma called on her during the morning and that she told him everything. '*Je disais tout à mon bon Talma.*'

9

TALMA'S suspicions had been aroused the previous evening at the theatre, where Georgina had arrived in her virginal attire of white muslin and lace, obviously dressed for some extraordinary occasion and hoping to be observed. She had been called for, had left the theatre looking agitated, and had driven away . . . where to? Talma had come to ask questions, because gossip and scandal were what all Paris lived for and he saw an opportunity for being first with the latest news.

Georgina had already told the excited Clémentine every detail of the night's events, but since she could think of nothing else she was glad to pour the story out again into Talma's attentive ear. She painted a pleasing picture of herself as she chattered, showing herself as modest, conscientious and full of creditable scruples. She assured Talma she was frightened by the prospect before her. The Consul was so great and powerful, and she was nothing but a simple actress! It was not easy to love such a man. She hesitated very much. . . .

'What! You hesitate?' said Talma. 'Are you mad? Think what a position you will have!' And he gave Georgina all the encouragement she was wanting, and helped her to thrash out the various aspects of the situation with such enthusiasm that she invited him to stay to dinner. 'We can talk about him,' she said. 'You know him so well, you see him so often with his wife, the charming Joséphine.'

But Talma replied, 'I cannot dine with you, my dear friend, to my great regret, because my wife is expecting me.'

And Georgina, who, for being loved by Jupiter himself, was the more mindful of her right to the admiration of lesser beings, took immediate offence. If Napoleon forgot his wife in her presence, surely it was the least other men could do? And she replied coldly, 'No doubt it looks well to get married, but at times it's not very convenient. Go along, then, my dear Talma, it's late. My compliments to Mme Talma.'

Talma drove away to tell the remarkable news to his wife, and it was soon known to all Paris.

Constant called on Georgina at three o'clock and received his orders; at eight in the evening he returned to take her out to St Cloud, this time coming to her own door. The valet, who had little to think of apart from this intrigue of his master's, was excessively friendly. 'The Consul is absolutely delighted with you,' he said. 'He thinks you're perfectly charming and he's waiting for you more impatiently than ever.' But Georgina, forgetting how she had encouraged such familiarity the night before, was cold and silent. What? The Consul had been discussing her with his valet? The thought exasperated her. But in all honesty she adds in her memoirs: 'After all, why not? I chattered enough with Clémentine!'

The Consul was waiting for her when she arrived at the palace. She describes his smile on seeing her as '*céleste*', his manner sweet, seductive and fascinating.

The affectionate greeting over, the great man showed that he had been making enquiries. 'Well, Georgina,' he observed, 'you told me the truth. The little ring I destroyed came, just as you said, from Mlle Raucourt; the other objects were from that handsome prince of yours, Sapiéha. You have, I trust, already requested him to put an end to his visits and his prodigalities?'

'No,' said the astonished Georgina, who had little anticipated that the honour of being called to St Cloud would bring with it such disadvantages. 'No, I confess frankly I had not dreamed of doing such a thing.'

'Never mind,' said the Consul, easily but firmly. 'He will understand. You will see no more of him.'

According to Georgina's account, the night was not unlike the previous one. The Consul was eloquent in declarations of love, sympathy and understanding, but was too gallant to force himself upon an 'innocent and modest young girl', as she calls herself. Instead, he implored, he pleaded with her.

'Yes, I love you,' Georgina said eventually. 'But I'm afraid of loving you too much and being unhappy. You are too great and powerful to give yourself up wholly to anything but politics. We poor women are taken up, then thrown aside and forgotten. We are only toys to amuse you for a little while; and although you're the First Consul, I'm not satisfied to be your toy.'

'But if you're my favourite toy, you won't complain, I hope? Come, Georgina, don't be so suspicious about me, or you'll annoy me.'

'Very well,' said Georgina, 'I'll come back tomorrow.'

'You see how I give way to you, letting you go like this without your giving me a proof of your love. . . . Go along, then, Georgina. Until tomorrow.'

'Oh, I had forgotten. I am acting tomorrow night.'

'Good. I will come and watch. Afterwards, the carriage will be waiting for you.'

'But I shall be tired.'

However, the Consul began to grow impatient, and he firmly demanded a solemn promise from her that she would not only come but would give way to his desires; and upon her agreeing to this, he took from his pocket two fine diamonds in the form of ear-rings and gave them to her. 'These are for you, my dear Georgina,' he said. 'I spoilt your jewellery last night, it's only right I should repair the damage I did.' He embraced her affectionately and they parted.

Cinna was the play performed at the Théâtre Français the following night. It was Napoleon's favourite tragedy; but when Georgina entered the scene as Emilie the Consular box was empty. At once she felt hurt and offended. After his promise to come, his protestations of adoration, she took his absence as an insult. If this was how he treated her, not on any account would she go to St Cloud again. She was thankful she had resisted him; he had had a passing whim for her and nothing more. Well, so much the better! She was free to do as she pleased. So her thoughts revolved in an agony of self-pity as she heard herself reciting her lines lifelessly and monotonously.

But at the end of her monologue there was a sudden stir in the audience, followed by a storm of applause. The Consul had arrived and the whole theatre came suddenly to life. 'Begin again, begin again!' cried the audience to Mlle George; and with bright eyes and a ringing, expressive voice the young actress went through her lines once more. With Talma in the role of Cinna and Monvel as Augustus, the performance was brilliant; and if the presence of the Consul inspired Mlle George, elated as she was at the prospect of being his mistress, it had hardly less effect on the other actors, so evident was his interest, his close attention to the meaning of every word. About Talma's performance in this play, Mlle George is at a loss for words when she describes it in her memoirs. Like so many others, she speaks of his superlatively great art. He could portray terrible emotions so perfectly, she says, that members of the audience would turn away at times, unable to look at him. On the stage one could see how he made use of every facial muscle. Future generations would never believe such emotional effects could be created. 'And they will be right,' she says, 'for they will never have seen anything like it.'

As far as she herself was concerned, admiring the marvellous acting about her and lifted up by its emotional atmosphere, she strove to surpass herself and gave an unusually good performance. She was applauded enthusiastically; but she little expected the roar of applause which she received at a certain moment in the fifth act. She spoke the line, 'If I have charmed Cinna, I shall charm other men as well.' And the audience cheered and turned its gaze suggestively from the stage to the Consular box. All Paris was interested in the gossip that was circulating about Napoleon and Mlle George. There were three outbursts of frenzied applause, and the actress felt herself turning scarlet. What would the Consul say to her, after begging her to be discreet? And yet she had told no one but Talma. . . .

Talma himself hurried into her dressing-room after the performance. 'Well, you heard?' he said, looking agitated.

'Yes, and I'm rather worried. So long as the Consul doesn't accuse me of indiscretion! But, after all, what does it matter? I suppose the public thought they were paying me a graceful compliment. Get along, Talma, someone is waiting for me.'

Once more Georgina drove out to St Cloud. The Consul received her eagerly, and was still under the spell of the play.

'It was a wonderful performance,' he said. 'Talma was really sublime. And Monvel is an actor of great profundity. Unfortunately, nature has not treated him well. No one can achieve a great reputation with a figure like that and such a poor voice. In the theatre all must be ideal. No one wants heroes who are not fine figures of men. Monvel combats these defects by his intellect; but charm is lacking. You gave a beautiful performance, too, Georgina.'

'I did my best to deserve your approval, which is more flattering to me than any other I could have.'

'Hullo! You're turning into a courtier!'

'I'm trying to make myself a fine lady,' said Georgina, laughing.

'You're trying to be tiresome, you mean. Be yourself. I prefer Georgina to any countess.'

He overwhelmed me with kindness [Georgina's memoirs continue]. 'Sit here next to me,' he said. 'You must be rather tired. Take off your shawl and your hat so that I can see you a little.'

Little by little he helped me off with my clothes. And he made himself my *femme de chambre* with so much gaiety, so much grace and tact, that it was impossible not to give in to him despite oneself. It was impossible not to be fascinated and drawn towards this man. He made himself humble for my sake. He was no longer the Consul. He was a man in love, perhaps, but it was a love without violence or abruptness.

I left him at seven in the morning. But feeling ashamed of the charming disorder the night had caused, I said,

'Please let me tidy everything up.'

'Yes, my dear Georgina. I will help you.'

And he was kind enough to make a show of straightening out that couch with me, the scene of such abandon and affection. . . . In order to know this great man, one had to see him in intimacy. There, rid of his vast thoughts, he took pleasure in all the little details of simple, human life; he relaxed from being himself.

They parted affectionately, but Georgina said: 'I'm afraid of loving you too well. You are not made for me, I know, and I shall be unhappy. . . .'

'Come,' the Consul replied, 'you're no good at all as a prophetess! I shall always be good to you. But we're not there yet. Kiss me and be happy.'

Georgina returned home, tired but elated. She was in love with the Consul, and the future looked as brilliant as those diamond ear-rings he had given her. At the age of sixteen, indeed, she could feel that there was little more for life to offer, so high she had risen in less than a season. She talked to Clémentine, looked in the mirror and refused to see visitors, 'except for my faithful Talma, who came round almost running'.

'Well,' said Talma, 'and did he say anything about that terrible applause after "If I have charmed Cinna . . ."?'

'He didn't say a word about it,' said Georgina. 'But he did say that your acting was sublime, my dear Talma. And how well he talks about the theatre! What good criticisms he gives!'

Talma asked Georgina when she was next going to St Cloud, and he observed that most women would give anything to be in her place. He urged her to be duly grateful, assured her she would find a better man nowhere, and advised her to be discreet in her conduct. 'Don't do anything for which you could be reproached,' he said. 'The Consul values decency above everything.'

While he lectured and advised, Talma, who was shortsighted, peered closely at his friend and suddenly stopped short. 'What on earth have you got on your ears?' he asked.

'Oh, I had forgotten to take them off. They're a pair of ear-rings the Consul gave me the night before last.' And Georgina passed them to Talma, who examined them with respect.

'These are superb stones you have here,' he said.

'Yes, they are certainly beautiful,' said Georgina. 'But it was his way of giving them to me that I appreciated most. How could anyone fail to love him? The fact is, Talma, I am wild about him.'

'You are right. Indeed, I would say that such an attitude is most reasonable! Are you coming to the theatre this evening?'

'I don't really want to.'

'Why not?'

'I feel I look very pale.'

'Oh, you never have any colour, and you know very well it suits you to be pale. You look much as usual. Come along, and we'll talk about him together. Ah, I love him well enough myself, you know.'

Georgina allowed herself to be persuaded and spent the evening at the theatre. In her memoirs she describes the room, half dressing-room, half sitting-room used by the actresses during the performance. As one actress left her chair to enter the scene, so another took her place. Here, in between their appearances, they discussed all that was going on and spared no one their criticisms. That evening Sedaine's *Le Philosophe sans le Savoir* was being played, and Mlle Mars was taking the part of Victorine. Mlle Mars, young and gifted, was already considered one of the finest of French actresses; between her and Mlle George there was no rivalry, for Mars did not act in tragedies. They were on good terms, and Georgina listened silently to the malicious remarks being made about Mars each time she left the room. Unable to assail her talent, her colleagues talked of her age. It was a mania of the times. A woman need only be past twenty to be the butt of everyone on the score of her waning charm. Mars was twenty-three at this time; Duchesnois, as a débutante of twenty-five, had been made to feel unbearably ill at ease and self-conscious on the score of her age. It is not surprising that Joséphine, now almost forty years old, felt that disaster was upon her.

Presently Mars came off the stage and threw herself on to a chair beside Georgina.

'Good evening, George,' she said. 'How's everything?'

'Very well, thanks. And you?'

'Me? So, so. I'm not in good form. I shall be glad when it's over. My God, George! Those brilliant rays shooting out from your ears make my head ache!'

'From my ears? What do you mean?'

'Those great diamonds.'

'Oh,' said Georgina, putting her hand up to one of her ears

and assuming the air of one who had forgotten the existence of the costly jewels.

'Take them off and let's have a look,' said Mars.

'I can't take them off,' said Georgina. 'You can see them well enough. Surely there's nothing so unusual about a diamond ear-ring?'

'But they're such a colossal size, your diamonds. It's a king's ransom you're wearing on your ears.'

'Neither king nor ransom,' said Georgina. 'They brought them round for me to see, they are allowing me time to pay— that's all. You'd have done just the same yourself, Mars. You know how you like pretty things when you can get them. Every-one does, of course, but women above all.'

'Quite, quite, my dear George. But they did right to give you time. You'll need a vast amount of it to pay for those diamonds!'

Georgina was thankful when the moment came for Mars to go back on to the stage; although very anxious that her ear-rings should be noticed, and satisfied to arouse envy, she did not enjoy Mars's evident amusement. But now Talma arrived, full of sympathy and admiration.

'Ah, at last, Talma!' Georgina cried. 'Come along, take me away from these envious, gossiping women.'

'Why, what's wrong?' said Talma, taking her arm and leading her away from the room.

'What's wrong? Nothing, except your *jeune ingénue* Mars has discovered my ear-rings, which I had left on under my hat because I'd completely forgotten about them. And she's been cross-examining me for half an hour, trying to find out where they came from.'

'Well, what do you expect? You must realize that secrecy is impossible.'

'You see, Talma, I was right to be afraid of such great happi-ness. It's a joy to think I'm loved by this man, but I can see I'm going to be worried about it all the time. I haven't any illusions, my dear Talma; it will be a difficult and hopeless existence. When I'm away from him nothing can please me, I care for no one else. He may be the First Consul, but when he's alone with me he's just a charming, unassuming man who makes me forget how powerful he is. I can't help feeling both proud and sad at the same time. My carriage is waiting; come and have a cup of tea with me and then it will take you home.'

Talma accepted the invitation, and Georgina gave vent to her irritation with her colleagues of the theatre. 'You've no idea how spiteful women are, Talma . . . a new piece of jewellery, and they're all on tenterhooks. They devour you with their eyes, they try to peer into the bottom of your heart. . . . Well, it's something I cannot understand and could never descend to myself. Would it annoy me if they were wearing valuable jewellery? Certainly not! I should be only too happy to see the envious creatures getting all they want. . . .' And so on.

The following evening, when she drove out to her fourth rendezvous at St Cloud, Georgina was still feeling the need to complain about the envy and malice she thought she detected in her colleagues. She tells us in her memoirs how kindly Napoleon listened to her grievances, being so full of love and sympathy, that she soon became happy and light-hearted once more.

'Tell me everything, Georgina,' he said.

'Well, yesterday I was really persecuted by Mlle Mars. I had on your ear-rings and neither curiosity nor questions were spared me. I'm so afraid they suspect where they came from. And yet I am most discreet.'

'Well, what can you expect? Let them talk, let them imagine. I shan't blame you for it. Continue to be good and kind, Georgina, no woman can be anything better than that.'

The night passed happily. The Consul was both amorous and light-hearted. 'The hours I spent with him slipped by uncounted, and the morning came to astonish us.'

Now there was no looking back. Georgina was committed to being the Consul's mistress and to all that went with such a situation. She knew that perfect propriety would be expected of her in her private life and that she must be entirely submissive to the will of her august lover. Prince Sapiéha had vanished, proud, it may be, to have been supplanted by one so glorious. He raised no protest, but repaired tactfully to his native land.

Napoleon's police, who reported on the movements of distinguished foreigners, noted: 'Mlle George has recently sustained a great loss. The Prince Sapiéha has left to return to Poland. He gave her, it is said, 5,000 francs a night. Even if we must reduce this figure by half, it still leaves her an honest profit.'

10

NAPOLEON was infatuated by Mlle George and sent for her whenever he had the time to spare. He and his wife changed their residence from St Cloud to the Palace of the Tuileries in Paris, and the nocturnal visits became easier. The old palace was well supplied with back stairs and convenient, silent rooms far away from the main activities of the lives of its occupants, and the young actress would be escorted from the theatre or her home by Constant and led furtively to a specially prepared suite of rooms at the top of the building.

The intrigue was intoxicating. Yet Georgina's daily life was less easily delightful than it had been. She had been a goddess whom the Prince Sapiéha had regarded as being entitled to every privilege and whose bills he had paid unasked. He had been the perfect attendant. The position was now reversed, and it was Georgina's turn to attend.

Napoleon was not the man to fling money about. He had given the costly ear-rings, and he kept his mistress well supplied with funds. But his gifts appear to have been intermittent and not excessive. She was undoubtedly less well off than she had been. Not that this mattered to her at the moment. Tradespeople were delighted to supply all she asked for; as Napoleon's mistress she had unlimited credit.

Her prestige in the fashionable world, too, had increased enormously. No one, it was felt, was more entitled to consideration and respect. Her parents, though making a stand for the

68

MLLE. GEORGE

NAPOLEON

The First Consul

moral code on a lower level, were swept off their feet by the name of Bonaparte and were proud of their daughter's triumph; if money was a little less plentiful they did not know it; attentions were lavished upon them as before and they basked in luxury and satisfied pride. In fact, family, servants, friends and the world at large looked on with that unreasoning and unqualified admiration which can be expected when a popular actress is having a love affair with the leader of a nation. 'Everyone,' says Mlle George, speaking of this time, 'knew what I wanted so much to hide.'

It was not true that Georgina wanted to hide an affair which made her so widely envied. But it was true that everyone knew about it.

Everyone knew, and therefore Mme Joséphine Bonaparte knew. Her husband had deserted her for several nights at St Cloud, making the excuse that he was hard at work in his study. Then the rumours that were beginning to circulate in Paris reached her, and she charged him with being unfaithful to her. Joséphine could never hide her feelings, and she shed tears, reminded Napoleon of her love for him and reproached him bitterly for changing towards her.

Napoleon was irritable and assured her he had not changed in any way. She was a silly, suspicious woman who listened to gossip, he said. Did she not realize that in their position unfounded gossip was inevitable? Naturally he cared for no one but herself. She knew that perfectly well. But he could not be tied to her at every moment of the night and day. He was extra hard at work just now, thanks to the machinations of unscrupulous men. He did not trust William Pitt at all, and there was a great deal he had to keep his eyes on. He begged her not to harass him further with idiotic feminine scenes. She knew how it worried him.

Joséphine, disarmed by this projection of guilt on to herself, dried her eyes and apologized. It was true, she reflected, that most of the gossip concerning her husband was wicked calumny coming from his sisters. These sisters were ladies of leisure who employed much of their time in making trouble between herself and her husband; their latest fabrication had been that Napoleon was the father of her daughter's child. Certainly it was wisest to ignore all rumours.

But as the days passed the rumours increased, and Joséphine was unable to escape from the sad realization that Napoleon's manner towards her was completely changed. He neglected her; he looked through her instead of at her, even when she had surpassed herself in the art of her *toilette*; and if she insisted on drawing him into conversation he was cold and irritable. At other times he would appear to be radiantly happy, but with an absent look in his eye; it was a happiness in which she had no share. She felt sure he was in love. Deeply distressed, she poured out all her feelings to Mme de Rémusat, her favourite lady-in-waiting, a woman much younger than herself but able and very ready to give her sensible advice. Mme de Rémusat did her best to reassure her mistress; but Joséphine's anguish was not assuaged for long, and in Paris she set her personal servants to spy on her husband. Her valets were soon able to report that a mysterious young lady was being brought into the palace at nights. And now there were many scenes between Joséphine and her husband, for she did not attempt to hide her despair. She heaped reproaches on Napoleon, refused to listen to his denials and wept helplessly.

Since coming to Paris, Napoleon had been as cautious as he could. Georgina was introduced into his private apartments with great secrecy, being brought in by an inconspicuous side-door and up carefully guarded staircases. She was usually sent for on the nights when she was not acting, so that she could come early and he could join his wife later on; and although it was always in the early hours of the morning that his mistress left, he would tell Joséphine that he had been at his desk all this time.

Joséphine, however, was no longer to be placated. Her valets continued their spying, and soon she had definite information that the unwelcome nocturnal visitor was her friend Raucourt's pupil, the innocent little Mlle George. In a frenzy, Joséphine sought to discover how serious the affair was. Had George any capacity to move Napoleon seriously? Her enquiries did not reassure her. Mlle George, everyone told her, was refined and charming as well as being so superlatively beautiful. No one was more fastidious than Napoleon, more ready to be thrown into a state of cold disapproval by the least imperfection of dress or person; Joséphine's days were spent in the attempt to please his over-civilized senses, and such was her taste, skill and zeal that so far she had never feared serious rivalry. But Georgina, too, was impeccable. People told her how greatly the actress loved baths, and, indeed, Georgina's passion for cleanliness was in time to become proverbial.

Joséphine, the supreme courtesan, felt herself threatened. Now forty years of age, she was struggling against a wrinkled skin and deteriorating teeth. She had no desire, no interest, beyond her sensual instincts. She lived for love and for nothing else, and all her happiness lay in charming Napoleon. Much of her day was spent in trying on and buying the finest and most elegant clothes the arts and crafts of France could produce, in trying new beauty preparations, having her hair dressed and being painted with cosmetics. The flowers, the gardens, the master-pieces of the cabinet-maker's art, the decorative schemes and all the beauty, created or natural, that she loved so passionately—all these were envisaged as the setting of her idyllic amours. Emotion now was permanently fixed upon her husband; for in him were centred all things; he was young and virile, he was sensitive and responsive to her charms, and he gave her the only position to which she could aspire. No lurking thought that someone else could give her more could lure her desires elsewhere; and so, in a world where all is in a state of perpetual change, and where she followed the path of the most changeable of all women, the courtesan, her emotions were in a curious way fixed and per-petuated by the combination of circumstances.

Joséphine wished always to renew herself and to renew her surroundings, so that her husband should never become accus-tomed to her, never indifferent. Love alone would enable her to hold her position. Napoleon's wish for a son was an ever-present excuse for divorce. She had countered the danger by claiming that, since she had had children by her first marriage, it was Napoleon himself who was impotent. None of Napoleon's mistresses, indeed, had had children, and he was somewhat worried on this score. But although Joséphine trusted she was right in her assertions, she knew that one could never be certain. It was essential, she felt, to keep his affections centred upon herself. Divorce had once been in his mind, and the question could always arise again; in fact, she knew her brothers- and sisters-in-law often brought it to his mind, although without making any impression, since he was devoted to her. Now she saw that she was in danger of losing her hold upon him; if that should happen, her security would be lost.

After a time, seeing that his wife had proof of his affair with Mlle George, Napoleon ceased his denials, though not his reproaches. He now charged her with lack of understanding. His delight with Georgina increased, and he would have liked to find a sympathetic ear into which he could pour his praise of his mistress. Truly Georgina was a woman apart! She was all goodness, discretion and devotion; and then she was so gay and lively, so sweet and unselfish; he was delighted with himself for discovering her; he might even marry her off to one of his generals some time in the distant future, as he did his sisters and their friends. He was exasperated by Joséphine's continual outbursts of weeping. He even expected approval and assured her he was entitled to any distraction he wished for. 'I am not like other men,' Mme de Rémusat quotes him as saying, 'and the ordinary laws of morality and rules of propriety do not apply to me.' Such declarations drove Joséphine to further tears and complaints, and her husband would then become so angry that at times he would speak to her with a violence which Mme de Rémusat says she would hardly dare to describe.

Joséphine always waited for her husband for dinner, the one meal of the day which they took together, and would never begin without him even if he did not turn up until ten or eleven at night. Nor would she go to bed until he was also ready to do so. Therefore she now had many sad and wearying sessions alone or in the company of one or other of her ladies. Mme de Rémusat describes one of these in her memoirs.

It was during that winter. Bonaparte was still in the habit of sharing his wife's bed. She had been clever enough to persuade him that this intimacy ensured his personal security. Being a very light sleeper, she said, she would be instantly alert if anyone made a nocturnal attempt on his life and could give an immediate warning. At night she never retired until informed that Bonaparte had gone to his rooms. But when he was caught by this passion for Mlle George, whom he would send for after he had finished working, there were certain occasions when he did not come downstairs until the night was far advanced.

One night, more troubled than usual by jealousy and uneasiness, Mme Bonaparte kept me with her and regaled me with a heartfelt outpouring of her troubles. It was one o'clock in the morning; we were alone in the salon. A profound silence reigned in the Tuileries.

'I can't rest,' she suddenly said to me. 'Mlle George is up there, I feel sure. I'm going up to see if I can take them by surprise.'

Not a little worried by this sudden resolve, I did what I could to dissuade her; but without success.

'Follow me,' she said. 'We'll go up together.'

I put it to her that such spying, unwise even on her part, would be quite intolerable on mine, and that if she should find what she suspected, I should certainly be *de trop* in the scene that must inevitably take place. But she would listen to nothing, and urged me so vehemently that, despite my repugnance, I gave way to her will, consoling myself with the inward thought that we should achieve nothing, since Bonaparte would have taken all precautions against surprise.

Here we are then, creeping silently up a secret staircase that leads to Bonaparte's rooms. Mme Bonaparte, exceedingly agitated, going first, and I following, lighting the way and feeling much ashamed of my role.

Half-way through our journey, however, the stillness was interrupted by a small sound. Mme Bonaparte turned to whisper to me.

'It's perhaps Roustan,' she said, 'Bonaparte's black servant, guarding the door. The brute is perfectly capable of cutting both our throats!'

At this, I was seized with panic. Without reflecting that I was leaving Mme Bonaparte in absolute darkness, I turned and rushed downstairs with the candle I was carrying, precipitating myself back into the salon with the utmost speed.

She followed me a few minutes after, astonished at my sudden flight. When she saw my startled face, she began laughing and this set me laughing too. So our enterprise ended. I left her, saying that I believed the fright she had thrown me into had served her well, and that I had done right to give way to it.

11

At least Joséphine could assist Mlle Duchesnois, who was having so sad and difficult a time, and was still being kept in comparative obscurity by the intriguers of the Comédie Française. She could express a desire to see her as Phèdre, and she could persist, however many specious reasons against such a performance were presented to her. The time was approaching for Georgina's first appearance in the title-role of Racine's masterpiece, and it would have been to her great advantage, as Raucourt and Talma knew, if all thought of Duchesnois's performance could have been kept out of the brief memory of the public mind. But Mme Bonaparte wished to see Duchesnois's Phèdre on a particular evening, shortly before the appearance of Mlle George in the role; and so there were to be two performances, two versions, of the great play, and the public regarded the event as a contest which would decide which of the actresses would take the leading place in the theatre.

Napoleon was not a forthright tyrant, or his mistress could have persuaded him to suppress the performance arranged for her rival. Although he considered the Théâtre Français was there for his use and pleasure, as it had been there, formerly, for the pleasure of the kings of France, he refrained from exerting his influence in any strictly personal matter. He had recently given M. de Rémusat, his Palace Prefect, the task of controlling the theatre, and the authority above was the Minister of the Interior, Chaptal. He did not interfere with the decisions of either of them. Mme de Rémusat was devoted to Joséphine and disgusted by the conduct of Mlle George. It must have been with some alacrity that M. de Rémusat, a man who lived in harmony and sympathy with his wife, insisted against even the most impudent protests that Duchesnois should appear as Phèdre.

The annual salary of beginners at the Comédie Française was about 4,000 francs. This did not allow an actress very much for her theatrical dresses, which she had to provide herself; and Joséphine, who knew Duchesnois had no rich lover to assist her, told her that she would provide a special costume for the performance. With her impeccable and conciliatory tact, she ordered one to be made for George also. Certainly that of Duchesnois was rather more costly and brilliant, but both were very beautiful. The dresses had wide bands of fine gold embroidery round the hem; Duchesnois had a scarlet cloak strewn with stars, and George had a blue cloak with simple embroidery. The Consul was equally tactful and sent each actress a present of 3,000 francs.

Raucourt and Talma took great trouble in preparing Georgina for the great task. Phèdre is one of the most difficult parts to play, and they knew she was incapable of reaching the level of her rival. Talma was ingenious in seeking to make use of every quality she possessed. Her voice had great volume, and what she lacked in depth of feeling was to be made up for by a series of shocks, by unexpected gestures and contrasts of tone.

On the appointed night Duchesnois appeared in the striking dress and gave a brilliant and finished performance. The extreme enthusiasm of most of the audience showed how pleased the public was to see her brought once more into prominence; but at the same time there was a fair amount of organized disturbance, for the friends and supporters of George had come in large numbers to wreck the evening if they could. None the less, in spite of the hostility of the leading critics, inspired by Geoffroy, the performance had been so remarkable that news of its excellence spread about Paris and there was small chance now of suppressing the actress altogether.

When the night of Georgina's performance arrived, the audience consisted largely of friends. The critics favourable to her were assembled and there was no likelihood of failure. Certainly she was radiantly beautiful; Joséphine's blue costume suited her, and her entry was greeted with prolonged applause. Thanks to Talma's coaching, she went through her difficult part with remarkable effect, electrifying the audience by her originality. Whereas Duchesnois had been restrained, emotional and touching, George was tempestuous and violent. Throughout, the methods of her rival were carefully avoided, and she declaimed and gesticulated furiously, silencing the few adversaries present and calling down a roar of enthusiasm from the rest. In the vanity of all her recent successes and her emotional satisfaction, she had become overweeningly confident and did not doubt for a moment that she far outshone her rival; hostility towards Duchesnois lent conviction to her declarations of love for Hippolytus; ambition and determination made her movements imperious. The presence of her lover, watching her attentively from the scarlet velvet setting of his box, made her eyes shine. Even Joséphine, smiling and inscrutable at Bonaparte's side, was applauding her.

Geoffroy pronounced upon the performance the following day in the *Journal des Débats*, and the triumph of Mlle George was confirmed. Yet many realized in retrospect that her rendering of Phèdre had been melodramatic; and when next Duchesnois appeared her superiority was evident and fierce arguments arose in the Press, the salons and the cafés of Paris. Duchesnois was at least in the forefront of the news, and Raucourt and her following had to resign themselves to seeing her on the boards from time to time.

Georgina, who took all the gossip of the theatre to her lover, found in him an ardent partisan in this quarrel, and he made it clear to M. de Rémusat that the more Mlle George was given the roles she wanted and the more Duchesnois was kept out of sight the better he would be pleased. Beyond this he did not go. He let his Prefect know his views, and that was all. Had all else been equal, M. de Rémusat would no doubt have done his best to forward Mlle George's ambitions; but as things were he and his wife disapproved of the little favourite, and he was glad that Joséphine was there to use her influence on the side of Duchesnois. There were, too, the older habitués of the Comédie Française, and the intellectual members of society in general, who must be considered. These people were of great importance in the artistic world and their opinion could not be ignored. The position of the Palace Prefect was not easy. 'On the one hand,' Mme de Rémusat writes in her memoirs, 'the public of Paris increasingly took the side of the plain actress. The beauty was often hissed. M. de Rémusat tried to give an equal protection to both débutantes; but whatever he did for one or the other was the cause of dissatisfaction either to the audience or to the Consul.' Napoleon does not appear to have been altogether deceived with regard to the two actresses, however. In a conversation with his brother Lucien which took place round about this time, he gave it as his opinion that Mlle George was the most beautiful woman in Europe; but he added: 'It is a pity this charming actress has not a talent proportioned to her beauty.'[1] In fact, Duchesnois performed before him very frequently, both during the Consulate and later.

A certain section of the public demanded the appearances of Duchesnois; there were newspapers that encouraged her, too, and ran down Mlle George. But Georgina's supporters were strong, and at every one of Duchesnois's performances they distributed about four hundred free tickets to those who were willing to hiss and make disturbances throughout the evening. This nightly assault on Duchesnois, so corrupt and brutal, aroused the inevitable reaction from the disinterested playgoer, and often there was turmoil in the theatre. Two factions were formed, popularly called *Georgiens* and *Carcassiens*, a poor play on words. The country of Georgia borders upon Circassia, and *Circassien* was changed to *Carcassien* as being suitable to a follower of the very thin Duchesnois.

The excitement in the theatre whenever George or Duchesnois appeared was so great that the police often had to be called in. Men shouted, argued and often came to blows; and one night emotion was so strong that fists were not enough and a column supporting the balcony was torn down as a weapon. This was the year of 1803; the world was engaged in a deadly conflict of ideas which was tearing the entire globe into political factions.

[1] Lucien Bonaparte, *Mémoires*, Vol. II, p. 290.

77

But Parisians saw no other conflict but this in the Comédie Française, and the battle between two rival débutantes was the most interesting event of the year to them.

Geoffroy, the learned critic, had gradually become the leader of the cabal formed against Duchesnois; he poured the most unmeasured and fulsome adulation on to George, and reserved for her rival all his skill in the expression of contempt and ridicule. Duchesnois was spared no humiliation by the venomous critic. Many have spoken of her as a touching figure, quiet and sad under the violence of the persecution she had called up by daring to be so superior in ability to George. The power of her acting increased with experience, and the intelligent habitués of the theatre refused to accept the verdict of Geoffroy. As time went by, her admirers increased in number; but the relentless underground struggle against her did not abate.

Georgina's acting improved with practice to a small degree, largely owing to the constant vigilance of Raucourt and Talma, both of them proud of the theatre's artistic reputation. Without their supervision she would have taken scant trouble. Surrounded by flattery, acclaimed by Geoffroy, she felt no need to improve, and she had no difficulty in believing that the adverse criticism she received in certain papers was due to malice or lack of discrimination.

Joséphine had some satisfaction in seeing Duchesnois's growing reputation, but her worries concerning Mlle George did not diminish. Her husband seldom failed to appear at the theatre when his mistress was playing, and this, she thought, created a bad impression. Even Mlle George says in her memoirs: 'No doubt he came too often.' His presence certainly did nothing to discourage the rumours that were going about.

Poor Joséphine's anguish reached a climax when Napoleon hinted to her that she would be very much more comfortable if, henceforth, they were to occupy separate rooms at night. She countered the proposal with her usual skill, but was certain she had not heard the end of it.

12

WHILE Joséphine was spending long and lonely hours repining, while she complained endlessly to Mme de Rémusat about the treacherous George, whom she had thought so innocent and candid, Napoleon enjoyed himself in a carefree spirit, as the memoirs of the erring actress show:

I can still see that suite of rooms in the Tuileries, with the little windows above the great apartments. There was a salon, and a bedroom in which was a kind of boudoir. My dear little windows, how often I looked at you! I was so attached to them that I always went for my bath to the *bains Vigier*, because I had a view there of my dear little windows when I was bathing. I was as sentimental as possible!

'Look, Clémentine,' I would say. 'Have a good look at those two little windows up there with the shutters. Those are my rooms —it's there that I am loved. Oh, I am in love with my good, handsome Consul. . . .'

To reach the pretty little suite of rooms, I had to climb a horrible staircase and go along dark corridors.

'Ah, Constant! What a height! I can't go any further.'

'Sh! Don't make such a noise!'

'Why "Sh"? You never said "Sh" at St Cloud. I get bored with all your hushing. There seem to be people everywhere here.'

Now we have arrived! I always entered by a small ante-room which led into the bedroom. The Consul had not yet come upstairs. I took off my cashmere shawl. I was in the habit of bringing an extra pair of shoes, because at St Cloud I had to cross the Orangery. I was about to change, when I noticed I had lost one of the shoes on those frightful stairs.

'Ah, my God, Constant! I've lost a shoe! Quick! Run! My name is in all my shoes. Whatever will the Consul say? Run! Run!'

While Constant hurried after the unfortunate shoe, the Consul arrived, kind and tender as usual; but I was extremely worried.

'What is wrong, Georgina? Come, child, tell me what it is.'

'I dare not tell you what's happened. It's something dreadful. I've lost my shoe on one of those horrible stairs.'

'Surely that's a very small disaster?'

'Yes, but that's not all. My name is written in all my shoes. You see how awful it is and how I'm trembling.'

'Well, dearest Georgina, your name will be read—and he who finds your pretty white shoe will keep it, the scoundrel, as having belonged to a beautiful woman. Don't worry about it, but be glad to see me.'

They were in love, and they were light-hearted. 'My Georgina, do you really love me? Are you happy?' the Consul would ask. 'He knew very well,' the actress writes, 'that I would have died for him.' But soon youth and high spirits would prevail over sentiment. One reason why Georgina found the Consul such an ideal lover was that he shared her taste for a good romp. They had, too, identical, and very youthful, sense of humour.

One night, Georgina arrived with a wreath of white roses placed on her dark and glossy curls. Napoleon promptly took it off and put it on his own head, pranced about the room in it, then stood before a mirror admiring himself, grimacing and making absurd remarks while Georgina watched, helpless with laughter. He would not part with the wreath, but made her sing a love duet from one of the operas with him; together they parodied the song until laughter overcame them so they had to stop. In such ways they would amuse themselves for hours on end.

On another occasion, Constant greeted Georgina on her arrival at the palace by telling her the Consul was waiting for her upstairs.

I went up, but no one was there. I looked in all the rooms. I called out, but there was no answer. I rang the bell.

'Constant, has the Consul gone downstairs again?'

'No, Madame. Have a good look for him.' And he made a sign to me, pointing to the door of the boudoir. The Consul was there, hiding underneath a heap of cushions and laughing like a schoolboy.

Having found the Consul, Georgina asked whether a miniature he had promised her was yet ready; and when he told her it was

80

not she demanded a lock of his hair as a souvenir, and this was a signal for more jokes and laughter as Napoleon rushed round the rooms pretending to be afraid and Georgina pursued him, snapping a pair of scissors. 'How he laughed, the dear Consul!'

Finally he allowed her to catch him. 'Ah, the little pest!' he cried. 'Get along, then, but make sure it doesn't show.' And Georgina, shouting with laughter, snipped off a substantial lock of hair.

The abandoned Joséphine in the state apartments below would have been surprised if she had known how much of these nights spent with the queen of classical tragedy were passed in the liveliest frolicking. Napoleon was thirty-three, Joséphine was forty. At forty she could offer him a love that was still intense, but quiet, restful, sentimental; she hardly wanted to play hide-and-seek with him. Napoleon had an immense amount of vital energy, a need to laugh and sing and shout. Joséphine could not vie with him in this respect; it would have seemed senseless to her. But the sixteen-year-old Georgina encouraged him and they played about like children.

One of the characteristics that have made Napoleon such an interesting figure to study is the capacity he had for changes of mood far swifter than those of ordinary men. He could live, when he wished to, very completely in the immediate moment; he would allow no useless emotions from the previous hour to linger on and cloud the present, although he forgot no useful information. So he could enter fully into enjoyment with Georgina, although the problems he had in mind as spring approached would have kept most men preoccupied night and day. Those problems were nothing less than what the destinies of the world were to be, for two paths lay before him now, that of compromising peace and that of war and conquest. The Peace of Amiens had not brought him what he wanted, and he was faced with great decisions.

Leaving his study, after hours spent among his maps and reports, he would enter fully into domestic life as though it was his only concern. Joséphine would reproach him once again for the affair with Mlle George, and he would give himself up to arguing with her. 'Bonaparte,' says Mme de Rémusat, 'was by turn imperious, hard, defiant to excess; then suddenly he would show some feeling; he would relent and become almost sweet-tempered, repairing with a good grace the harm he had done—although he showed no sign of mending his ways.'

It seems that at this period of his life, the time when he was at his greatest, he had the power to remain inwardly untroubled by his own outer actions, and that these actions were always willed by a mind fully under control. This was shown by an event that now took place, and by which he intimated to a helpless world that he was about to plunge it anew into war.

It was March 1803. Once a month he held a reception for the diplomatic corps; it was normally a formal and insipid function; the diplomats and their wives gathered in a salon, and then Napoleon and Joséphine, followed by a lady and gentleman of their suite, would enter and address an amiable word or two to each of those present. Then, bowing and smiling to the assembly, they would retire.

On this occasion Mme de Rémusat, who was to accompany Joséphine, joined her mistress in her dressing-room a few minutes before the ceremony was due to begin. She found Napoleon in a charming humour, sitting on the floor and playing with the baby son of Hortense and Louis Bonaparte, the two-year-old Napoleon. At the same time, he critized his wife's dress, and then turned to Mme de Rémusat to see what she was wearing. He was very knowledgable about women's dress, and he gave them both his studied opinion of every aspect of their costume and appearance, doing so with his usual attention to detail, talking with the greatest amiability, making jokes and continuing all the time to amuse the baby on the floor beside him.

Now the Palace Prefect came in to say that the ambassadors were all assembled. Napoleon jumped up from the floor and all trace of gaiety dropped from him. He turned pale, he assumed an air of cold severity, his features became tense and contracted. '*Allons, mesdames!*' he said curtly to Joséphine and her lady, and he marched into the salon with a grand air. He went straight to

Lord Whitworth, the English ambassador, and fixed him with a stern, accusing look. 'So you wish for war!' he thundered. Hard, violent words poured from a mouth trembling with rage. His anger appeared to increase with every word, until it filled those present with horror. 'Mme Bonaparte and I,' says Mme de Rémusat, 'looked at each other in silent astonishment, and everyone about him was agitated.'

Nothing now could save the Peace of Amiens, and diplomatic relations with England were broken off in May. Joséphine was deeply distressed by the resumption of war, though mainly for selfish reasons. War for her meant a real possibility of divorce. A royalist herself, she would have liked to see the Bourbons restored to power, while she and her husband, great and honoured but unambitious, lived quietly and happily enjoying love and leisure. Such had been her dream and her hope; but Napoleon preferred to gamble. She knew the mentality of the exiled Bourbons and of the kings of Europe; her husband could now prevail only by subduing them all. It was a question of all or nothing. Either Napoleon would be destroyed or he would be master of the world; in the latter case he would be, as she knew he often dreamed of being, another Emperor of a United Europe, and consequently he would wish for an heir.

Ever since he had been made Consul for life he had been tempted by the possibility of taking possession of the vacant throne of France; Joséphine, when such a mood was upon him, had always urged him to adopt an heir. This Napoleon was ready to do, for the Roman emperors had been allowed to adopt their heirs according to their choice. Yet all Joséphine's hopes that Napoleon would adopt her grandson, the child of Hortense and Louis, were coming to nothing. The malice of his family was against it. She would complain about it regretfully to Mme de Rémusat.

'It is a great misfortune for me,' she said, 'that I haven't given Bonaparte a son. It would have been a sure means of keeping off all the enmity there is towards me.'

'But, Madame,' said Mme de Rémusat, 'it seems to me that the child of your daughter, Mme Louis Bonaparte, has done much to put right this disappointment; the First Consul loves him and will perhaps end by adopting him.'

'This, indeed, is what I could most wish,' Joséphine replied, 'but the suspicious, jealous character of Louis Bonaparte makes it impossible. His relations are all so malicious—they have taken good care to repeat to him all the outrageous rumours that have circulated about the conduct of my daughter and the birth of her child. Our enemies pretend the child is Bonaparte's, and that is quite enough to keep Louis from coming to an arrangement with him.'

It was true that the Bonaparte clan had taken a most violent dislike to Joséphine soon after her marriage to Napoleon, and in unison they had fanned the flames into a ferocious hatred the more remarkable when one considers the otherwise universal affection and esteem which Joséphine won by her kindliness, good temper and unassuming manner. Joséphine was silly in many respects, but no more so than her sisters-in-law, and she had at least the grace to know her failings; no one could say she did Napoleon the least harm, and yet the desire of her sisters- and brothers-in-law was to bring her low at all costs, and above all to see that her husband divorced her. To this end they were continually scheming.

Napoleon himself was much concerned with the question of providing himself with an heir. His brother, Louis, whose son he would otherwise have adopted, was an intensely disagreeable and difficult man to deal with, and if he only knew for certain that he was capable of paternity he would be strongly tempted to seek a new wife. Regarding his own capacities in this direction, his thoughts naturally turned to Georgina, so young and splendidly healthy. He had broached the subject with her and she had responded enthusiastically. She would be mad with joy, she assured him, if she were to have a child of his; and she chatted gaily about the fine bonnets and robes in which she would dress their son.

Napoleon was much attracted by the idea; how fine a child such a one would be, the son of Georgina with her pure Grecian beauty and himself, the heir of the Caesars! Surely another and more splendid race of Europeans would be begun! Georgina, though, had shown no sign of becoming pregnant, and he now sent her off, she records, 'to a woman who lived in the Faubourg St Antoine and who indicated means of becoming a mother'. Should this objective be achieved, Georgina was promised a brilliant and secure future.

Joséphine, indeed, had every reason to fear divorce at this time. Mme de Rémusat writes:

> I well remember one particular day when Bonaparte asked me to have dinner with his wife and himself. Mme Bonaparte was exceedingly agitated and excited just then because he had announced that in future he intended to spend his nights alone, in a separate apartment. No doubt he wished to avoid dining alone with her; but in the course of the meal he saw fit to take me as judge in this strange question. Was a husband obliged to give in to the fantasy of a wife who never wanted to sleep in any room but his? I was little prepared for such a question, and I knew very well that Mme Bonaparte would never forgive me if I did not take her side. I tried to avoid replying by saying that it was not possible, let alone decent, that I should take any part in determining the question. But Bonaparte, who rather liked to put me in embarrassing situations, pursued the question with great vivacity. And I could do no better to extricate myself than to say that I did not know precisely what limits there should be to the demands of a wife and the compliance of a husband, but that it seemed to me that anything which gave the impression that the First Consul was changing his mode of living was likely to give rise to undesirable gossip. The least change that took place in the Palace of the Tuileries was certain to be noted and discussed. Bonaparte began to laugh, and he pinched my ear. 'Aha!' he said. 'You are a woman, and the whole lot of you hang together.' But all the same, he adhered to the course he had decided upon, and made arrangements to use a different apartment from then onwards.

Joséphine was becoming deeply alarmed for her future, and still more jealous of Mlle George. Had she known of the actress's visits to the Faubourg St Antoine she would have been still more distressed. Probably, too, she would have said that with a girl of Mlle George's character a state of pregnancy would prove little as far as Napoleon was concerned. Napoleon, however, believed in the devotion and sincerity of his good Georgina. Besides, he had her watched very closely. 'I saw very few people, I paid very few visits,' the actress writes. 'When I went out, there was always a frightful cabriolet behind my carriage, following me. I amused myself by leading it a pretty dance and making it stop in some queer places.'

Napoleon complained at times to Mme de Rémusat that Joséphine's reproaches and tears bored him; but the young lady-in-waiting was outspoken and loyal to her mistress; she made it clear that she considered Napoleon was very much to blame and that she sympathized with his wife. On the other hand, she admitted that it might have been wiser on Joséphine's part not to employ her valets to spy upon himself and Mlle George. And this last admission was enough to send Napoleon hurrying off to his wife to tell her that her *dame du palais* thoroughly disapproved of her conduct, whereupon Mme de Rémusat would have to submit to Joséphine's reproaches. Arguments would follow, and in a frenzy Joséphine would defame her husband's character, although she was so passionately in love with him, charging him with the most extraordinary vices and insisting that, if she did not keep an eye on him and try to check him, he would gradually abandon himself to the most shameful excesses.

The court moved out to St Cloud for the summer months, and Napoleon proceeded to make his plans for the impending conflict. Two possibilities lay before him: either he must defeat the British on the Continent, or he must cross the Channel with an army and fight them in their own island. Though later events were to force him to change his plans, he was for the moment determined upon the latter project, and he had the country solidly and enthusiastically behind him, for it had long been a popular French illusion that England could easily be conquered by sea invasion. Innumerable flat-bottomed boats were already available, and others were now being made in vast numbers.

It was with terror that the neutral nations looked on; far from sharing France's easy confidence, they saw the two belligerent nations as so equally matched that they might threaten each other endlessly without being able to strike effectively; and such a situation would ruin everyone in the course of time.

Napoleon's eyes shone. Having convinced himself that war had been forced upon him, he forgot his former plans for universal peace. He went frequently to Boulogne, from which the invasion of England was to be launched, studying the tides and the weather. The more he thought of it, the more simple a matter the conquest of the neighbouring island seemed. What William the Conqueror had done, he could surely do. And in conquering England he would become master of the world.

Joséphine saw these growing ambitions with increasing depression, though her fears were all of George the actress and not of George III. The enemy was Mlle George, and Joséphine still kept her spies stationed near the entries to her husband's bedroom, with never a thought of danger from England. What harm could England do her? She could not understand what sense there was in setting forth in flat-bottomed boats to murder a lot of poor men whom one did not know and therefore could have nothing against. The contests of nations seemed to her fantastic and unreal; but Mlle George was real enough and close at hand.

Her spying valets reported that Mlle George was coming to St Cloud despite the intensive diplomatic activities on which her husband was engaged. One night, indeed, Prince Talleyrand, who was carrying on the most delicate negotiations with Russia, was sent away because the First Consul was otherwise engaged. The gossip of the servants spoke of loud laughter coming from the Consul's bedroom on these occasions, and the romantic Joséphine felt impatient. What did her husband see in this silly, empty-headed girl? Napoleon would be singing, perhaps, or pretending he was an actor. Often he and Georgina would spend their time in his library, and sometimes he would get down a volume of Corneille or Racine and go through an act or two with his mistress. Usually their abounding energy and cheerfulness was such that these rehearsals ended in the wildest merriment. Napoleon would decide to declaim from the top of the library steps, which were on wheels, and his mistress would give him a sudden push and send him flying across the room; or they would chase each other about madly.

Joséphine's nights were tormented when she knew that Mlle George had arrived, and in the morning she would renew her reproaches. Napoleon was now less angry on these occasions, however, for he was less intoxicated by the pleasures of love than by the lust for power.

'Love!' he exclaimed gaily on one occasion. 'Don't you see that love is nothing to me? What is love? It is a passion which balances the entire universe against the person loved and finds it lighter. You surely don't think I'm the man to give myself up to any such exclusive passion? What do my little distractions matter to you, since love doesn't enter into them?'

There was little consolation for Joséphine in such words, and there would have been equally little for Mlle George, had she heard them.

Joséphine, therefore, continued to feel sad and distressed until, one fine day half-way through June, she learned to her astonishment that she was to have a long holiday with her husband. Flat-bottomed boats in sufficient numbers were now ready for the invasion of England, and Napoleon was to make a detailed inspection of coastal regions combined with a diplomatic visit to the Low Countries.

To Joséphine's great delight, her husband requested her to spare no expense in the preparation of suitable clothes; and for the first time he asked the Treasury to allow him to make use of the Crown jewels for her adornment. He intended to appear as a sovereign—a sovereign, moreover, who upheld the Catholic religion and all the virtues of domestic life. He desired that Joséphine should be seen everywhere at his side; furthermore, the Papal Legate, the venerable Cardinal Caprara, was to accompany them to certain places. Thus there was no fear of any scandalous intrusion of the mistress, Georgina.

The Consul was to make his progress through the provinces and the Low Countries as a respectable man, and Georgina would be left in Paris for many weeks. It could only mean that Napoleon's infatuation was much diminished; and Joséphine, greatly relieved by this pleasing thought, and charmed by the prospect of wearing the Crown Jewels, prepared for the journey with renewed hopes and a light heart. Her rival, on the contrary, heard of the coming journey with dismay.

13

NAPOLEON was many men in one, and Georgina had come to know the most likeable and attractive of them all. It is not surprising that she had become deeply attached to him. The Consul whom she knew and who made love to her was always affectionate and good-humoured, attentive and considerate. About the stage, the central interest of her life, he was hardly less intelligent and knowledgeable than Talma himself; then he was interested in clothes and appreciated her efforts to please his eye, and he was as fond of gossip and small talk as she could wish. By now he was the centre of all her thoughts and preoccupations; throughout her days she saw each small occurrence in relation to him and was impatient to be with him and share with him her experiences and thoughts. She relied on him for all her happiness and turned to him in everything.

He had not warned her in advance that he would be leaving Paris, and she was completely taken by surprise. When the moment of parting came, Napoleon appeared to be as moved as she was herself. 'He was more affectionate that evening than I had ever seen him,' she writes. This did not make the parting easier, and Georgina wept. He seemed overjoyed by this proof of her devotion to him, and she was consoled by his heartfelt assurances that their happy evenings would be resumed on his return.

But in this world of incessant change it is seldom the same person who returns. Georgina was never to see again the lover who now left her. Napoleon was changing; the idealistic young Consul was fading into nothingness, and the Emperor, the tyrant, the conqueror, was beginning to dominate his mortal frame. He set off upon his travels bent on maintaining a royal dignity and impressing all beholders—his own family first of all. He called with his suite at Mortefontaine, the residence of his brother Joseph. All the Bonapartes happened to be there, including Mme Laetitia, mother of them all. An hour or two was spent in admiring the gardens, and then dinner was announced. Joseph, as host and eldest son, prepared as a matter of course to escort his mother into the dining-room and to place her at his right hand, while offering Joséphine the seat on his left. And it was now that Napoleon showed signs of the extraordinary megalomania that was about to take full possession of him. Flying into transports of rage, he declared it was an unheard of thing that his wife should take second place; and he ordered Joseph to place Joséphine on his right and Mme Mère on his left. The two women concerned cared little where they sat so long as the dinner could be eaten in peace, but they were allowed to express no opinion. A fierce argument ensued in which Joseph refused to be ordered about in his own home by his younger brother, and Napoleon became increasingly insistent in his demands. The outcome was that Napoleon marched firmly to the head of the table himself, placing Joséphine on his right, Mme de Rémusat on his left, and leaving Joseph and the rest of the company to sit below him where they would.

In the confusion the hostess, sister of the Désirée Clary of Marseilles whom Napoleon had once wished to marry, found herself obliged to sit at the wrong end of the table, among the least of her guests. A dreadful silence fell upon everyone except Napoleon. Napoleon was perfectly happy now that he had had his own way. He chattered gaily to his wife, who, in her ardent wish to win back his affections, was perfectly willing to keep him in countenance though she felt inwardly sad and embarrassed. She had tried so often to live in love and friendship with this extraordinary family; and now here they were once more, these handsome, brilliant young men, looking like a company of Corsican brigands despite their silk knee-breeches and their richly embroidered coats.

The rest of the day passed coldly, and the following morning the journey was resumed. The Consul had treated his family exactly as he proposed to treat Europe now that war with England was resumed. He was in the good spirits of a man who has discovered an infallible trick for getting his own way, and Joséphine found him a charming companion as they drove towards Amiens. She was happy to respond, feeling thankful for this unhoped-for opportunity. He was committed to many weeks in her company, with no occasion for dallying with other women; and she used the idle moments to such effect that Napoleon, feeling, perhaps, that it was the best way to relieve the tedium of the journey, soon became affectionate. By the time he and his wife reached Amiens they were on the best of terms.

In Amiens, triumphal arches had been set up, flowers were strewn in the road before them, and finally the townspeople unharnessed the horses of Napoleon's great carosse and themselves drew their hero and his wife round the town.

In Paris, Georgina saw the four beautiful swans presented by her home town to Napoleon and which now floated gracefully in the pond of the Gardens of the Tuileries. She heard much about the brilliant reception her lover received wherever he went: in Ghent, Antwerp, Malines and Brussels. But he sent her no message. Her life had suddenly become empty. She writes:

Acting was my chief distraction. But looking across the crowded auditorium I saw only a desert. The box from which the Consul had so often watched our tragedies was always empty. Even my good Talma could no longer act with the same emotion. At night, after the performance, I seemed to hear the carriage arriving to take me out to St Cloud. So everything, then, goes wrong in life?

I made up my mind that if the Consul did not send for me when he returned I would go away. I would not on any account remain in this frightful Paris if I was not to see him again. . . . I felt how insecure my greatly envied position was. At any moment the fine edifice might collapse. Could I flatter myself that my brilliant position would not come to an end?

I had only Talma to listen to me, and he showed an angelic patience while I poured out all my troubles to him, though I must have bored him at times.

'Come,' he would say, 'you have a splendid future as an artist, you will always be secure and independent. Don't dream of impossibilities, therefore. Enjoy yourself. I only hope that if the worst happens, as you fear, it won't lead you into becoming a Carmelite, like La Vallière. You would really be somewhat ridiculous in religious robes, and I'm certain you'd never get through your year as a novice.'

'No,' Georgina replied, 'I don't suppose I should. I should cut a poor figure, and, moreover, no one would show the least desire to snatch me out. They'd all be delighted to see me shut up in a convent.'

It was not until the beginning of August that Napoleon returned to St Cloud. He did not send for Georgina straight away. He was occupied with intensive diplomatic efforts to force all Europe to his side, and particularly with a bitter difference of opinion with Spain. When at last she was invited to his rooms she found him kind and affectionate, but she knew at once that the intensity of his passion was gone for ever. He could live perfectly well without her. She tried not to admit to herself this painful truth; but even when he was at his most amorous she knew that all was changed. He loved her while they were together, but he really would not mind a great deal if he never saw her again. He was different. He was older in spirit, he no longer sang and lost himself in uncontrollable laughter.

Mme de Rémusat speaks of a renewal of the actress's visits to St Cloud during the autumn, and Georgina herself describes an October day which she spent there, notable because it was the first time that she and Napoleon had seen each other in any light but that of candles.

One day the Consul said to me, 'Georgina, if you would like it, Constant shall come for you at nine in the morning, and we'll go together to Butard, the hunting lodge near St Cloud.'

'It's surely very early!'

'You lazy thing! It will do you good to get up a little sooner than usual. Besides, I want to see you by the light of the sun.'

'Yes? Well, the sun doesn't usually shine very much in October.'

'It will shine the day you come.'

'Good. I'll come, since you promise me the sun.'

So I was called for at nine in the morning, and it was a lovely day, though very cold. I put on a quilted wrap of padded white silk, and shoes of black satin. Boots were unknown to us in those days, and we were wrong not to wear them, for they are attractive and very useful. And on my head I put a veil of English lace.

'But, Mademoiselle,' said Clémentine, 'do put on a hat. Take this one, it suits you so well.'

'Do you think so? I think it makes me look like some pretentious creature in her Sunday best. I don't want a hat. Besides, the Consul wants to see me in the sunshine. I won't hide my face from him.'

Napoleon entertained Georgina to breakfast, and then took her for a walk in the woods.

He took me by the arm, and we passed before his four aides-de-camp who stood in a line, their hats off, in the courtyard: General Junot, Governor of Paris, and the Generals Caulaincourt, Bessières and Lauriston. I was walking along, arm-in-arm, with the greatest man on earth! Yes, my pride should have been satisfied, and it was. How often, in the midst of all my troubles, I have remembered that walk in the woods! Whatever has happened since, no one has been able to take away that memory from me. For more than two hours I walked arm-in-arm with the master of the world. . . .

My dear Consul! How charming and gay he was! It was cold and he made me run. The route was encumbered with branches and dead leaves, and he stooped down to clear them away for me . . . there are so few men capable of such attentions! Certainly I have never met anyone like him since. And then, in another it would appear simple and natural enough. But that *he* should do such a thing for me—that was very different.

After their long walk they returned for tea and sat together for an hour or so, talking. And then the carriage came and Georgina was driven back to Paris.

'Good-bye, Georgina,' said the Consul. 'I'll see you at the Tuileries. I'm leaving St Cloud tomorrow.'

He leaped on to his horse to follow the carriage a little way; coming up to the door he said, 'We'll see each other soon.'

They met, indeed, from time to time, but Napoleon was now much at Boulogne, and Georgina was never asked to join him there. Scanning the white cliffs of Dover through his telescope he gave her little thought.

14

NAPOLEON had intended invading England under cover of the November mists; but preparations were not completed in time and the project had to be delayed. He was now seen more frequently in Paris, and again watched his favourite tragedies at the Comédie Française. Georgina was sent for, though rather infrequently. The First Consul's attentions were absorbed just now by a royalist conspiracy that had been discovered; behind it were the Comte d'Artois and the Duc de Berry, who were living in exile in England; their agents had entered France and had planned to waylay Napoleon's coach on the route to Malmaison, to kill him and thus remove the chief obstacle to the return of the Bourbon kings. Napoleon, so free from fear on the battlefield, was unnerved by the threat of assassination and had lost his habitual calmness of spirit.

Georgina was unhappy. The winter seemed interminable. The visits to the mysterious woman in the Faubourg St Antoine had led to no interesting result, and the hopes she had had of being established as a kind of left-handed member of Napoleon's family had by now faded. She had disappointed Napoleon and she feared he was drifting away from her. Although there was much enjoyment in her theatrical life, she was in a mood to feel keenly anything that went wrong. The contest with Duchesnois continued to annoy her. The hated rival could not be shouted down; it was evident that she had too much support from Mme Bonaparte and other highly-placed patrons to be driven off the scene.

Still obedient to Napoleon, she refused to see visitors. She writes:

> I was obliged to be exceedingly discreet. I did not live at all and was really terribly bored. Talma, though, saw a lot of me, and he was always horribly nervous, my poor Talma.
>
> 'Be very discreet, my dear,' he would say. . . . 'Don't risk losing the Consul's devotion by any indiscretion. No sudden impulses, mind! Avoid being talked about at all costs!'
>
> 'I have everything I could desire, Talma, except a happy home. . . . I have to wait until he wants to see me. I have no place in the life of this great man, and in spite of all you say I am very lonely. . . . In the first place I was just influenced by vanity, but then I let myself fall in love with a man I ought only to admire. This is how I feel when I'm separated from the Consul, though when I'm with him I'm the happiest woman in the world.'

In the early weeks of 1804 rumours were flying round Paris about the Cadoudal-Moreau-Pichegru conspiracy against Napoleon, and Georgina's seventeenth birthday came in a season of widespread arrests and great public agitation. Alarming reports spread as to the extent and complexity of the plot and the number of would-be assassins still at large; but other rumours that reached Georgina's ear caused her considerably more uneasiness. People were saying that the Consul was much attracted by one of the ladies of court society. It was even said that he called on her secretly at a little house she had taken at St Cloud. Georgina anxiously questioned Constant about his master's private life when next she saw him.

'*Dame!* I don't know whether the Consul is very faithful,' Constant replied. 'But what I do know is that whenever he gives me the order to fetch you he's a different man. On these days he's so light that I lift him right off the ground when I'm helping him on with his breeches. And what do you expect me to say, anyway? I think the truth is that all the respect and deference he gets from these fine ladies really bores him and makes him yawn. Whereas with you he's always cheerful and happy. I can tell you this: he's glad to leave the salon as soon as possible to join you.'

Such words were hardly reassuring. So it was true! Well, it

was altogether too much, Georgina told herself, that she should be expected to sit moping at home wondering what he was doing and who claimed his attention. And we now find her saying: 'In spite of all the gossip there was about my intimacy with the Consul, admirers did not fail to seek me out. Decidedly I had no wish to lead the life of a recluse.'

She began to encourage visitors, and one of the first she received at this time was an elderly man who was announced as the private secretary of the Prince of Wurtemberg. He came with a valuable diamond ring and a velvet purse full of gold coins which he begged her to accept from his master as a small token of esteem.

'Monsieur,' said Georgina, 'tell the Prince that I accept the ring he is kind enough to offer me with pleasure and pride. As for the purse, I must decline it. He can make a better use of it by assisting those in need. French artists are not in the habit of receiving presents of money.'

'Mademoiselle,' replied the visitor, 'I am sure the Prince will offer you his apologies, for the last thing he would wish to do would be to offend you. But I know he would be greatly honoured if you would take the money and yourself distribute it to the poor.'

'Please thank the Prince, Monsieur, and be kind enough to tell him that I make my own modest gifts to the poor from my small purse.'

The Secretary asked if the Prince might call on her, and she replied that she would be pleased to receive him.

When the Prince of Wurtemberg called he turned out to be the very man who had posed as a secretary. He told her he had not dared to come in any other way. Georgina was affable but self-righteous. Speaking of the offered purse, she said, 'You don't know me, Prince. Gold is not a good passport to my house. I don't like money.'

She waved a beautiful white hand on which the accepted diamond ring was flashing; the donor could do not more than apologize profoundly for having failed to divine from afar the high-minded character of Mlle George.

Napoleon, it turned out, had not relaxed his vigilance. When next she visited him he said, directly he had greeted her:

'Well, Georgina! You have allowed the Prince of Wurtemberg to call on you!'

'Yes,' said Georgina. 'I'll tell you all about it.'

'A great deal can happen in a week,' said the Consul, suspiciously.

'You are becoming much too rare,' said Georgina. 'So listen to what I say. I'm bored. Yes, I received the Prince and I shall receive other visitors, too. You know very well that we actresses are obliged to receive visitors in our rooms at the theatre. Surely we can have visitors at home in broad daylight!'

'I see, my dear Georgina, that you have a taste for princes and high life!'

'If so, it is you who have given me the taste,' said Georgina. 'You know very well,' she added, 'that as long as I'm lucky enough to feel that you take the least interest in me I shall never do anything that could make you think less well of me.'

'And after? When you no longer feel I'm interested in you?'

'I don't know what might happen.'

'You are a fool.'

'Well, listen to what I have to tell you. First of all, here is my ring.'

Georgina showed Napoleon her ring and told him the story of its presentation, and also of the offer of the purse full of gold. No doubt she spoke with some complacency, for she really saw herself as a disinterested woman. But Napoleon was not impressed.

'*Fi donc!*' he said, frowning. 'You have taken this ring a great deal too easily. It was in the worst possible taste to accept it. I insist absolutely upon your receiving no more presents offered to you on the pretext of complimenting your art. It is neither right nor proper.'

'All the same,' said Georgina, indignant that she had not been praised for refusing the purse, 'there are plenty of artists who don't mind accepting presents from foreigners. In fact one sees

97

it every day. What else can they do? Frenchmen only show their admiration by fine words. It costs less, of course.'

'Georgina, you don't please me at all this evening,' said the Consul. 'I don't like the way you talk. I think the best thing I can do is to get you married.'

'Get me married? My God, whoever to?'

'Oh, I'll do well for you. I'll give you to one of my generals. You will have to leave the theatre, of course, and you'll have to lead a respectable life.'

She thought at first that he was joking; but he assured her he was perfectly serious. 'I was deeply hurt,' she writes. 'Ah, Constant! You have been clumsy enough to tell me the truth! Some fine lady has passed this way!' For the rest of the evening the Consul was affectionate and Georgina responded gratefully. But decidedly the rapture of love was over.

What had become of that once blissful and seemingly real state of love they had enjoyed? Napoleon had swallowed it and forgotten it; Georgina, though her own feeling was, she says, a cult, a passionate adoration which time could not change, was reduced to inward criticism, to feeling hurt and disappointed, to swinging over to love's habitual opposite. Normal human relations are intermingled with uncertainty and mistrust, veiled hostility and much deception; love is an illusion that one is no longer in such base circumstances but is raised to a brighter sphere of peace and understanding. Exalted moments took possession of Napoleon very easily, but the clamour of ordinary life soon reasserted itself. Life was proving very hostile to him just now; men, scores of men, were planning to murder him; he felt ill-humoured and exasperated, and his troubles had affected his feelings for Georgina.

This did not mean that they were not happy when they met. When they were together they usually enjoyed themselves, for they were too well adapted to each other not to do so. But Napoleon no longer greeted Georgina with the former rapture, and she felt the difference. It was enough to make her feel she was justified in amusing herself, and she began to give herself up to the normal pleasures of an actress's life.

There was plenty to distract her. She received many proposals of marriage; anonymous letters came inviting her to mysterious interviews; men of fashion called on her with flowers and jewels gracefully and tactfully offered. Some of those who came were eccentric, but they were usually respectful and nearly always wished her to receive some costly gift which her fame had led them to crave to lay at her feet. One of them begged to be allowed to set her hair in curl-papers, and when he had gone she found he had used bank-notes for the purpose. Another, a certain Captain Hill, came with tempting offers from the Prince of Wales, who proposed to keep her in unheard-of luxury if only she would abandon France for himself and England.

Such tales sound utterly far-fetched; yet Mlle George does not appear to have had much of an imagination, nor to have been a deliberate liar; and a little later on she was to have an adventure no less fantastic for the truth of which there is good evidence. For the attempt of the Prince of Wales to lure her over to London, which she describes in some detail, we have only her word, so that the reader can believe it or not as he pleases. The Prince of Wales, we are told, possessed a portrait of her and was madly in love. He sent her a portrait of himself, together with other gifts equally calculated to charm and please her.

> That same night I was to see the Consul, and I hastened to tell him all that had happened.
> 'I was horrified, I assure you, when I heard the name of the great person. I have told you all, and you mustn't accuse me of idle chatter. No, I suspect this may hide something more serious.'
> 'They were perhaps hoping to make another Judith of you, my dear Georgina,' said the Consul, smiling.
> 'Well, you will never be a Holophernes.'
> 'No, don't worry. I knew all about it. You won't see him again.'

Napoleon referred to Captain Hill, the supposed intermediary of the Prince of Wales. Georgina believed she had narrowly escaped being dragged into the great Cadoudal conspiracy for which England and the Bourbons were now being vilified. But the affair was perhaps one of those pleasing English hoaxes in which a wealthy society was able to indulge: the English were busy hurling defiance at Napoleon as he prepared for the great invasion; it would have been a nice touch to rob the great man of his mistress and Paris of its most fashionable ornament.

In the early spring of 1804 the public saw Mlle George and Mlle Duchesnois admitted as Associates of the Comédie Française. The long contest had ended in a draw, and from now on they were both to take their part in the company on equal terms, playing the same roles: twin stars who were to be perpetually uneasy. Popularly, the feud between them was supposed to be at an end. In fact this was not so, but the public had at last grown thoroughly tired of it. There was even a public reconciliation staged for the benefit of the theatre's clientèle; but it was a more than usually theatrical show.

Soon after, on March the 21st, Napoleon made the fatal mistake that changed the course of history for the worse, that made universal war to a finish inevitable, that made him Emperor, tyrant of Europe and then prisoner of St Helena, that made France first expand and then shrink, and that, last and least, effectively lifted him from Georgina's small world. Acting on suspicion, he murdered the young Duc d'Enghien, descendant of the *Grand Condé*, an innocent man whom he had condemned in his mind as being responsible for the conspiracy against himself.

15

THROWN into a dark humour by unexpected events, Napoleon had resolved to give a lesson both to royalists abroad and to those within France who might secretly desire to bring about his downfall.

Of all the Bourbon princes, the young Duc d'Enghien alone was within reach. He was at Ettenheim in the Duchy of Baden, leading the life of a country gentleman and taking no part in politics. Napoleon sent troops one night to surround his house and take him by surprise. The young man was dragged over the frontier, taken to Vincennes and executed forthwith.

After committing this crime Napoleon was a changed man, doomed to a perpetual self-justifying. He had become what the world commonly regards as 'strong', a ruthless man moved by self-will. It was seen that he was to be feared, and a wave of horror swept across Europe. Inside France the immediate impression created by the execution of the Duc d'Enghien was that Napoleon had strengthened his position; many who envied his successes now realized for the first time that he was too powerful to be opposed; and whereas they had hoped in the past to undermine him they now felt it more expedient to replace envy by cupidity, to exploit his vast ambitions, to help him upwards and enrich themselves as his favoured supporters. M. Fouché, the former Jacobin, hurried to Malmaison to point out to him the advantages of accepting a hereditary monarchy, and only a week after the murder at Vincennes the Senate by a large majority asked him to accept the crown.

Joséphine, who had pleaded in vain for the life of the Duc d'Enghien, unexpectedly found herself restored to the old terms of affection with her husband as a result of the tragic event. Nepoleon had called her a fool when she wept and implored him to be merciful, and had told her that women knew nothing about political affairs. It was necessary, he said, to choose between a decisive action now and an endless succession of conspiracies in the future. In politics, he assured Joséphine, a death which led to public security was far from being a crime.

Yet now the deed was done he needed reassurance and turned for it to his wife. Joséphine had condemned his action, but he was prepared to bribe her with his love to set his mind at rest. Joséphine was all tolerance and goodness of heart. If she thought well of him, he felt himself absolved. And he had his way because the craving to be loved and to enjoy herself was far stronger in Joséphine than any other consideration whatsoever. She never seriously reproached Napoleon for anything except neglect of herself, and now the crime she had done her best to prevent was in fact committed she wanted to forget it and find happiness once more. She listened to her husband's flatterers and hoped that he had acted as wisely as they said, and that her premonitions as to the disasters that must follow were entirely wrong. In truth Joséphine's premonitions were not usually wrong, as she knew well enough; but she drove them from her for the benefit of her husband. Let him only love her and forget the detestable little Mlle George and she would forgive him for any number of political crimes. Joséphine could do right, but could make no stand for it.

Mme de Rémusat was a witness round about this time of Napoleon's renewed affection for Joséphine. One evening at St Cloud he became involved in a bitter quarrel with his brother Lucien, who by now was married to Mme Juberthon. He had found a more suitable wife for him, the Queen of Etruria, but Lucien angrily refused to listen to the proposition. After a stormy interview, Napoleon came into the salon where Joséphine was sitting with M. and Mme de Rémusat, threw himself into a chair and complained bitterly about Lucien, for whom, however, Joséphine, although she had every cause to dislike him, put in a good word, trying, as usual, to find excuses for him and to make peace.

Napoleon looked at her thoughtfully and said, 'What a good woman you are!' And getting up he took her in his arms and stroked her hair while he gave an account of what had taken place between himself and his brother. Mme de Rémusat was struck by the contrast between Joséphine's elegantly dressed shining hair and the sombre, unhappy face of her husband, so close to it. When he had finished his account, Napoleon said how hard it was for him to meet with so much animosity in his own family. He felt himself isolated from everyone else, and always obliged to count on himself alone. 'Well,' he ended by saying, 'I am well able to stand alone. And you, Joséphine—you console me for everything.' And as he spoke his eyes filled with tears. He had never seemed so united with his wife.

With a man of such changeable character, these emotions could not be expected to last for very long. Having been assisted by Joséphine to stifle the voice of conscience, he soon forgot his uneasiness and resumed his dallying both with Georgina and the society woman of whom rumour had already spoken. Flattery, too, was having its effect, despite his keen intelligence. With everyone about him begging him to accept the crown of France, he had little need to entertain doubts about his own morality. Those who were not flatterers were alarmed by the deterioration of his character. Talleyrand urged him to take the title of King and not of Emperor. Empire was too suggestive of Charlemagne and ancient Rome, whereas a king might be expected to keep within his kingdom and respect the Concert of Europe. But Napoleon grew angry when anyone ventured to guide his choice. It was precisely as a new and greater Charlemagne that he now saw himself.

In May the great question was settled, and in a ceremony at St Cloud he accepted the title of Emperor. It was a difficult time for Joséphine, despite her recent reconciliation with Napoleon. The assumption of royal power brought to view again the question of divorce which the Bonaparte family never forgot for very long. Napoleon again turned his thoughts to the adoption of the son of Hortense and his brother Louis. But Louis, incited by Caroline Murat, showed himself more vindictive than ever on the subject and refused to take a place, as he put it, behind his own son. Unless the matter was dropped forthwith, he swore he would create a public scandal. Napoleon was forced to give way; he would not, however, pay attention to the demand of his brothers and sisters that he should divorce his wife. The Bonaparte ladies in particular would have given much to keep Joséphine from sharing the Imperial glories of the family, and with this end in view they harassed and importuned Napoleon without mercy; but they only succeeded in confirming him in his affection for his wife, and he announced that both he and she would be crowned at the end of the year in Notre-Dame. Joséphine was thankful; the danger of divorce seemed to be over, and the prospect of dressing up for a coronation was decidedly pleasing.

Throughout this time Georgina had seen little of Napoleon. When he sent for her she found him as affectionate as ever, though by no means so light-hearted. She had shared with all Paris the alarms of the plot against his life, and was greatly chagrined that he had not shown more inclination to seek relaxation in her society from such striking and terrible circumstances. She would have liked to think his first thought was for herself. His life had been threatened, might not the fear of their final separation have upset him a little? The less she saw of him, the deeper was her craving for his love; and his new monarchical grandeurs added very considerably to his glamour.

During the summer he spent much of his time at Boulogne, for he intended to conquer England before his coronation, and to be crowned as master of the West. Again he was thwarted, for one of his admirals died on the eve of bringing the French fleet up to the Channel from Toulon. The chosen moment was lost, and the invasion had to be postponed. His absence in Boulogne was followed by a diplomatic tour of the Rhineland which he made in the company of Joséphine, and he did not settle down in Paris again until October.

Georgina anticipated a resumption of her happy intimacy with him; but she was to be disappointed. If she had leisure to keep in mind their past pleasures, Napoleon had not. He saw her at this time, according to her account, but it must have been on very few occasions, for he had heavy preoccupations. Quite apart from the war which he had on hand, his domestic life was growing stormy. As the coronation drew near, the Bonaparte family (or such of them as were in France), half crazed with greed and ambition, schemed for their own places and for the exclusion of the detested Joséphine. Having given up hope of bringing about the divorce they had so often recommended, they were now doing their utmost to persuade Napoleon to exclude his wife from the coronation ceremony as one whose past was unworthy of such Christian solemnities. There were many loud and frantic family scenes, and they culminated in one caused by Joséphine herself when she surprised Napoleon alone with the unnamed society woman who had attracted him.

Flying into a violent temper, Napoleon stormed at poor Joséphine as she wept in disappointment and loneliness. He was wearied of being spied upon, he said, and he was determined to get a divorce. Yet, often enough, his violent tempers left him as suddenly as they came, and so it was on this occasion. The gloating satisfaction of his sisters distressed him, and he saw how much more true to him were Joséphine and her son and daughter. He asked Joséphine's pardon and wept sadly in her arms, wondering how it was that these strange quarrels arose with this kind and devoted woman. He gave orders at once for the fullest participation of his wife in the coronation ceremony, and she forgot her troubles in the delightful discussions she had with the painter Isabey on the subject of ceremonial dress.

Georgina, who heard rumours of all that was going on, could be certain of one thing: that she had long ceased to be the centre of Napoleon's thoughts. Deeply offended, she retaliated when she could with a series of slights, although she knew that, having ceased to care much about her, he would hardly notice them.

On one occasion she sent a curt refusal when Constant came with the carriage to take her to the palace. On another she sat in her box at the theatre and refused to make the least sign of recognition to Napoleon, who was also present. 'I did not once look at his box,' she says. 'I was much too hurt to do so.' On this particular evening Joachim Murat visited her in her box, and remarked to her that Napoleon was looking at her far more than at the stage.

'It's very flattering, no doubt,' said Georgina coldly. 'But in the circumstances I am not particularly interested.'

'Why? Has there been a quarrel?'

'You're laughing at me. No one has a right to quarrel with the Emperor, but one has a right to keep oneself to oneself, which is what I am doing.'

She left early to take a drive in the Bois de Boulogne with Joachim Murat. 'I was delighted to leave before the departure of the Emperor,' she writes. 'It satisfied that pride with which I tried to smother the feelings of my broken heart. Oh, how unfortunate women are!'

'Well, General,' she said to her companion as they drove

along, 'What do you expect me to do? You see well enough that it's all over. For two weeks he hasn't asked to see me.'

'But what does that signify? You surely don't think he's a man like others, you silly woman?'

'Silly? You should say mad! You say he's not a man like others and you're right. He's great and wonderful and far above all others. But as far as women are concerned he's a man like other men.'

Joachim Murat, according to her memoirs, persuaded her that Napoleon was still attached to her, and therefore on the following evening she accepted the invitation that came to her to go to the Palace of the Tuileries. Napoleon received her affectionately, but she reproached him for having neglected her so much.

'One cannot do all one would wish to do, my dear Georgina,' he replied. 'But whatever happens you may be sure I shall always have a tender attachment to you, and that I shall not lose sight of you.'

'But what you say is very sad,' Georgina cried, greatly distressed. 'Do you mean I shan't see you again?'

'Yes, my dear, you'll always see me, I promise you that. Have no fears. Now that's enough. No more questions today. Be good and natural, and count on me.'

Within a few days she was sent for again. She describes their meeting:

He took my hands with great kindliness and made me sit down.

'My dear Georgina,' he said, 'I'm afraid I have to say something that will upset you. For a time I shall not be able to see you. Well? You say nothing?'

'No, I expected it. I should have been senseless to think that I, who am nothing, could have any place—I won't say in your heart, but even in your thoughts. I have provided you with a little interest, that is all.'

'You are just a child, and a very charming one when you speak like that, for I can see you're attached to me, and I love you for loving me. In a position like mine one is loved so little. But I will see you again, I promise you.'

'Thank you for your kind words, but I am going away.'

'I don't believe that. You mustn't make such a mistake. It would ruin your future.'

'My future? I haven't a future any more. Anyway, nothing matters to me, and I shall go away.'

Napoleon became affectionate on seeing her tears and for the time forgot he had ever loved anyone else. In spite of herself Georgina felt reassured by his loving words, and he kept her with him until five in the morning. But at that chilly hour her courage failed her and she wept as she went home.

'Everything disappeared before me,' she says. 'Everything seemed to be dead. . . . Oh, it is in these moments of separation that one feels all the happiness one is losing. I was another woman, weighed down with misery.'

'Well, Clémentine,' she said on arriving home, 'you won't have to wait up for me all night any more. It seems I'm not going to see the Consul again.'

'Is it possible!'

'It is possible, though he said it was just for a time.'

'Then you must believe him, Mademoiselle. A man of his kind doesn't beat about the bush, and if he wanted to break with you he'd have said so.'

The devoted Clémentine, far from getting an hour or two in bed now that her mistress was back, had to sit and talk to her until Talma could be brought round. The great actor arrived in haste and out of breath, after being given an urgent note from Georgina. She describes his arrival:

'Good Lord, my dear young friend!' he cried. 'What on earth's happened that you send for me at this hour of the day?'

'What's happened is that I'm never going to see the Consul again!'

'How's that? It's impossible!'

'Oh, all things are possible, my dear Talma. . . . All the same, he was tender and angelic with me. What he said was, "My dear Georgina, for some time I shall not be able to see you. A great event is imminent which will occupy all my attention. But later on I will see you, I promise you that".'

'Well, my dear, believe what he says. And the great event! You know what that is, of course! They are talking of the Consul's coronation, and they even say the Pope himself is coming to Paris to crown him, though I don't think it's yet official.'

'Well, Talma, at least it won't be on my account that the Pope will refuse to come!'

'No,' said Talma. 'But, seriously, in the circumstances, it's natural enough that the Consul should feel he must put a stop to all gossip.'

'Say rather that his infatuation is over. And now, I suppose, he wants to attend to his devotions with suitable humility, and without being distracted by the senses. So much the better! You see? What had to happen has happened as I told you it would a hundred times. Well, I can't complain; it has all been my own fault, and so it's just that I should suffer. And I am very unhappy. I don't lend my heart for the interest it will bring—I have given it loyally, without calculation. I have never thought of making a fortune out of him, as he knows. I have just been happy to be with him, and now I'm very wretched.'

'You're letting it get the better of you,' said Talma. 'You've no common sense. You can't imagine that a man like Napoleon is going to transform himself into a romantic, fairy-tale lover for you? When one has the good fortune to attract a man of such stature, one should be able to respond with a little dignity oneself, my dear, and not indulge in senseless daydreams.'

'You're right. I won't say any more. . . . I'll be gay and indifferent. Let us have lunch, Talma. Then if you want to be kind to me we'll go out and have a walk in the country.'

'What? But it's devilishly cold, my dear.'

'*Dame!* The cold will do us good. It calms you down. Ice is good when one has a fever. You must let them know at home that you're dining with me. I won't let you go, I want to spend the whole day with you. And tonight we'll go to the theatre and hear Brunet. . . .'

'It's all very well to dispose of me like this, but I have a lot to do. There are visits I must make——'

'Oh, you'll do all that tomorrow! By tomorrow my attitude will be fixed and I will restore your liberty.'

'Well, do as you like with me—I am your slave until tonight.'

Taking Talma's advice, Georgina made the most of her opportunities for amusement and allowed herself no time for dwelling on her disappointment. Without doubt she was deeply attached to Napoleon; but she did her best to deny this to herself and found relief in discussing her deceptions with her friends as if in the hope of talking herself out of her real feelings.

Napoleon left Paris for Fontainebleau, where the Pope arrived a few days later, and she imagined him, as she had said to Talma, keeping his emotions intact for his impending devotions. But such was far from being the case, for Napoleon had again fallen in love, and even the presence of the Pope had no power to raise his mind to less worldly matters. He was certainly as discreet as possible; but Joséphine, who knew him so well, was suspicious because he had suddenly become strangely elated. Though a devotee herself, and uplifted by the visit of the Pope, she had no illusions as to the possibility of her husband being similarly rendered happy by their holy guest. No, he must have been attracted yet again by some woman, and she must have smiled at him. 'When the Pope retired to his apartments,' says Frédéric Masson in *Napoléon et les Femmes*, 'Napoleon remained with the Empress to talk with the ladies who were with her. Joséphine began to worry; her jealousy was aroused; his manner did not seem natural, and she imagined some intrigue was taking place.' Nor was she wrong.

Joséphine, however, had certain cards to play in this great struggle, this unseen war for the possession of Napoleon's heart. She had confessed to the Pope that she and her husband were not married in the eyes of the Church; they had merely contracted a civil marriage, and she wanted above all things to have their union blessed by religion. The Pope, greatly edified by this proper frame of mind, and little suspecting the reasons behind it, promised he would demand of the Emperor that the ceremony of marriage should be gone through before the coronation.

Napoleon was furious when faced with the Pope's request. It looked, he felt, ridiculous to go through a wedding ceremony when one had already been married eight years. Then it was distasteful to him to marry his wife at a moment when his heart was filled with visions of a woman with gold hair and blue eyes, Mme Duchâtel, who was only half the age of Joséphine. . . .

However, he had no doubt he was properly caught. It had been no light task getting the Pope to Fontainebleau, and he had only come on condition that Christian laws were to be kept in mind very much more than had latterly been the case in France. He had, indeed, from his own point of view, every right to require that the man and woman he was to crown as Emperor and Empress of the French were married, and he was equal to refusing to officiate if the wedding did not take place. The scandal would be intolerable if the Pope suddenly returned to Rome accusing him of living in sin.

There was nothing for it but to submit with a bad grace; and therefore on the last day of November, or as they had it in those times on the 9th Frimaire, he was privately married to Joséphine by Cardinal Fesch.

Joséphine, though her eyes were heavy with a night of weeping, due to her husband's anger, was none the less charmed by the turn of events. She knew Napoleon's displeasure would blow over, and she felt herself secure at last. She was Empress of the French, she was indissolubly married to the man she loved, and she was to be crowned and anointed by the Pope.

16

THE coronation day arrived, December the 2nd, a cold but bright and calm Sunday. Georgina was depressed. During the last few weeks she had managed to keep Napoleon out of mind, but on this occasion it was impossible to do so. All Paris was thinking solely of the Emperor and she could seek distraction in no one's company. 'I ought to have been overjoyed,' she writes, 'to see the great Napoleon raised to the rank which belonged to him and which he had conquered. But one never escapes from selfishness.' However, the day had to be gone through, and although she had no wish to see any of the spectacle and rejoicings, she had hired a room on the route of the procession for the benefit of her family.

The windows of the room overlooked the Pont Neuf and the Quai des Orfèvres, along which the procession was to pass. Georgina's valet de chambre was sent in advance to see that a fire was lighted and make arrangements for the meals that were to be served. He set out while it was still dark and bitterly cold. It was six o'clock when Georgina rose, and all the bells of the capital were pealing. No private carriages were allowed out, and she and her family were obliged to go to their room on foot, a circumstance which caused many complaints, particularly as it was foggy. Already the streets were thronged with an immense number of spectators, and they could only make their way a few steps at a time. On seeing these difficulties, Georgina would have liked to remain at home, and she was only persuaded with difficulty to continue the long walk. It took the Weymers two hours to reach their destination. A bright fire blazed in the well-furnished sitting-room awaiting them, and Georgina sat close to it, shivering and irritable and quite unable to share her sister's enthusiasm.

'Oh, Mimi, do come and look.' Bébelle kept calling out from her place by the window.

'All right, all right, there's plenty of time,' said Georgina. 'You keep opening the windows and I'm frozen. Leave me by the fire. I may have to act tomorrow and I don't want to catch cold, I'm going to sleep. You can wake me up when you see the horses.'

It was not long before she was roused, for the Pope left the Palace of the Tuileries at nine o'clock and passed by soon after. Splendidly attired, escorted by detachments of the Imperial Guard, he drove in a coach drawn by eight grey horses and ornamented with the attributes of his state. Despite the influences of the revolution, he was saluted with an awed respect, although many smiled without comprehension at the ecclesiastic who preceded him in all simplicity, riding on a mule and carrying a cross.

The excitement died away and nearly three hours passed by before the main procession arrived. Now, however, salvoes of gunfire announced that it was on its way; the Weymers hurried to the window; Georgina sulked again by the fire until the immense acclamations, growing nearer and louder, drew her in curiosity to join the others. The fog of early morning had cleared and the sky was now blue; the swords of the soldiers who lined the route were flashing in the sunlight. The cortège, she saw, was crossing the Pont Neuf, and at its head was her friend, Joachim Murat.

Then came squadrons of mounted troops, and after them, preceded by heralds, a dozen carriages, each drawn by six horses and containing the high officials of the Empire. They were followed by the Emperor's coach, massive and resplendent.

The painted gilt and glass coach, surmounted by a crown upheld by eagles, glittered and sparkled in the clear and chilly air. Four allegorical figures supported its roof; eagles interlaced with garlands and medallions decorated the panels. It was drawn by eight bay horses, caparisoned in white, red and gold, and led by footmen at a walking pace. A groom sat on one of the lead-horses, and on the coachman's box was a magnificent figure of pride and earthly splendour, César German, who had so often driven Georgina out to St Cloud from the Théâtre Français. In a plumed hat, his heavy figure adorned by a scarlet suit and white silk stockings, César was superb and complacent. And within the coach was that other Caesar, Napoleon.

Crowned at Napoleon's side, where Georgina herself would have been had the world been a place where all went exactly as she desired, was Joséphine, about to be united anew with her husband by the most solemn and splendid Christian rites. Georgina gazed at her sadly, but admiringly and without envy. She had always had a good opinion of Joséphine.

We were on the first floor [she writes] and nothing escaped our gaze. We looked straight into the carriages. The Emperor was calm and smiling; but the Empress Joséphine was marvellous to see. There was the perfect taste always evident in her dress, her air of nobility, and the benevolent expression that drew everyone to her. Underneath her attire, with its diadem which she wore without giving any suggestion of its weight, she remained the most unassuming and ravishing of women. She saluted her people with so much kindness and sympathy that she won them all. Not that she was anything less than imposing, but her smile drew you to her and you felt you could meet her without any fear, knowing she would never repulse you. She was so genuinely kind, that charming woman. And power made no difference to her: she was a woman of infinite goodness of heart. What a misfortune, the divorce, both for the Emperor and for France!'

Georgina scarcely seems to have noticed her lover, so fascinated was she by his wife. Napoleon, however, cut a fine enough figure in his costume designed by Isabey in the style of the sixteenth century. He was in red velvet, embroidered in gold, with a mantle strewn with bees (an old emblem resembling at a distance the fleur-de-lis which it had been thought wiser not to revive). He was much adorned with diamonds, and his hat was trimmed with white ostrich feathers. While he wore a hat, for he was only to put on Imperial attire at the cathedral, Joséphine wore a diadem of pearls and diamonds of immense value. Her hair was dressed in innumerable curls as in the time of Louis XIV, and her face had been made up by Isabey. Her dress of heavy white satin was embroidered with the Imperial bees in gold thread, the corsage strewn with diamonds. It was cut very low, like an evening dress, and with it went a white velvet court mantle. Her shoes were made of white velvet embroidered with gold, and her gloves and white silk stockings were also gold-embroidered. Infinite care had been taken by Isabey in the make-up of her face, at all times a successful art where the standard of dress-making is high; and even to her ladies, standing close to her before they left for the ceremony, she had the appearance of a woman not more than twenty-five years old. So she passed the actress, George, and the dazzled crowds in the streets: a woman displaying dress and jewels worth millions of gold francs, yet perfectly beautiful and in no way hampered by the weight of wealth.

Now they were out of sight with their accompanying cavalcade, and after so brilliant a spectacle there was little interest in the carriages that followed them with the members of the Imperial family and the ladies- and gentlemen-in-waiting. The Imperial coach went its way down the old sand-strewn streets of the city, narrow and historic: the rue St Louis, the rue du Marché Neuf, the rue du Cloître-Notre-Dame. It was almost midday, and as the Emperor and Empress entered the Archbishopric where they were to put on their Imperial robes, the Weymer family sat round the table to the meal prepared by their valet. The hours passed by, wearying to Georgina, exhilarating to her brother and sister.

Not far off, the great ceremony was slowly and splendidly conducted. Napoleon placed the crown of France upon his own head with great composure; Joséphine knelt before him and he bent forward to crown her also, doing so with an expression of such love and devotion that all onlookers were deeply impressed. Tears sprang to Joséphine's eyes; after so many storms, so much anxiety and dread of loneliness on her part, after such jealousy of the successful little actress, Mlle George, she felt that she and her husband were now eternally drawn together by this solemn and ancient ceremony.

With her husband she now walked down the nave to the sumptuous thrones awaiting them. Pius VII , who had been so many hours in the chilly cathedral, raised his hands with unruffled benevolence to bless them, and then kissed Napoleon on the cheek. And now he turned towards the assembly and chanted the words which had rung through St Peter's in Rome when Charlemagne was crowned: *Vivat in Aeternum Semper Augustus!* and in response a thousand voices shouted *Vive l'Empereur!*

At the same time, Georgina listened to the guns firing a salute and watched the lights appearing round about, for it was already dark.

17

'I WENT home with a heavy heart, saying to myself that everything was at an end,' says Mlle George. 'I had heard nothing from the

Emperor and had not attempted to see him. I was in the habit of sending him a little note from time to time; but I felt now that I could no longer do so. There were fêtes, illuminations and fireworks in plenty, and certainly I had no desire to see any of them. But Mars came round with Armand, Thénard and Bourgoin, and insisted on my going with them to the Tuileries. It would have looked unfriendly to refuse; besides, my sister was dying to see everything, and as she was a great friend of the daughter of Mars I had to resign myself. So off we went to the Gardens of the Tuileries and were nearly suffocated in the dense crowd.'

The Emperor, the Empress and all their court came on to the balcony from time to time, bowing and smiling at the crowds below and watching the fireworks that were being let off. Napoleon had dined alone with his wife; he had insisted upon her keeping on her crown throughout the meal and had been affectionate and appreciative, complimenting her repeatedly for the grace and dignity she had shown throughout the day. It was as though they had reached the happy ending of a novel, for no happier climax, no happier situation, could have been imagined. Unfortunately, there are no tidy endings in life, and one reaches such harmonious hours, if at all, only to be hustled out of them again by the passage of time.

The actors left the Tuileries and drove in Georgina's carriage through the crowded streets to the home of Mme Thénard. Everywhere people were dancing out of doors, although it was a cold winter night. Food had been distributed to the poor, and the main fountains flowed with wine.

A few days later Napoleon asked for a performance of *Cinna* at the Théâtre Français. Georgina appeared in the role of Emilie. 'I went on to the stage with the determination to be Emilie only,' she writes. 'I did not turn my eyes once towards that box which I used to rejoice so much to look at. I did my best, helped by Talma who never ceased to encourage me.'

'Don't give way,' Talma said. 'The theatre is crowded, all the highest in the land are here. My dear child, think of your future. . . . With the Emperor here, your pride should make you surpass yourself.'

The Emperor vigorously applauded Georgina's appearances, the Empress smiled benevolently; and after the performance both of them sent Georgina messages of congratulation. It had been a brilliant evening; the audience had acclaimed the new monarch and his wife joyfully on their arrival; ministers and ambassadors had been present, and most of them went behind the scenes when the play was over to talk to the actors. Georgina says:

They enjoyed seeing us in our dressing-gowns, deprived of our splendour, our maids saying to them:

'Excuse me, gentlemen, let me pass, I have to let down Madame's hair.'

'You will allow her to relieve me of these ornaments, gentlemen? They are making my head ache.'

'Why, of course. We don't want to be in your way.'

And Prince Talleyrand, leaning against the mantelpiece, said, 'Oh, you won't be in her way. She's a coquette, our beautiful Georgina; she only wants to be seen in all her simplicity.'

Talleyrand was one of the admirers whom Georgina, now eighteen years old, encouraged at this time. She says of him: 'M. de Talleyrand, whom I saw much of, liked me well enough —inasmuch as such very great persons can like anyone else— that is to say, being very witty and quite dried up in all his grandeur, he was amused by everything and interested in nothing, and he both took possession of you and left you without really giving you a thought.'

With such admirers about her, and with all the varied interests of the stage, she managed to enjoy herself in spite of her disappointments. One day, however, about, five weeks after the coronation, she received a visit from Constant.

'What brings you here after all this time?' she asked.

'The Emperor asks if you will come this evening.'

'Ah! He remembers me? Tell the Emperor I will obey his orders. At what time?'

'Eight o'clock.'

'I will be ready.'

All day she was impatient and excited; yet feelings of resentment were uppermost. She had heard much just recently about the beautiful Mme Duchâtel with whom Napoleon had fallen in love at the time of the coronation. She spent the day in arranging her dress, bent upon outshining her rival. The Emperor received her kindly, but without the former sparkle of pleasure in his eye.

'How beautiful you are, Georgina! And what a dress!'

'Can one be too well dressed, Sire, when one has the honour to be admitted into your Majesty's presence?'

'Ah, my dear, what fine style! What affected language! Come, Georgina, these preposterous manners don't suit you at all. Be as you always were, a frank and simple person.'

'Sire, one changes in five weeks; you have given me time to reflect and to forget my old ways. No, I'm not the same as I was. I shall always be honoured when your Majesty deigns to receive me, but I can say no more. I feel depressed. I feel I want a change of scene.'

Napoleon assured her he loved her as much as ever, but she knew that this was not so; and, although they enjoyed their few hours together, a dark mood fell upon her when she returned home. His manner had been entirely different, he seemed to have grown old. Never again, in fact, was Napoleon to forget his power and glory. 'The Emperor had driven away my First Consul,' Georgina says. 'Everything was bigger and more imposing now, but there was no space for happiness.'

All the same, in spite of her feeling of loss, she was to be sent for more frequently during the next few months. Napoleon's passion for Mme Duchâtel collapsed suddenly one day, and he resumed not only his affectionate relations with his wife but his interest in Georgina. Though he had changed, the charm he exercised on her was always there, and the animosity she had built up in her mind against him vanished.

It was a happy, brilliant year that followed the coronation. It was marked by the fêtes that inaugurated the Empire, and later was to be notable for great victories on the Continent; and although it was to be the year of Trafalgar and the invasion of

England had to be abandoned, there were to be conquests enough to dazzle the multitude and persuade them that their Emperor was invincible.

The arts were held in high esteem, and Georgina was often called with her colleagues to perform before the court at the Palace of the Tuileries, St Cloud and Fontainebleau. In March she played with Talma in *Nicomède* at St Cloud; and in May she was there again to play in *La Mort de Pompée* and *Polyeucte*. In May, too, she acted at the Comédie Française in one of the plays that marked the beginning of Romanticism on the stage, *Les Templiers* by Reynouard. Reynouard, Alexandre Duval and Gabriel Legouvé had broken away from tradition, and instead of writing plays about the classical world they dramatized scenes from French history, an idea that was to be fully exploited later in the century by Dumas and Victor Hugo.

Les Templiers, with Georgina in the role of Jeanne de Navarre, was performed during Napoleon's absence, for he spent several weeks of the early summer in Italy, which country he had resolved to make a province of France; and on May 26th he went through a second coronation ceremony in Milan Cathedral, being anointed by Cardinal Caprera and then placing on his own head the ancient crown of the Lombard kings.

In all this splendour, however, with all his political preoccupations, with his plans for annexing the other Italian states and creating satellite kingdoms everywhere for his brothers and friends, he yet had time to keep the Comédie Française in mind. He had read Reynouard's play before it was produced and in his usual manner had criticized it well and suggested alterations, which the author, somewhat to his annoyance, had not thought fit to make. Hearing about the play's success, he wrote to his Minister Fouché a few days after the coronation, showing that he was not entirely pleased by the new trends of drama. The success of *Les Templiers*, he said, would draw the attention of the public to their history in medieval times, to which he had no objection. But he did not think that plays should be shown which dealt with a time too near to the present. He had just seen in the papers that there was talk of performing a tragedy whose subject was Henri IV (sixteenth century), and which was close enough to the present to arouse political passions. 'The stage has need of a little antiquity,' he said, and he asked Fouché to prevent the performance of this play if he could. None the less, the Comédie Française was proud of its independence, and the play in question, *La Mort d'Henri IV* by Legouvé, was performed some months later.

On his return with Joséphine from the brilliant weeks in Italy, where the light, the glowing palaces, the dark blue sky, the rigid shadows, the statues and fountains had dazzled him and filled him anew with the love of the world and his own fortune, he held his court at the Palace of St Cloud and there enjoyed the pleasures of the theatre. The actors of the Comédie Française were again sent for, and Georgina now played before him in *Les Templiers*, *La Mort de Pompée* and *Andromaque*.

She describes the performance of *Andromaque* on a hot summer night. While waiting to enter the scene, she was alarmed to see bats flitting about the corridors behind the stage. As Mlle Bourgoin made her exit she enquired anxiously of her, 'Have you seen any of these frightful creatures in the theatre?' Mlle Bourgoin replied that she had not, and Georgina made her entry reassured. But now, during her scene with Orestes, a large bat appeared and began to fly round her in circles, and with a loud shriek she rushed away through the exit, while Napoleon and all the audience laughed heartily.

Talma hurried after her to tell her severely that she was out of her mind and to order her back. Summoning all her resolution, and encouraged, no doubt, by the interest of seeing Napoleon's reactions to her anguish, she allowed herself to be led on to the stage again, where she bowed to the monarch and his wife as a sign of apology. 'I resumed my acting, or, rather, I did not act at all, my eyes being all the time on the point where the bat had appeared. But it had changed its direction and now flew straight at our beautiful Joséphine.'

Joséphine, interested in all the world of nature, did not share Georgina's fear, but merely laughed and waved the bat away with her fan. But the poor creature, lost, flew wildly round among the bejewelled courtiers, and the play had to be suspended while lackeys chased it away.

Polyeucte was also performed before Napoleon, and a translation of *The School for Scandal* which pleased him so much that he did not fail to enquire who the translator was and to reward him handsomely. Napoleon was extraordinarily punctilious in praising and rewarding people who had pleased him in the arts, and was so generous in this way that he must have thought it outrageous had he been able to foresee his general reputation today as a tyrannical, selfish character. To playwrights and actors he was particularly kind and generous.

18

HE had changed, however, and had come back from Italy hardened in his pride; his gaiety had left him altogether and he was full of the sense of his own power. His despotic will showed itself more and more, silencing those about him who had formerly treated him as a friend. In Milan Cathedral he had placed the iron crown of the Lombard kings on his head in all seriousness. It had been with the utmost energy that he pronounced the sacramental words as he did so, giving them a significance that had made the assembly shiver as though in anticipation of a dreadful future. '*Dieu me l'a donné, gare a qui la touche!*' What he did not believe, as was clear from his tone of voice, was the first half of the phrase.

His notorious fits of rage were becoming more violent, and he had one of them during August at Boulogne, where he went to await the arrival of his fleet for the long desired invasion of England. Once more his admirals disappointed him. He railed at them in terrifying terms and fell from wrath into despair; then, unexpectedly, he recovered his composure in a flash and returned to Paris with a bold conception in mind of a campaign against

Austria which would break the coalition raised against him on the Continent.

Tense and ready for the prodigious military efforts he was about to make, Napoleon greeted Georgina after their separation. But it was not long before he again left Paris for an indefinite period, taking his army to the East. Though missing him sadly, Georgina's patriotic zeal was aroused by news of his victories which soon began to reach Paris, and pride in his achievements outweighed any sense of personal loss.

How great the victories were that Paris celebrated as the brilliant year of 1805 came to an end! They culminated in the Battle of Austerlitz, in which he defeated the Emperors of Russia and Austria. At the Comédie Française, the play would be interrupted at any moment by the dramatic arrival of the Commissaire de Police with the latest bulletin from the theatre of war. Coming on to the stage with a candle in his hand, he would read out the news in an atmosphere of tense excitement.

News of the Treaty of Presbourg was followed by the arrival of captured standards—more than a hundred of them—which were paraded through the streets of Paris while the populace looked on, intoxicated with joy. The naval victory of the sublime Nelson, the Battle of Trafalgar which had taken place in October, had been falsified and practically ignored by the papers by order of Napoleon, who fancied that the more his people believed in the inevitability of French victories the more French victories there would be.

Towards the end of January the Emperor himself returned, the great victor of Ulm and Austerlitz. It was not long before he visited the theatre to see his favourite play, *Cinna*. He received a rare ovation; there were cries of joy and tears were freely shed. 'And he, always so unassuming,' says Mlle George, 'bowing with his charming smile, and then taking his place in his armchair and listening with such engrossed attention to the masterpiece he had asked for. . . .'

His achievements had been extraordinary, somewhat comparable to the feats of Marlborough, whose campaigns he carefully studied. But he did not return home as Marlborough did to a country which had learnt to protect itself from exclusive and immoderate powers; he had the misfortune—though it looked to many like good fortune—to return to a country ready to deify him and forget all greatness apart from his. The Senate decreed that a monument should be erected to Napoleon the Great, and his birthday was proclaimed a national holiday. Triumphal arches were to be built in his honour, and it was even proposed that his sword should be solemnly blessed and placed in some commemorative building. Endless were the addresses of senators, bishops, prefects and mayors, wringing from the French language the last ounce of unctuous flattery. 'How was it possible,' says Mme de Rémusat, 'for any human mind not to become somewhat deranged by the excesses of all this praise?'

Napoleon's mind did not stand the strain, and those who knew him well could see his despotism increasing day by day. It was now that he planned to place his brothers on thrones, to create kingdoms and have them as his vassals; and it was now that he introduced ceremonies into his court which placed a barrier between him and other men. The ladies had to learn to curtsey, and at certain times the entire court, enlarged now by many foreigners recruited in Italy and the German States, had to file before him and his wife and make obeisance, a procedure which the growing megalomania in him had ordered, and which after a time exasperated the more normal side of him profoundly, for he was by nature a sensible and rational man. But there was no going back, and he would sit scowling at the curtseying ladies and ordering them to hurry, furious with them and self-persuaded that it was they who were forcing him to endure the ritual. In the pompous and artificial atmosphere pleasure withered away; even Joséphine's love for her husband, which had been so lively a passion, now wilted like a flower deprived of water. She endured all with perfect patience, but her boredom was extreme and she regretted the simple court of Consular days and the lost attractions of her husband.

Everything and everyone changed. And it was as though Napoleon had wrought the universal change by becoming a different and worse character himself. It was now, some time in

1806, so far as one can tell, that Georgina's love affair was suddenly terminated. The climate in which it had begun was dissipated, and it could hardly continue, though she had grown confident of late and little dreamed that the end of her connection with the Emperor was near at hand.

Her memoirs give the impression that she and Napoleon drifted apart gradually, and she gives as the cause her disappointment in him as an Emperor. She says nothing of a certain episode about which the gossips of the time spoke in low voices, and which was later referred to by Lucien Bonaparte.[1] One night, according to this episode, when she was with the Emperor in the private rooms he used for these pleasures, he alarmed her in the early hours by losing consciousness and even foaming at the mouth. He had had one of those fits which were from now onwards to overtake him from time to time.

Always impulsive, Georgina pulled desperately at the bell-rope and called for help without any thought of putting on a little clothing. The palace was aroused, doctors and surgeons were sent for, and the commotion did not fail to reach the ears of Joséphine, always a light sleeper. Joséphine, far from showing annoyance with Georgina, at once joined her in trying to help, and when Napoleon came to it was to find himself in the arms of both his wife and the undressed George, with doctors, servants, and ladies-in-waiting all about him: a sight which promptly caused him to faint anew.

He did not forgive the actress for her indiscretion. She was hardly to blame for calling for help in such an alarming situation; but she probably realized when she was being hurried out of the palace by Constant that it would have been wiser to have summoned assistance in less resonant tones. Constant would have dealt with the situation. But she was so accustomed to throwing the whole volume of her voice across large spaces that she had automatically acted in the same way now.

Whether the interesting story is true, no one could now say, but it was certainly believed in Paris at the time and was the subject of indiscreet engravings and caricatures after the fall of

[1] *Table Talk of Samuel Rogers*, 1952, pp. 222 and 240.

the Empire. Nothing could have infuriated Napoleon more than such indiscretion, and Georgina was not invited to spend a night with him again. He gave her up, whatever the truth of the matter might be, although as an actress she continued to be favoured by him.

19

DECISIVELY abandoned by Napoleon, Georgina rearranged her life. 'Not happy anywhere,' she says, 'I felt I must leave my apartments in the rue St Honoré. I could no longer bear them.' She moved to a flat in the rue Louis-le-Grand, and the rent was paid by M. Ouvrard, a financier who was well able to do so. Sometimes she stayed in his villa at Le Raincy, where the food was excellent and she could bathe in his marble swimming-pool. Life was easy and luxurious. But keeping a mistress was just a part of fashionable life; Ouvrard was courteous and amusing but cared nothing about her, and she missed the sympathy she had had from Napoleon, the interest he took in her career and in all her personal affairs.

At the age of nineteen she had tasted most of the pleasures of a luxurious society, and she was left feeling empty and dissatisfied. And if Napoleon had grown despotic, she was no less so in her own world. She had been haughty at the theatre ever since she was first invited to St Cloud. Flattered continually by men of rank and wealth, it seemed to her the most natural thing in the world that all she desired should be humbly offered to her by an admiring society. And while she played the part of a gay and charming woman among men of high society, she had many enemies among her colleagues, for whom she reserved her slights and cold airs of superiority. The actresses in particular had never forgiven her for her complacency over the great love affair, and were not a little amused by the story of her fall from favour. That fall, however, had not made her more bearable to live with; on the contrary, her complacency had hardened into an attitude of permanent arrogance.

The financier Ouvrard received no consideration from her but was exploited to the full; while paying her bills and doing her bidding, he had to respect the host of courtiers continually offering their homage. Among her admirers was Prince Clément de Metternich, with whom she was much seen; Ouvrard had to be thankful to be seen with her when she was not too busy.

Her success as an actress increased during the summer, when it was decreed that Raucourt should form a company of actors to go to Italy and there create a taste for French drama. The pupil now took her teacher's place as the leading actress of tragedy, the superior gifts of Duchesnois being, as usual, overlooked.

Yet Georgina was unhappy and cast about her for some compensation for her lost pleasures as Napoleon's mistress. There was no emotional satisfaction in her life, and she craved for some repetition of the affection that had made the days so easy and delightful for her. And in this state of mind she was easily captivated in the course of 1806 by the wiles of a man of letters called Souriguère Saint-Marc, who greatly desired to foist a play he was writing upon the Comédie Française.

Saint-Marc was turned forty but well preserved and youthful in appearance. More ready, perhaps, to be dotingly amorous than her princely admirers with their sense of personal splendour, he swept her off her feet and she fell into a deep and joyful infatuation.

His five-act tragedy, *Octavie*, was decidedly mediocre; but here he was, in a good strategic position, and he soon had it in rehearsal with a splendid cast, and Georgina as the heroine.

'Another favour, my good little Saint-Marc,' writes Mlle George (in a letter quoted by A. Augustin Thierry in his biography of the actress). 'Come to dinner this evening and help me to work on the first act. Your excellent and experienced lessons are of great value to me. If I have a success with it you will be able to say: "This is my work". And then . . .'

Octavie had its first performance—and its last—on December 9th 1806. Its failure was complete and catastrophic.

Deeply chagrined, Georgina lost interest in the handsome author as rapidly as the run of his play had come to an end. The grand passion vanished and its place was taken by resentment, for her credit was much diminished by the affair. Her enemies could hardly fail to smile. The worst aspect of the situation was that Ouvrard, tired of her infidelity, abandoned her for a rival actress, Mlle Volnais.

Now indeed she had cause for unhappiness. To be considered lacking in judgement was a blow to her conceit; she thought more regretfully than ever of the lost association with Napoleon, and yet without the consolation of having kept her faith and love intact. She had strayed from her true feelings and given way to the most unrestrained passion for a few weeks; now she regretted it and the old love for Napoleon swept back upon her in full force. And she was left, for the first time since the days of her début, with no regular and certain addition to her salary as an actress. And, indeed, by comparison with the amount of her debts it was but a small sum. If only fate had not denied her the child she had wished to have, the child of Napoleon, the Emperor's son! Napoleon had promised her everything she could desire if only this event could be brought about: a settled fortune, a great establishment, her own estate. In that case he would not have abandoned her. He would have visited her in her own home, and she would have been happy, perpetually happy and affectionate, making Napoleon happy and everyone else about her happy.

20

THAT lavish provision of which Georgina's ambition had once caught sight was about to be made to another. Without rhyme or reason a woman less clever, less beautiful, less charming—in fact, with no charm at all—was to have the glittering prize, the gratitude and the wealth. Only a week after the fall of Saint-

Marc's play, the first child of Napoleon was born, the illegitimate son of a certain Eléanore Denuelle.

On his return from Austerlitz, the Emperor had dallied for a week or two with the young and frivolous Mme Denuelle, a lady-in-waiting to his sister Caroline. She had not interested him or even pleased him, but she had provided distraction for a few idle hours. She had become pregnant, and now a son was born whose resemblance to the Bonapartes was striking. Napoleon thus had proof at last that he was not incapable of having children. Great was his satisfaction. Though he never saw Mme Denuelle again, he provided lavishly for her and settled a fortune upon the child.

Napoleon was abroad at the time of his son's birth. War had broken out between France and Prussia during the autumn and, the victor now of Iéna, he received the news at Pulstuck. The following day, January 1st, 1807, he was in Poland on his way to Warsaw, and fate brought him face to face with Marie Walewska. Joséphine, Georgina, Eléanore Denuelle—every woman who existed or could exist, faded into nothingness. For Mme Walewska he felt anew all the romantic passion he had once felt for Joséphine.

This year which opened with his meeting with Marie Walewska was the year of Eylau and Friedland, victories which made him the conqueror of the whole continent. Paris was in a frenzy of excitement and enthusiasm; two hundred conquered flags were paraded through the streets during the spring, and great packing-cases brought masterpieces of art to the Louvre, booty from the museums of defeated capitals; and at the end of July Napoleon returned to St Cloud after nearly a year's absence, having signed the Treaty of Tilsit which ended the war on the Continent and appeared to put him on the friendliest terms with Alexander of Russia.

The events had been prodigious. England once more stood alone against the Continent. Napoleon greeted his wife joyfully. 'We are sure of peace on the Continent,' he said, 'and peace on the seas will inevitably follow.' And he added that he was weary of the life of a general and was ready now to enjoy life at the head of civil affairs. Somewhere in Paris Marie Walewska was living in discreet obscurity; whenever he could escape from the splendours of the Tuileries and St Cloud he would drive off in secrecy to spend an enraptured hour or two with her.

He gave thought, too, to his recently born son. He was greatly elated by the event which inflamed his ambition to be succeeded by a Napoleon II and so brought the question of divorce to the forefront of his mind. In gratitude, he could not do enough for the mother and the child, and he gave orders for a luxurious and privileged upbringing for the latter; everything was to be made smooth for this favourite of fortune. Yet in spite of his self-seeking plans, in spite of his intention of discarding her, Napoleon was very affable with Joséphine at this time, not wishing her to suspect the truth. He was well pleased with the summer months.

The court moved to St Cloud. The Comédie Français came out to act before him and Georgina saw him frequently. With Talma she acted for him in *Rhadaminte et Zénobie*, *Mithridate*, *Nicomède* and *Rodogune*. Talma was still the Emperor's personal friend, able to talk freely to him; but Georgina, though she received friendly smiles and compliments from him, as from Joséphine, was kept at her proper distance.

Since Napoleon, as Emperor and master of Europe, had the dignity and confidence of his vast position, he was more than ever an impressive figure, and Georgina felt herself no less in love with him than in the past. Never had a man looked so noble and heroic; and surely no one could have been better matched in Imperial splendour with her own Grecian beauty? But Napoleon felt nothing of this, being satisfied with the frail and puny form of Mme Walewska. There was nothing Georgina could do for herself, and she went away from each performance feeling unhappy, so unhappy that she thought more and more frequently of going away from Paris.

Her life during the summer was as luxurious and extravagant as ever, but no one had come forward to take the place of Ouvrard and her debts were mounting. To add to her troubles, it was no longer as easy as it had been to ride roughshod over her colleagues at the theatre; since the failure of Saint-Marc's play she had had to endure many a veiled slight. 'I did everything I could to amuse myself,' she writes, 'but I was horribly bored. Even the theatre no longer attracted me as it used to. When all was said and done, it was a life of monotony. One played the same thing over and over again.' And she began to assure her friends that she intended to leave Paris, to abandon her position as an associate of the Comédie Française. They listened incredulously.

'Leave the Théâtre Français?' said the actor Florence. 'What are you thinking of? What about your pension, your reputation? The idea's demented. If you leave you'll lose everything—and a lot more as well!'

'Well, that's exactly why I want to go,' said Georgina. 'And I'm determined I will go.'

'But why? Are you not happy here?'

'Don't ask me. I'm tired of the emptiness of my life.'

The idea of leaving France, foolish and extraordinary though it was, gained upon her, and it received encouragement from the many foreigners she met and from whom she heard so much about foreign capitals. Her discontent made her criticize everything about her, and she persuaded herself that she would be far better understood and much happier in some other country. In France salaries were very low and an artist had no status. To be an actress in France meant living in misery, she told her friends. She recalled the recent funeral of Mlle Chameroy, a young dancer of the Opera whose remains had been refused admittance to one of the Paris churches by its vicar. The Paris clergy, indeed, showed the greatest objection to giving Christian burial to those actresses and dancers who ignored the moral code of society. Yet in England there were noblemen who married actresses. 'Actors such as Garrick,' she said one day to Talma, 'are buried among kings. But you, Talma, will not be allowed Christian burial here in France, though you are the pride and glory of our theatre.' And at times she was almost ready to fly off to London itself, the seat of the enemy's government.

In the autumn, the ambassador sent by the Czar Alexander, the Count Tolstoy, arrived in Paris; and since all ambassadors quickly found their way behind the scenes at the Théâtre Français Georgina's enthusiasm for foreigners received new encouragement. Nothing seemed so desirable now as a visit to Russia. The Russian noblemen were all that was distinguished and charming, and their manner was flattering. They watched her act with uncritical rapture and thought her a genius. No one ever heard these elegant persons speaking Russian to each other; they spoke in French and regarded France as the only source of culture. Their ruler, Alexander, had told Napoleon at Tilsit how eagerly he desired to visit Paris, 'the capital,' as he put it, 'of the most civilized empire in the universe'; and if he himself was not yet able to do so, his embassy had come in advance to enjoy the privilege and pay their homage to its actresses.

Count Tolstoy often called on Georgina; Count Maurice Benckendorff called more often still and made love to her. Their flattery helped to restore her *amour propre* after the disaster of Saint-Marc's failure. They talked much of Russia and of their handsome young Emperor, Alexander, who was so gallant with women. 'Count Benckendorff,' she writes, 'urged me to go to Russia. I said yes, but the next day I said no. It was at a masked ball that the affair was decided. Count Tolstoy would not leave me until I had promised to sign the next day.'

Count Benckendorff had forced her decision by asking her to marry him; it was an offer not to be refused. It was arranged that she was to travel to Russia at the earliest possible moment and meet him at St Petersburg; there she was to give performances and receive the homage of a court which knew better than the Parisians how to appreciate such gifts as she could show. And then the wedding would take place.

In all respects this was an exciting and exhilarating time. Wonderful French victories were constantly celebrated, and all things seemed to be possible. Why should she not marry a Russian nobleman and surpass her previous successes as the Venus of St Petersburg? There she would forget the ungrateful Napoleon and be rid of her tiresome creditors at the same time. Secrecy was necessary, for it was illegal to leave the national theatre when one had once been admitted to it. She told no one of her plans except Talma and the actor Florence, both of whom assured her that she was out of her mind. But they could not shake her resolution. The spring had arrived, the spring of 1808, and she made her preparations for the long journey. She did not dare to tell her family of her plans, but eased her conscience by promising herself she would send for them as soon as she had a home of her own.

21

DELRIEU, head of the Central Administration of Finance, who wrote plays on Sundays, had produced a tragedy for the Comédie Française, *Artaxerxes*, in which Mlle George, as Mandana, was the chief attraction. It was first performed on April 30th, and all seemed to be in train for a satisfactory run. On May 11th, however, the author arrived at the theatre to find it in confusion. Mlle George was missing and no one had news of her. The play had to be performed without her, while messengers went forth in search of information. She was not to be found, and her alarmed family could not account for her disappearance.

All Paris was in a state of excitement over the missing actress and little else was talked about. To add to the interest of the affair, another well-known theatrical figure had disappeared at the same time, and it was assumed that they were together. The *Journal de l'Empire* wrote on May 13th: 'The news which occupies the whole of Paris just now is the sudden disappearance of Duport, dancer of the Opera, and Mlle George, actress of the Comédie Française.'

The days passed, Mlle George did not return, and the play was withdrawn. Napoleon, as curious as any other Parisian, told the police to inform him as soon as they had news. In due course he learnt that his former mistress and the dancer from the Opera were on their way by coach to Russia. But it was too late to catch them at the frontier.

In flight from the creditors who were beginning to press her, from the theatre which had come to bore her, and the Emperor who had abandoned her, Mlle George raced eastwards. Awaiting her at St Petersburg was the Count de Benckendorff, the man whom she believed was shortly to be her husband.

The noble Count, as it happened, had no intention of marrying Mlle George. His proposal had been a ruse to entice her away from the Comédie Française. Once in Russia, she was to be offered to the Emperor Alexander as a diversion. Alexander had long been attached to Mme de Narishkine, whose family and friends enjoyed political favour. Men of the opposed party, who were in eclipse, desired nothing so much as the end of Mme de Narishkine's reign. But the Emperor was deeply devoted to his mistress, and so far all attempts to dislodge her had failed. Now, however, the Russian embassy had seen the celebrated Mlle George and had been dazzled by her charms. Surely Alexander could not resist the Venus of Paris, the mistress of Napoleon, of Talleyrand and Metternich? And the monstrous plan to place her in the limelight before their monarch, in rivalry with Mme de Narishkine, was concocted. Mlle George was lured to St Petersburg by a proposal of marriage, and it was hoped that Alexander would only have to see her to fall under her spell.

Georgina travelled along foreign roads with a light heart, and in the general game of deception she was holding her own. Louis Duport, the handsome young dancer from the Opera, was with her to ensure that the journey should not be tedious, and to add to the amusement of the adventure he had disguised himself as a girl and was travelling as her *femme de chambre* with the name of Julie.

'Why did I go?' asks Mlle George in her memoirs. 'Why did I leave Paris and the Comédie Française? Dear Heaven, do I know why? No. My capricious departure was brought about by my meeting with Count Tolstoy, the Russian ambassador. For some time I had not seen the Emperor—it was my own fault, no doubt. Ah, yes, without the least doubt it was my own fault. I was bored, I was in debt, and I could not bring myself to ask for help. I justified myself in every way; but the chief reason for my going was that I wanted a change, I wanted to go abroad. Ah, how stupidly a young artist can behave!' But these were the regrets of a later time. In the summer of 1808 the light-hearted Georgina gave herself up to the enjoyments of the hour, and as their coach rolled eastwards she and Duport laughed heartily at the thought of the consternation they had left behind in Paris.

The journey to Vienna took a week. Awaiting Georgina in this agreeable city was a letter telling her that she had been sentenced to pay a fine of 3,000 francs and that her name had been struck off the list of members of the Théâtre Français. About this she cared nothing, for all Viennese society was alert to meet her, and her arrival was equal, in its own sphere, to the arrival of the conquering Napoleon in foreign cities. She received a flattering welcome from everyone of note, and the most exclusive salons were open to her. The Princess Bagration seized her for her receptions, Mme de Staël made a cult of her and would hardly leave her side. 'She was very enthusiastic, Mme de Staël, and decidedly noisy,' say the memoirs. 'I was overwhelmed by her compliments, which it would be fatuous to repeat, but which were most flattering coming from such a witty and extraordinary woman.'

Two weeks flew by, and now it was time for her to leave, in spite of the many invitations she received to prolong her visit. She must leave, hurry along the roads to still greater triumphs and her wedding at St Petersburg.

Eastwards the horses trotted towards Vilna; magnificent scenery was passed, and at the inns and villages there was no one who understood a word of French. Georgina and Duport lived by signs, imitating a hen when they wished for eggs, a cow if they wanted milk, or a woman with a churn if they wanted butter. For a young actress of twenty-one and a ballet dancer who was not much older, making themselves understood without words was the easiest thing in the world, and no doubt they aroused much interest and admiration with their French wit and grace. 'I laughed until I was nearly ill,' Georgina says. 'And for payment, we simply held out our hands filled with ducats and they took all they wanted.'

Sometimes, however, the inns were detestable, and then Georgina would be filled with sombre doubts. 'My poor Paris, how I regretted having left it, and how I cursed the ambassador!' But at last Vilna was reached, and here again was an elegant society speaking French, with the governor of the town hastening to call on her and invite her to dinner and a great reception. Again she enjoyed extraordinary attentions, though she did not linger long in the town but hurried onwards towards St Petersburg.

There she and Louis Duport arrived early in June, the time of perpetual daylight. From the last relay-station, where the Grand Duke Constantine had his summer residence, the route was lined with the country houses of the nobility, houses built in a curious medley of international styles according to the taste of the owners. Georgina's dazzled eyes caught sight of Chinese pagodas, Greek temples, Swiss chalets and Italianesque towers, as well as French villas and Gothic mansions. These houses stood in brilliantly green gardens, where silver birches shone in stone vases, and vast heated conservatories were filled with the fruit that would not grow outside in such a northern climate.

At St Petersburg Georgina alighted at a luxurious hotel near the Winter Palace of his Majesty Alexander I, and there her supposed fiancé hurried to meet her. Duport joined a group of French dancers already established in the city, and Georgina was soon installed in the Klenovaïa. Count Benckendorff, in agreement with the Minister Spéranski (who particularly dreaded Mme de Narishkine's influence on Alexander) set about arranging for her introduction to court circles.

Napoleon's ambassador to Russia was M. de Caulaincourt, the Duke of Vicenza. The Duke's memoirs quote the reports that passed between St Petersburg and Paris on the subject of Mlle George. The first of them, sent to Napoleon on June 12th, 1808, records a conversation he had with the Czar just after the actress's arrival. Alexander, who had not yet seen her, was greatly displeased, for he realized she had been persuaded by members of his embassy to come to Russia.

'What,' he asked, ' is one to do with a single actress without actors? Besides, she's not the type who would have any success here. I am very displeased that having left the Paris theatre she should come to St Petersburg, where we have no use for her. It is in Paris itself that I hope to see all its attractions, and it is not at all my way, as you know, to wish to rob that capital of any of its advantages. Narishkin [his *Grand Chambellan*] thinks some love affair has brought her here. Well, she would have done better to conduct it elsewhere. . . . This is between ourselves; but if you think it proper to say a word to the Emperor [Napoleon] you may do so. You know what store I set by a due consideration of others, and I shall not overlook this lack of regard in those who are responsible.'

Napoleon replied indulgently to Caulaincourt's report. 'I have written to you regarding French actors and actresses at St Petersburg,' he said. 'They are welcome to keep them there for their entertainment as long as they please, although the Emperor is quite right to object to his agents enticing our actors away from their duties. It is M. de Benckendorff who encouraged the flight of these two. However, if a suitable moment arises for referring to the matter again, say that, for my part, I am charmed to think that anything we have here in Paris should amuse the Emperor.'

Napoleon was confident that Georgina would please Russian society, whatever Alexander's first thoughts on the subject might be; and although he was displeased with her for going away he felt that she would serve him well abroad, for he was doing all in his power to spread the taste for French culture everywhere in Europe. In Russia above all he wished his country and all its ways to be respected. The amicable terms established between himself and the Czar at Tilsit still prevailed. In his present mood, brought about by the birth of his illegitimate son Léon, his passion for Marie Walewska and the attendant diminution of his sentiment for Joséphine, he even envisaged marriage into the Russian Imperial family following upon the now almost inevitable divorce. He was most anxious to maintain his alliance with Russia for England's undoing, and he sought to impress Russian aristocrats by all the show and splendour his embassy could contrive to present. On a previous occasion he had written to Caulaincourt: 'I give you a free hand. . . . The French court must not appear to be small or mean. Our brother of Russia enjoys luxury and festivals. Be as magnificent as possible. Let them have their money's worth.'[1]

So the French embassy gave banquets that were second to none, and French actors and actresses were accorded protection and helped to maintain a good standard of living; for there was a French theatre at this time in Russia. When Alexander spoke of 'one actress alone' in his conversation about Mlle George, he was referring to her as a tragic actress; those already established in Russia played in comedies. Among them, Georgina found her colleague Thérèse Bourgoin, always well disposed towards her, though an implacable enemy of Napoleon, whom she could not forgive for failing to fall in love with her.

Of the French actors Frogère was the most celebrated, and he enjoyed the friendship of all the Imperial family. It was the habit of Alexander's brother, the Grand Duke Constantine, to receive friends while he was dressing; and on one occasion, when Frogère was present, he made some objection to a new pair of knee-breeches his valet had just helped him into. They were uncomfortable, he said, and he took them off and ordered his man to fetch another pair. The Grand Duke was a plain man but had a very good figure. And Frogère, who had been watching silently, suddenly said,

'Ah, you can't take *me* in.'

'What do you mean?' asked the Grand Duke.

'All you want to do,' said the actor, 'is to show off your fine legs and let us see that you own two pairs of breeches.'

There were shouts of laughter from the Grand Duke and everyone else in the room. Napoleon, says the Duke of Vicenza, who tells the story, would have had a man thrown out of the window if he had ventured upon such familiarity; but Alexander himself was equally unassuming in his manner with the actor.

France and everything French was the fashion in Russia. Alexander was mistaken in thinking that Mlle George would not be successful. She was from Paris, and that was enough.

[1] Vicence, *Souvenirs*, I, 30.

22

AN enchanted life opened out before Georgina. At that time St Petersburg was the seat of court life and appeared to exist solely for the pleasures of the mighty. Everything there spoke of wealth, and excessive wealth, a state of affairs very gratifying to the luxurious Georgina. All was elegance and beauty. The marble palaces, the blue canals with their pink granite quays and wrought-iron bridges, the fine avenues and parks: all this made the city unique in Europe. Moreover, it was June and the light was magical. It was very warm, and yet all day there was a singular calm and purity in the air as in the early hours further south when the sun has just risen. On the Neva were yachts, the reflections of whose coloured sails appeared to be varnished on to the translucent water; and Georgina was taken out on Venetian gondolas on the endless summer evenings and heard the music of primitive horns in the distance. In July there came the fête of Peterhof where the fountains were so splendid, and soon after she made her début at the court theatre in *Semiramis*.

Since her memoirs do not take us as far as Russia, it is only here and there from others that we find information about her life at this time. Hector Fleischmann quotes from letters she sent to her mother, letters signed 'George Benckendorff'—a sure indication that she seriously considered herself as being engaged to marry the Count. On August the 5th she writes describing her appearance at the royal theatre at Peterhof:

'All the Imperial family were present. In order that I should not be disconcerted, I had been told beforehand that it was not the custom to applaud the *entrées* of an actor. But in spite of this, as soon as I appeared I was received as at Paris—I swear it. Imagine how astonished everyone was! No one applauds until the Emperor has done so. It was therefore he who began at each of my entries. Just imagine, dear mother, what a brilliant success!

No one had seen anything like it before. And the whole family sent me their compliments afterwards. You can have no idea of the enthusiasm. The Emperor, above all, was in ecstasies. Her Majesty the Empress Mother said at dinner: "I was in Paris in the times of Mlle Clairon and I went very often to see her. But she never produced such an effect on me as Mlle George has done." '

After describing her successes at length, Mlle George says that the Grand Duke Constantine visits her every day and loves her like a sister, and that she herself is more than ever in love with Benckendorff and that everyone is jealous of her happiness.

The Emperor Alexander was momentarily dazzled; and before long Count de Benckendorff and his fellow schemers had their reward. Just as Mlle George had been asked one night to St Cloud by Napoleon, so now she was called to Peterhof. But neither she nor Alexander have left any comments for posterity on this interesting *tête-à-tête*, and it did not lead to enthusiasm on either side. It would have been surprising if Alexander and Napoleon could both feel attracted by the same woman, so entirely different were they in character. Alexander was exceedingly gallant and most anxious to please attractive women; but he so exalted the idea of love that to him it was more a spiritual than an earthly thing, and he could find no true pleasure in it if he did not feel that body, soul and intellect were all involved. He had sent for Mlle George, perhaps, because it had seemed the kind of thing he ought to do—that all his aristocratic subjects would do. Or perhaps it was because he was really curious to have a close view of the fine new toy imported from Paris. Or it may have been because Mme Narishkine, so frequently unfaithful to him, had recently hurt his feelings and left him with a kind of inner desolation that he often experienced, so that, clutching at straws, he listened for a moment to those who praised the famous George and swore her charm and understanding were equal to her beauty. Might she prove to be the ideal woman he was seeking, longing for a profound and eternal love such as he had it in him to bestow? No doubt it did not take many moments to find out that Mlle George had no such aspirations. Behind her beauty there was none of the depth of feeling that he sought.

Georgina, in any case, was in love with her Count de Bencken-dorff. No doubt she was exceedingly pleased to display her perfection of form to the Autocrat of all the Russias. But she went to him as a vain though obliging woman, accustomed to dissipation and more ready at all times for a good laugh than for the exchange of eternal verities. It was not in her that the Czar's melancholy depths of longing, his desire to find reason and meaning in life, would obtain satisfaction. He sent her a magnificent set of diamonds and turned back to Mme de Narishkine. However inadequate Mme de Narishkine's response might be—and he knew it was hopelessly inadequate—he saw more in her than in anyone else and he did not wish to dissipate his feelings in the company of other women. 'The Emperor,' the Duke of Vicenza writes, 'loved Mme de Narishkine like a true knight.'

Georgina admired her flashing diamonds with much complacency and felt no regrets; and Alexander prepared himself for another friendly meeting with his brother of France, Napoleon.

23

THE famous meeting at Erfurt took place in September and October of this year of 1808, and Georgina, had she remained with the Comédie Française, would have been present, for Napoleon, the host, profited by the occasion to put on a dramatic festival and took his players with him. Every night there were performances at the theatre of Erfurt; and the visitors to the festival were kings and reigning dukes, summoned to improve their minds and take their second place in world affairs. Napoleon had promised his friend Talma he would one day give him the chance to act before a parterre of kings, and it was now that he kept his word.

Acting with Talma was Duchesnois, who had come into her own on the departure of her rival. For this actress life had suddenly taken a happier turn. Talma had been dotingly attached to Georgina; but now that she was out of sight he had time to notice Duchesnois, who was left as the leading actress of the company and now acted with him in George's place. His old animosity towards her quickly faded as he began to enjoy the pleasure of constantly working with someone so intelligent and conscientious. He helped her as he had hitherto helped George, and he took pride in her performances. There were qualities, after all, that were more desirable in one's close associates even than beauty.

Erfurt brought the divorce so greatly dreaded by Joséphine a step nearer, for Napoleon had given further thought to the possibility of marrying one of Alexander's sisters, and he hoped now to make some definite arrangement for himself. In his pride he could not risk a rebuff in the form of a refusal, so Talleyrand was called on to broach the subject with the Czar. No one was so expert as Talleyrand at making men say the things he wished them to say, and Alexander, although it was not his true feeling, soon found himself intimating to Napoleon that he would like nothing so well as to have him as a brother-in-law.

No one could fail to notice the evident contentment of the two Emperors, nor to be struck by their show of affection for each other. The conference ended on this happy note. Thanks perhaps, to the atmosphere of festivity produced by banquets and plays, it had run easily from start to finish. Kings and princes had been placated and reassured by Napoleon's attentions and affability, and they all dispersed with a great exchange of gold snuff-boxes, miniatures, Sèvres and Dresden china and graceful compliments. Yet even the stormiest and most frustrating conferences of a later and less polished age could scarcely be less productive than this one was to be. Of all that was planned, nothing was to come about; and Napoleon and Alexander, who seemed to divide the world between them and had promised it peace, were never to see each other again. Only war and enmity lay ahead.

The Czar returned to St Petersburg and its winter pleasures. The close alliance with France intensified the passion for all that had the stamp of Paris, and Georgina had become an idolized favourite. Somehow or other a French company was assembled to play with her at the Imperial Theatre, where French tragedies were now regularly given. No one was over-exacting with regard to the standard of acting. That Mlle George should be on the centre of the stage reciting French verses was enough in itself to send the fashionable audiences into transports of delight.

In January 1809 the actress wrote to her mother and told her how she was situated financially. She was receiving a salary of 16,000 roubles, she said, and two benefit performances had brought her in an additional 20,000 roubles. She assured her mother that she was now living an orderly life, and that she was almost married to her dear, good Benckendorff.

In fact, she was living a life of supreme self-indulgence and luxury, and the conceit which had been tempered in Paris by criticism was now increased a thousandfold. Here there was no Duchesnois, with a following of discriminating admirers; there was no malicious gossip about her sudden dismissal from the Emperor Napoleon's favour. She was the great attraction of the city, peerless in the eyes of all and free to do as she chose.

There was only one flaw in the situation. The Count de Benckendorff could not be brought to the point regarding their marriage, and as the weeks passed the truth dawned upon her: he had no intention of marrying her. He even grew noticeably tired of her, and eventually he managed to slip away from her altogether. However, she had much to distract her and did not feel the disappointment for very long. Princes and grand dukes were there by the score to flatter and make love to her, even if no one among them was rash enough to propose to marry her. And the great families, the Strogonoffs, the Galitzins, the Dolgoroukis, strove for the distinction of having her in their salons. A recitation by Mlle George was an immense attraction, and the guests at an evening reception would be enraptured by the official manner of the Comédie Française which had blossomed forth in her to perfection.

The winter season was as delightful as the summer had been,

and social gatherings were brilliant. The Strogonoffs, for instance, held receptions in their conservatory. This conservatory, of an immense size, heated by stoves and pipes which were hidden from view, contained large trees forming beautiful alleys. Birds flew about among them and sang from their branches, and bright tropical flowers were in bloom. Fruit hung on smaller trees, some of it growing there, and some produced at immense expense, suspended in ornamental baskets for the guests to eat. The perfumed air was that of a hot summer day; yet when you looked at the vast glass walls you saw large snowflakes whirling by; you saw snow and ice on the ground, and perhaps a coachman passing by, his long hair and beard white with frost.

The Neva, the canals and lakes were frozen. Snow covered the ground for about eight months. But the weather was calm and sunny for much of the time, and there were parties on the ice and excursions into the surrounding countryside on sleighs. The forest trees were white with frost, and the branches sparkled like diamonds. On the Neva, avenues of pine trees were set up and beneath them a fair was held. Here the finest food was on sale at a very high price: pineapples costing several pounds each, and whole animals, killed but otherwise untouched and standing upright. All was frozen as in a refrigerator and so would keep in perfect condition for weeks on end. Georgina, well covered with superb Russian furs, was able to glide round in a *troika* drawn by fine Ukrainian horses; sometimes the Czar met her, and he would invariably stop his horses and descend from his own vehicle in order to bow to her as she passed.

Of her place in Russian society, a brief picture has been given by Tolstoy in *War and Peace*. He is describing a party given by the Countess Besonkhow. Anatole Kouragine, earlier described as being on terms of great intimacy with Mlle George, is present with the intention of flirting with Natacha, the daughter of Count Rostow:

While Mlle George withdrew to change her costume, the chairs were placed in rows, and everyone found a seat; Anatole was about to take a place by the side of Natacha when the count, who kept his eyes on his daughter, took the chair, so he was obliged to find one close behind them.

Mlle George soon reappeared, draped in a crimson shawl fastened on the shoulders so as to display her fine though large dimpled arms; she stood in the middle of the space left for her facing her audience, struck an affected attitude which was hailed by a murmur of enthusiasm, and after gazing round her with theatrical gloom began to declaim a long soliloquy in French (from *Phèdre*) describing her guilty passion for her stepson. Raising and dropping her voice by turns, she lifted her head in defiant pride or, rolling her eyes, she gave utterance to deep, hoarse chest-notes.

'Exquisite! Divine! Delicious!' was shouted on all sides. Natacha, with her eyes fixed on the stalwart tragédienne, neither saw nor understood. She was only conscious of having been suddenly plunged once more into this strange, mad world, immeasurably remote from reality; a world where good and evil, folly and reason, were all mingled in confusion. Startled and painfully excited, her nerves were quivering with expectancy. The monologue being ended, everyone rose and applauded the actress.

'How beautiful she is!' Natacha exclaimed to her father who, like the rest, was trying to get through the crowd.

'I cease to think so when I look at you,' Anatole murmured in her ear so that she alone could hear. 'You are too bewitching. From the first moment I saw you . . .'

'Come, Natacha,' said the count, turning round.

She followed her father with a dazed look in her eyes.

Mlle George recited several more pieces, and then bid the countess goodnight. The rest of the company were asked to adjourn to the ball-room.

Georgina's acting was hardly likely to improve in Russia. She had learnt the traditional conventions of the Comédie Française, and she was now content to go through her roles mechanically, gesticulating and declaiming and posturing with ever-growing exaggeration, and convinced herself that the performances were superb, since they always met with the applause a superb performance would deserve. Nor was there ever anything new to be learnt. During the five years of her residence at St Petersburg, the old tragic roles were repeated endlessly.

From France there came news of Mme Weymer's death; she had been ill for some time and did not long survive her daughter's flight. Other news, coming at the end of the year, was hardly less saddening; it told of the Emperor Napoleon's divorce from Joséphine. Poor Joséphine, after many terrible scenes, in which tears were shed and consciousness was lost, had been defeated at last in her long battle to keep the husband to whom she was so strangely devoted. Napoleon, still in love with Marie Walewska, was now able to feel sufficiently detached about Joséphine's feelings to face the emotional stress of the event he had so long put off. The old attachment lingered still, however, and when it came to the point he wept only less than Joséphine herself; moreover, he ordained that at all court ceremonies Joséphine was to take second place after his new wife (when he had found her); she was to have palaces to live in, an immense revenue and the highest honours. But all this was little consolation to Joséphine, who was exceedingly unhappy and also alarmed for Napoleon's future. She always believed it was she who was responsible for his good fortune. To her influence in the first place he had owed the Italian command that brought him to fame; she felt that when he strayed from her he was no longer safe. The Bonaparte family, outshining each other in pride, were gloating over her divorce, when most probably her own lack of pride would have kept all of them from falling, had they befriended her instead of working to bring her down.

Georgina, who had always admired Joséphine, was dismayed by the news. Russians coming home from their visits to Paris described the excitement and the rumours flying about concerning Napoleon's second marriage. Most people supposed it would be with the Grand Duchess Anne, the Czar's sister.

Napoleon had, indeed, recently asked Alexander to give him a decision on this point immediately. Forthright Napoleonic words had been put into the French ambassador's mouth in an order from Paris: 'His Majesty wishes you to bring up the question frankly and simply with the Emperor Alexander, speaking to him in these terms: "Sire, I have reason to think that the Emperor, urged by all France, has decided upon a divorce. May I report that he can count on your sister? Will your Majesty think about this during the next forty-eight hours and then frankly give me his reply?" '

Alexander, who had his *amour propre* as well as Napoleon, disliked being ordered to make up his mind within a given time. He replied that he must consult his mother and that family discussions could not be hurried. Napoleon, who regarded himself the superior of all princes, believed that his hand ought to be accepted the instant he deigned to offer it. He took offence, he waited a few weeks with the utmost impatience, and then he broke off negotiations, preferring to offer a rebuff himself rather than risk receiving one. Other courts were more than eager to offer him a wife, and he wasted no time. Three months after the divorce he was married to the Austrian Archduchess, Marie Louise.

24

In Russia, the affront offered by Napoleon's conduct in the marriage negotiations had been felt, and there was a decided chill in the air. But Napoleon, the recent victor of Wagram and the husband of Marie Louise, was in a position of unusual power and appeared to be solidly and for ever established as the arbiter of Europe. Deference was paid to him, therefore, and Mlle George continued to enjoy her status as priestess of Parisian culture. The time passed, she took little note of political events which had no effect upon her life of endless pleasures. She had settled down, and she sent for her father and sister, who came to share the ease of her pleasant home.

Gossip from Paris was more interesting than news of battles and the continental blockade. One learnt that Marie Louise was unpopular. She did not enjoy spending, and the tradesmen were in despair. Napoleon treated her like a spoilt child but appeared to be rather afraid of her. He seldom slept in her room because she loved draughts and cold air and had no notion of considering his tastes. She would order the fire to be extinguished and the windows opened on a cold night; she was only eighteen years old and had soon become pregnant, a state in which a girl so lusty had nothing to complain of regarding circulation. Napoleon, of Mediterranean race and rather frail, felt the cold intensely. This was his first experience of cold bedrooms and he did not enjoy it. It was equally his first experience of intimacy with a being as selfish as himself.

Joséphine was living at Malmaison, consoling herself with her flowers and trees; Duchesnois was the leading tragedienne of the Comédie Française, working quietly and modestly, appearing with Talma night after night and enjoying the best reputation. This was not welcome news, for Georgina had not ceased to detest Duchesnois. The rival had a lover, too, and even a child. But this lover was a mere nonentity, a young man named Harel, illegitimate son of the writer Luce de Lancival. Georgina had seen him at times at the theatre but had paid him no attention. News came of magnificent festivals in Paris. Now that Napoleon was married to a Hapsburg there was surpassing splendour in all the ceremonies of court. Wonderful fêtes were given by the nobility in honour of Marie Louise; but at the one given by the Austrian ambassador fire broke out. The walls of the ballroom were hung with tapestry and gold and silver gauze; elegant light draperies, ribbon, flowers and wax candles made the scene a delight to the eye; but a draught lifted a muslin curtain towards a candle, and soon all the inflammable decorations were ablaze. Marie Louise was hustled away without ceremony, but many lost their lives and the Russian ambassador Kouragine, who had succeeded Tolstoy, was seriously injured.

Most of the gossip reaching St Petersburg, however, was of splendid and happy events in the favoured capital, Paris, and it culminated in accounts of the birth of Napoleon's heir, the child on whom he immediately conferred the crown once offered by Antony to Julius Caesar.

Yet, unseen by the majority, things were going wrong with the Emperor Napoleon; still kind to those about him and most indulgent towards his selfish young wife, he was increasingly susceptible in political affairs. One reason for this was certainly the absence of Joséphine, who had looked after him so well. He was by no means an independent man, but had great need of someone to turn to when he was depressed, someone who understood all the best in him and would patiently and cheerfully talk him into his better moods. Now he was irritable and suspicious; he regarded lack of deference as an insult, and the least assault on his vanity appeared to him to warrant a battle. All had gone askew, and even while Georgina basked in her illusion of perpetual security Alexander had come to fear Napoleon and to regard him as an enemy.

And one day, unexpectedly and astonishingly, there came news that Napoleon was marching into Russia with a colossal army. Well, he would score some fine victory, of course, dictate his terms and then at last give Europe that conclusive peace so often promised. So the French in St Petersburg confidently believed. But it was Russia who won the day, and soon there came news of the French disaster, the retreat from Moscow and the rout of the Grand Army. In London, in the House of Commons, men wept with relief, so terrible had been the strain of many years of desperate danger. In St Petersburg every house was illumined at night, apart from that of Mlle George, where the shutters were drawn.

Georgina was stupefied. She had thought little about politics and knew nothing of history; her ideas had been formed in Consular Paris, where everyone had worshipped Napoleon. At the time when he was her lover, he had seemed to her not merely a successful man but the very embodiment of success. She had spent those delightful nights which she would never cease to miss with the god of good fortune himself, and she had never envisaged the possibility of his meeting with failure. Such he had seemed, too, to Marie Louise. But Joséphine was not surprised. She had always felt that it did not do to be fortunate to excess, and had told him so many a time. If he had listened to her, how different everything would have been!

The blow had been sudden and the French colony in St

Petersburg was thrown into confusion. Some fled at once, others stayed. War was still limited to armies and battlefields, and there was no animosity between the civilians of enemy countries. The Weymer family hesitated for a few weeks, uncertain whether to remain or leave. Then, the news becoming more disastrous every day, they decided to return to Paris, and they set off on the long journey at the end of January 1813, accompanied by most of the French actors in the town.

They left on sleighs *en route* for the Gulf of Finland; further south the roads were blocked by the desperate remnants of the French army. Georgina and her sister, wrapped in padded clothing and heavy furs, sat in the front sleigh, and their postilion, she says, was no more than eight or ten years old. Between them, the sisters grasped a large bag containing money and diamonds worth 300,000 gold francs. It is Alexandre Dumas, a friend of Georgina's at a later time, who gives this figure. Not an altogether agreeable picture, this, of the pampered actress fleeing with her spoils; nor is the picture of Napoleon's flight from Russia any more pleasing.

It was on January the 5th that Napoleon left for Paris, abandoning a disorganized army which was without food or shelter and in the enemy's country. Mme Choiseul-Gouffier, in the vicinity of Smorgoni, describes his arrival there at midday. His lunch was served in his carriage, and as he ate his coachman fell dead from the cold. That night, in the greatest secrecy, he set off westwards, incognito, in a sleigh, accompanied by his servant Roustan, by the Duke of Vicenza, the Count de Lobau, Marshal Duroc and General Lefevre-Desnoëttes. Drawn by three fast horses, the sleigh swept across the vast, icy plains of Lithuania and Poland towards Saxony; and Napoleon reclined among his furs, hidden from view. Had his name been mentioned anywhere where there were men to hear it, or had his face been recognized, he would have been torn to pieces. And this, perhaps, was all a man could acquire inwardly when he fought to gain the whole world and acknowledged no power above his own: the certainty that if at any time he was caught at a disadvantage he would be torn to pieces as by a pack of wolves.

Two weeks later he was in Paris; and still on the frozen plains were thousands of young men struggling on foot towards Poland. They walked in groups, silent and in despair; there was nothing for them but to walk until they fell. And they fell in thousands daily; first they would lose their sight, then their hearing, and then, mercifully, their consciousness. But the man who had fought for power over them and had forced them to march into Russia was comfortably in his warm rooms in Paris, if not in the best of humours.

25

THE flight of the actors was not easy, but they surmounted its difficulties in the high spirits habitual to them. Napoleon had long since forgotten the gaiety of his youth and had travelled an easier route white and frowning; but Georgina laughed as readily now on a snowy night in Finland as she had laughed with him ten years ago when they loved each other.

Immense tracts of silent and deserted land had to be traversed. Wolves howled incessantly, as hungry as the remnant of the Grand Army; often they came close and had to be dispersed by gunshot. There were relay stations and primitive inns along the route where the actors spent the nights—usually sleeping on the floor—and changed their horses. They passed through sheets of icy rain and through blizzards; they went down rivers on blocks of shifting ice, and at times they swept over ice so thin that they could see the water rushing along beneath. Bébelle fell out of the sleigh one day into the mire and could not rise because of the heavy weight of her furs, boots and jewels. 'And I was so overcome with mirth,' Georgina says in her notes on the journey, 'that I was unable to help her. Fortunately our caravan arrived at a gallop, their guns ready to meet the danger of wolves.'

Great was their relief when, after crossing to the Island of

Aaland, they reached Sweden, where the inns were clean and cheerful and they had beds to sleep in. But it took three weeks to reach Stockholm, the capital, where they were sure of being welcomed and intended to pass some time.

They entered this city in their sleighs, shabby and weary with travelling. By now, the splendid furs Georgina and her sister wore were bedraggled and stained by the harsh weather; their heavy bonnets, trimmed with swansdown, which had been so attractive when they set out, were splashed with mud and looked grotesque. They were glad to hurry into a hotel and remove their travelling clothes.

Visitors soon appeared: Mme de Staël, who was living in the town, and Prince Bernadotte. This last placed a carriage at Georgina's disposal, and she and her companions were begged to give a series of performances at the theatre. The actors agreed, and decided to remain in Stockholm until the approach of spring, when travelling would be easier.

As usual, Georgina was entertained by all the rich and influential citizens of the town, and dinners and receptions were given in her honour. The King and Queen attended her first performance at the theatre, and she was asked to give recitations in private houses. Once more Mme de Staël pursued her, begging her to attend her parties. The Queen often asked her to call, and not only talked about St Petersburg and the Russian court, but read the works of the great French playwrights with her.

Three months passed very agreeably in Stockholm, and now it was time to leave. The Queen gave Georgina an enamelled watch as a parting gift. Prince Bernadotte provided her with a handsome travelling carriage, and asked her to deliver a letter for him to King Jérome in Brunswick. The war had reached a critical stage and a courier might be caught by the enemy and searched; but no one would molest an actress travelling with her company.

Once again Georgina set off, travelling very comfortably now in fine spring weather. She called first at Brunswick, where she placed Bernadotte's letter in the hands of King Jérome, and then went on to Dresden, which she reached on June 20th. The Duke of Vicenza called on her as soon as he heard of her arrival, and she learnt that Napoleon himself was in the town. Not only that, he was arranging another of his theatrical festivals. The comedians of the Théâtre Français had reached the town only forty-eight hours ago. The Emperor, said the Duke, was eager to see Georgina and had sent him to make an appointment.

Unfortunately the rendezvous was fixed for the respectable hour of seven the following morning; and if Georgina hoped to arouse the former passions of Napoleon she was to be disappointed. Napoleon was gracious and had forgotten his past displeasure with her. He was pleased to see again a woman he had once enjoyed loving and whom he found more beautiful than ever. He was almost affectionate, but in a way no more than friendly. Moreover, he was turned forty and now lived as a respectable man. His liaison with the Polish countess, Marie Walewska, was not frivolous; he loved her well enough to regard her as the woman who would have been his wife had he been a private citizen. He treated Marie Louise with all possible indulgence, and he adored their son, the King of Rome, as in some way a more Imperial extension of himself, born to the purple. He wished to behave as a man this son could grow up to admire, and his private conduct was such as befitted an Emperor and a father.

Since his flight from Russia to Paris, he had been trying to hypnotize his people into thinking they were extremely well off, and had been conscripting more men to replace the many thousands lost in Russia. The mothers of France were beginning to despair, but they were of no account and it appeared that every young man could be claimed for a never-ending war. Momentarily, however, there was a truce. Napoleon had scored two victories recently, those of Lutzen and Bautzen, and had then signed an armistice. This he had done merely to gain time in which to prepare his armies for still more battles. The presence of the Comédie Française was to help to throw dust in people's eyes. All Europe, weary of war, was ready to give him peace on very reasonable terms, and he was pretending that he was ready to negotiate. In fact, however, it was intolerable to him to accept a peace, however reasonable, whose terms he himself could not dictate, and he was preparing to avenge the defeat in Russia, so injurious to his pride. With another theatrical festival to divert attention he could the better hide his plans. Moreover, his passion for the theatre was as great as ever and he looked forward to the coming performances. Even in the darkest moments he could turn his thoughts to the affairs of the Comédie Française, and it was in the Kremlin that he had recently drawn out a complete set of rules and regulations for the company, the *Décret de Moscou*. This work had been done with the ruined city of Moscow still smouldering about him after the great fire, at a time of catastrophe that would have driven such minor concerns as the welfare of the theatre out of the mind of anyone less extraordinary.

Georgina found him a changed man. He had grown very fat, complacent and self-assured. His eye had lost its former penetration, its capacity for seeing into the thoughts of others, and was clouded with constant suspicion. He had lost his gay spontaneity, and yet had become more talkative. The thin young man, sometimes lively and amusing, sometimes lost in thought, but never tedious, had vanished altogether. Georgina was surprised to find him so wordy; he talked hard about the theatre and asked about her life abroad, though without paying much attention to her replies. However, he was obviously well disposed and pleased to see her, and he insisted that she must take part in his festival. It had been his intention to have only the comedians at Dresden; but since she had arrived so opportunely he would send for Talma and the rest and they would put on the works of Corneille and Racine.

Napoleon was staying at the Marcolini Palace, and here a theatre had been specially constructed for the comedies. But the tragedies were given at the elegant public theatre of Dresden, so admirably designed to display the uniform, the evening dresses and jewels of the period. Georgina appeared with Talma in *Phèdre* and subsequently in other tragedies of the repertory. Duchesnois was not asked to be present on this occasion, and the omission must have appeared insulting. For five years she had been the leading actress of Paris; but now, it seemed, she was to be discarded since the Emperor's favourite was back.

The festival lasted for six weeks, and was brilliant enough although in no way comparable with the festival of Erfurt. At Erfurt the parterre of smiling kings had believed Napoleon invincible; but behind the polite smiles at Dresden were thoughts that no one would have wished to make known to the host. The snows of 1812 had cast their chill on diplomatic friendships. And here only one king was present, the old King of Saxony.

Talma felt the difference, but Georgina and the actors of comedy who had not been at Erfurt found the occasion very brilliant. The actor Fleury describes in his memoirs the delight of himself and his colleagues on being ordered to Dresden. The immensity of the disaster in Russia had been carefully hidden from the general public, and the actors had no notion of the extent to which the Empire was now undermined. They set off, he says, 'proud to take part in the Emperor's promenades'. Besides, everything was organized so lavishly that there were no grounds for doubting the power and solidity of the government. Each actor was given 3,000 francs for the expenses of the journey, and, if he had no travelling coach of his own, the Government provided one for him and arranged the transport of his servants and luggage in the public diligences. And when they arrived at Dresden they received a flattering welcome and their rooms were waiting for them in the best hotels.

'What a theatre!' Fleury says. 'And what an audience! One of the great kings of the north, a prince royal, twenty princes from the Baltic and the Rhine, illustrious confederates and sovereign dukes, and the conqueror himself: always awaited and arriving last of all.' Georgina referred to all these princes as *les chambellans de l'aigle*.

Among the Dresden flatterers was a German scholar named Ritterstein who had devoted much time to researching into the ancestry of Napoleon. He now came forward with his thesis, which proved, with the fullest reference to documents, that Napoleon was descended from the minstrel Blondel, that touching and devoted figure who accompanied Richard Cœur de Lion on his crusade, who played soothing music to him when he was stricken with malaria at Jaffa, and then discovered his whereabouts when he was imprisoned in Germany. It appears that Blondel was an Italian named Buonaparte, who changed his name on marrying a Norman lady to one more easily pronounced in his country of choice. Napoleon, while acknowledging the genealogical work with great politeness, would probably have preferred descent from King Richard himself.

The armistice expired, Napoleon left for Mayence, where he had arranged to meet Marie Louise. Soon after, the Comédie Française left for Paris. Georgina had had innumerable conversations with Napoleon and had once more felt the old attraction. She would have given much to have him at her feet as in the past, but she had to realize that he was now no more than a warm friend. She had certainly made the fullest use of the interest he took in her. She had confided in him her fears for the future. She was returning home, she pointed out, with no prospect of employment. What would become of her if she had to rely on the uncertainties of the ordinary commercial theatres? Napoleon had responded by ordering that she should be reinstated as an associate of the Comédie Française. He did more. He ordered that arrears of payment should be made to her as though she had been present and working all these five years at the theatre, instead of playing truant at St Petersburg. He also paid her at the highest rate for her performances at Dresden.

Georgina now travelled on to Paris very cheerfully. She was still to be the queen of the Comédie Française, the great George, the leading tragic actress of France. And had Napoleon known how to compromise with Europe she would no doubt have kept this fine position all her days. The majority of her colleagues, however, exasperated by such blatant injustice, only awaited a suitable moment for revenge, and the moment was nearer than anyone thought.

26

DUCHESNOIS learnt with alarm and depression that her old rival was returning to the Comédie Française. But Talma, who had been shocked by Georgina's acting at Dresden, wrote to a friend: 'Duchesnois would be wrong to be anxious. She has advantages which George cannot equal, and I think the latter cannot do her any possible harm, especially if the newspapers refrain from interfering.'

But the newspapers were all ready to whip up the former rivalry between the two actresses. They were not allowed to talk of the political facts of the day, of the menace from abroad and the growing discontent of the mass of the people, so they were only too delighted to interfere in the doings of the Comédie Française. The actors from Dresden arrived at the end of August, and the Press was full of the great event of Mlle George's reappearance.

She began to perform at the end of September, and the leading critics were loud in her praise. In all the official papers of the Empire she received glowing homage; the influence of Geoffroy was still on her side. Elsewhere, indeed, many criticized her freely, but in an undertone, in newspapers of no account. All was well; Duchesnois, who had played the leading roles for so long, now had to give way to herself, and she did not doubt that she would soon win complete supremacy. All Paris was talking of her resplendent beauty; for it was agreed that, although she was now approaching the age of twenty-seven, she was more attractive than ever. It could no longer, indeed, be said that she resembled the Grecian statues of Venus or Psyche, but she could now be compared with the goddess Juno.

The autumn was mild and there were public fêtes and cele-brations as usual, for Napoleon tried to disguise the truth from his capital by providing such pleasures. Yet conscripts were being called up and uniformed men walked about the streets. The country was being bled to death, the working classes were in misery and even the rich were less well off than formerly and were inclined to complain.

Georgina established herself in the rue de Rivoli and settled down to the pleasures of the capital. But the year ended dismally, with terrible rumours of impending disaster passing round the salons.

1814 opened more dismally still, and the rumours spoke of Napoleon's outbursts of rage on January 1st when certain deputies had dared to murmur against the war and the distress it was causing. People were hiding away their gold, and even in the foyers of the Comédie Française one might often hear the Emperor openly abused. As Talleyrand said, it was 'the beginning of the end'.

While the majority of Napoleon's admirers were cautiously silent in the presence of those who now criticized him, Georgina displayed plenty of courage at this time. She was a pampered favourite, enjoying privileges that were blatantly unjust, but at least she was not ungrateful. If anyone spoke against the Emperor in her presence she would turn on him, pale with anger, and pour eloquent wrath upon his head. The Emperor, in her opinion, had restored France and worked unremittingly for the good of them all; it was despicable to turn against him in times of misfortune. If the country stood by him, all would still be well.

At the end of January Napoleon joined his army and shortly afterwards couriers reached Paris with exaggerated news of minor victories. Once more, the play was interrupted nightly at the Théâtre Français so that reports could be read out from the stage. For six weeks or so the papers described the successful contests of Montmirail, Château-Thierry, Vauchamps, Montereau and Troyes, and all criticism was for the time being silenced. The theatres put on pieces of topical significance and were crowded every night. Georgina was frequently cheered, in sentimental recognition, no doubt, of her former association with Napoleon. Shrove Tuesday, with its carnival, was lively and joyful as usual; no one understood the true position; no one knew that the Czar

Alexander was marching towards the unprotected capital. Paris was still reading victorious bulletins when the enemy was at its gates.

During March, however, wounded French soldiers began to pour into Paris, followed by terrified peasants, driving their sheep and cows along the boulevards, or pushing a few possessions in a hand-cart. And from these peasants the real situation was learnt. Great foreign armies were bearing down on Paris, the countryside was filled with Russian cavalrymen too numerous to count. There followed the news that in the south the English had entered Bordeaux.

On the 27th of the month, the Empress Marie Louise left the capital for Blois with her son, the King of Rome, escorted by more than a thousand mounted guards. Joséphine left Malmaison for the château of Navarre, which had become one of her domains when she was divorced. And on the 31st Paris capitulated.

At ten the previous evening King Jérome Bonaparte had given the order from his headquarters at Montmartre that Paris was to be defended to the last gasp; at eleven he was in flight. Paris in any case had not been given the means of defence, so little had Napoleon imagined defence would be necessary. And at midday on the 31st the Russian and Prussian armies entered peacefully through the Porte Saint-Martin.

The Parisians as a whole were too stunned to express any opinion; but the royalists, silent for so long, found their voices and openly rejoiced, waving their flags from balconies and windows, and cheering the conquerors with much enthusiasm. And Georgina, as in a nightmare, watched the Emperor Alexander riding gracefully and politely about Paris, with just such an air of gallantry as he had always shown in his own capital.

'Long live Alexander!' cried an excited young woman as he passed. 'He has given us back the Bourbons!' She was kneeling on a balcony with outstretched hands, beneath a large white flag adorned with the fleur-de-lis.

The autocrat of all the Russias raised his plumed hat and bowed to her, calling out cheerfully, 'Yes, Madame, you will soon see the Bourbons. Long live your king, Louis XVIII, and long live the young ladies of Paris!' And he went his way, smiling and courteous as Georgina had always seen him in St. Petersburg.

Napoleon was at Fontainbleau, hesitating between abdication and a continuation of the war. He had armies intact, and the Allies were in a vulnerable position. But although he was perfectly capable of scoring another great victory and driving the invaders out of France, the time had come for him to desist. His generals were beginning to desert him, and France preferred a peace imposed by foreigners to a continuation of war. Europeans were not attuned to war, to such continual bloodshed as there had been under his rule. Now that he seemed to be defeated, people dared to speak and he was denounced as a monster engaged in devouring whole generations of young men to satisfy his insane love of militarism.

In Paris he was being freely and vigorously cursed by the people, as Nero and Robespierre had once been cursed. Georgina had cause enough now to quarrel with her enemies at the Comédie Française. Talma and Mlle Mars alone were loyal to Napoleon; the others either hid their feelings out of fear or had been royalists all along. Raucourt, back from Italy, delightedly helped to tear down the Imperial eagle from the Emperor's box at the theatre.

Georgina did not waver in her loyalty. Despite the years of dissipation and self-indulgence through which she had lived, she had retained a certain integrity. The more Napoleon was vilified, the more loudly and obstinately she defended him. She was certainly indiscreet, and perhaps a little lacking in sympathy for the many who mourned because of his wars; but her character is seen at its best at this time when she so freely expressed opinions which few shared and hardly anyone dared give voice to.

She was exasperated by the open rejoicing of the royalists; she had been brought up to fear and dislike the Bourbons, and she could scarcely believe that they would come to power again. Yet the whole population of Paris was changing before her eyes. It was a phenomenon as confusing as it was alarming and unexpected.

The truth was that people were utterly weary of war. Europe had never before seen such wholesale slaughter; on scores of battlefields, hundreds of thousands of men had been driven into destroying each other, and bereaved parents execrated Napoleon, who had doomed the young men of France in his insatiable lust for conquest. Everyone preferred to make peace, though it meant being subject to the Bourbons, rather than settle down to a war which might never end at all.

On April 4th Napoleon offered to abdicate in favour of his son, and the Duke of Vicenza hurried to Paris with documents. During the day, Georgina happened to drive through the Place Vendôme with a friend. A large crowd was assembled round the triumphant column set up in Napoleon's honour, the column in the Roman manner on which the hero stood, carved in bronze. A placard had been placed against the pedestal, displaying a verse which can be roughly translated as follows:

> On this tall column deified,
> Tyrant, if all the blood you've shed
> Were here you need not bend your head
> To drink until you're satisfied.

Ropes were fixed round the statue's neck, and excited men were tugging at them, regardless of the danger to all if the statue should fall as they wished. Fortunately it was strongly and firmly erected and resisted all assaults; there was time for engineers to arrive and remove the offending figure without harm to the angry crowds beneath.

'And I,' says Mlle George, 'when I saw this frightful spectacle, became pale and cold. I was jumping out of my carriage, in my madness, to oppose the ferocious act—I, a woman alone against them all—when the friend who was with me seized me and pulled me back forcibly and took me home. It was time, for I felt I was dying.'

On the 6th of the month, hearing that a whole army corps had gone over to the enemy, Napoleon resigned himself to the inevitable and abdicated unconditionally. Georgina records that she visited the Duke of Vicenza that same night. From him she learnt that Napoleon's mind was acting as brilliantly as ever and that he was perfectly detached and murmured against none of

those who were deserting and cursing him. He was very dignified, asking nothing for himself, but only urging his emissary
to see that his family and servants were provided for. The Duke
walked home with Georgina, and they passed through the Place
du Carousel where they found themselves in the midst of troops
from Russia, Austria and Prussia.

'Ah, my dear Georgina,' the Duke said, 'what a pretty walk
for two French citizens to be taking!'

A few days later Napoleon, assured that his family were to be
provided for, decided in his Roman manner to put an end to his
days. He had carried poison on him for some time in case he
should find himself in a tight corner, and on the night of the
11th he drank it down. Yet his resolution came to nothing, for
the dose proved insufficient. It did no more than render him
violently ill; he had steeled himself in vain.

'Destiny has decided for me,' he said to the Duke of Vicenza.
'I have to live and await what Providence sends me.' And at
the end of the month he left Fontainebleau for the Isle of Elba,
the small kingdom provided for his exile by his victors.

At the beginning of May the Bourbon kings were restored and
Louis XVIII made his ceremonial entry into the city in an open
carriage drawn by eight white horses. The public wore white
cockades, lilies decorated the buildings, and a white balloon,
decorated with the fleur-de-lis, ascended above the capital, containing the celebrated Mme Blanchard, who waved a couple of
royal flags. Georgina watched all that was taking place with
increasing indignation, but those who shared it with her could do
nothing. Paris had become a city of royalists. The Polignacs,
the Montmorenceys, the Choiseuls and Fitz Jameses were suddenly in evidence. The revolution was at last over.

All this time the theatres were active, for the Allied princes
and officers wanted to see the French plays which were so
renowned. Once again Talma and his troupe acted before a
parterre of kings. Only this time the kings had to pay for their
seats and came of their own accord. Royalist actresses came on
the stage wearing white lilies; but Georgina made no pretence of
cordiality.

May the 18th arrived; it was on this day ten years ago that the Senate had officially proclaimed Napoleon Emperor of the French. Mlle George appeared on the stage ostentatiously dressed in deep mourning. For this piece of bravado she was summoned to appear before the Duc de Berry. Her beauty saved her from any undue severity.

'Well, fair Bonapartist——' the Duke began, smiling at her.

She interrupted quickly. 'Yes, Prince. I stand under the Bonaparte flag, and I shall always do so.'

She was sent away with a polite warning, and put under the surveillance of the police.

Outwardly, at least, she displayed more loyalty to Napoleon than Joséphine herself. Joséphine had returned to Malmaison from Navarre and was now leading a brilliant social life. The royalists had nothing against her, for she belonged to the *ancien régime* and had always befriended them to the best of her ability. The Allied princes regarded her as one of Napoleon's victims, since she had been repudiated, and were exceedingly courteous in their manner towards her. Monarchs and diplomats attended dinners and receptions at Malmaison; the Emperor Alexander spent much of his time there, and members of the English aristocracy were often at Joséphine's table.

Joséphine, fifty-one years old and always struggling against the onset of age, made herself exceedingly attractive at this time. Now, in the spring of 1814, as though it was the spring-time of her life, she bought the most delightful embroidered muslin dresses in pale colours from Leroy, and endless care was taken in the dressing of her hair and the painting of her face. Yet it was not indifference to Napoleon's fate that made her play this role, although there is no doubt that the great social occasions were a consolation to her. Her diplomatic sense, her instinct to please and reconcile all parties and to bring about peace even by insincerity, was always uppermost. At the moment she strove to placate Napoleon's enemies for the sake of her children and grandchildren. It was good for France, too, and for Napoleon himself that she should look charming at the head of her table, that her chef should excel himself and the wines from her cellars be of the finest quality. She could not follow Napoleon to Elba, since he had a wife; but here at Malmaison she did the best she could, not defending him, as Georgina did, but quietly smiling at his conquerors and helping them to keep their minds on all that was peaceful and enjoyable.

Yet suddenly, on May 29th, Joséphine died very quietly. A fortnight earlier she had caught cold while strolling in the moonlight at Malmaison with the Emperor Alexander. The evening was chilly. Alexander was in his warm uniform, but Joséphine wore one of the transparent, fragile dresses made by her ingenious couturier. It was cut very low, a sleeveless evening dress of the flimsiest character. But vanity kept her from covering the charming masterpiece with a shawl. Walking gracefully at Alexander's side, arm-in-arm with him and almost certainly enjoying a sentimental and very personal conversation, Joséphine suppressed her shivers and became badly chilled. She had always enjoyed good health, and there seemed to be no real reason for her death. But, living for love and its pleasures alone, and having outlived the age when these are easily obtained, she had probably no great desire to continue her existence. She had stretched youth out to the uttermost by every artifice, but she could do little more. It was better to be gone.

Now Georgina, with many other citizens of Paris, went out to the village of Rueil, near Malmaison, to watch the funeral procession. She felt very sad. The passing of Joséphine seemed to mark the end of her own youth. Even at the height of her love affair with Napoleon she had deeply admired Joséphine, and she was convinced that the divorce had been the beginning of France's troubles and of her own.

The first and surely the most happy part of her own life was over. Now the circumstances that had brought her so much success had vanished, like snow in a sudden thaw. She was twenty-seven years old, and she was no longer in the fashion. The critic Geoffroy had died just before the collapse of the Empire; the newspapers had all changed their editors; she was under the eye of the police as a suspicious character. She took pride in ignoring the Duc de Berry's warning. She and Mlle

Mars, disgusted by the sight of sycophantic actresses carrying white lilies on and off the stage, had taken to appearing with bouquets of violets in their hands, the emblem of the King of Rome. The theatre would be thrown into an uproar and they were constantly in trouble. Life had become difficult, and Georgina was no longer the Venus of Paris. The title given to her now by the newspapers was 'the Corsican Widow'.

27

THE Allied troops had gone and Paris gradually resumed its normal life under Louis XVIII. In January 1815 Georgina attended another funeral, that of Mlle Raucourt, an event marked by typical altercations. The clergy tried to keep Raucourt's coffin out of the church of St Roch, ordering the cortège to go direct to the cemetery. The actors who followed would have acquiesced, but a few thousand spectators had assembled who forced the doors of the church, and the funeral service took place under their menaces. It was an old grievance in Paris, this reluctance of the clergy to treat the actresses of the city as Christians. Raucourt's life had certainly been marked by a complete absence of Christian morals, but the Paris crowds, who loved their theatres, insisted that she should be treated with indulgence.

March came, and with it the astonishing news that Napoleon had left Elba with 1,200 men and was marching towards Paris, everywhere catching the enthusiasm of the people. The Congress of Vienna was in progress, and all was at once thrown into confusion. On the 29th of the month Louis XVIII retired to Ghent, and the following day Napoleon entered the capital. Throughout the afternoon and evening of the 20th, Georgina and Mars sat in a window in the Champs Elysées. News had come that he would enter Paris this way, and the two actresses had joyfully secured a window. There they were conspicuous in white dresses, carrying immense bunches of violets. Violets were also on the brims of their straw hats and in their sashes. This day was the King of Rome's birthday (his fourth), and these flowers had somehow become associated with the event. The waiting crowds below gazed much at the actresses, and the fashion for carrying violets was started; from now onwards the Bonapartists took to wearing violets, and pictures of violets intertwined with portraits of the Imperial family were soon on sale.

The crowds were disappointed, for Napoleon did not arrive in Paris until after dark, slipping in unobserved by a different route. Georgina and Mars drove down to the Palace of the Tuileries and strolled about the gardens and the courtyard. The tricolour was flying; and in the courtyard enthusiastic Bonapartists, most of them very young, were singing and dancing. Hortense, Napoleon's stepdaughter, was in the palace, and by her orders wines and liqueurs were sent out to the assembled crowds. After this the singing and dancing were wilder than ever, and no one seemed in the least aware of the dangers of the situation.

Napoleon was not much seen by the public in the days that followed, for he had much to do. He had to appoint Ministers, draw out a new constitution (for he knew Europe would not again accept him as an autocrat) and prepare his armies for battle and himself for the diplomatic negotiations he believed would still be possible. No one could approach him but members of his family and his closest associates. Georgina, however, longed to see him and contrived to bring herself to his mind. Frédéric Masson records that she sent a message telling him she had certain papers in her possession which he ought to have, papers which compromised his former Minister of Police. Napoleon sent a trusted secretary to call on her, and when he returned asked:

'Did she say if she was in difficulties?'

'No, Sire. She only spoke of the papers, and said that she desired your Majesty to receive them from her own hand.'

'Well, I know how it is,' said Napoleon. 'Caulaincourt has spoken to me about her and told me she's short of money. Give her 20,000 francs out of my funds.'

Whether the papers were of any interest and how she came by them is not said; but by means of them she had her interview. Only Alexandre Dumas, to whom she talked so much about her relations with Napoleon, gives any account of the meeting. On arriving, says Dumas, she found Napoleon concerned by the neglected state of the palace rooms, always kept in the most perfect order in his own time. In the dining-room he had even noticed asparagus stalks thrown carelessly about, and he complained that the tapestry worked by Marie Louise and her ladies had been stained and spoilt. It was his only criticism of the Bourbons.

Of other things discussed no trace remains. No doubt Napoleon treated the actress with his habitual indulgence; but he must have been preoccupied by the difficulties and dangers that were rising up against him on all sides. He kept Georgina in mind, however, for in April she was made by his orders a member of the *comité de lecture* of the Comédie Française.

Again her position was enviable. Once more she saw the *Journal des Débats* in the hands of its Imperial editors, while the servitors of the Bourbons were sent packing. The Corsican Widow was once more the Venus of Paris, and whenever she appeared on the stage there was thunderous applause. By her known loyalty she had come to represent the Bonaparte cause.

By the remarkable feat of leaving Elba and rallying the army to his side, Napoleon had gained immense prestige; and the delirium of delight continued among his followers, and particularly among those, like Georgina, whose fortunes had left them with the return of the Bourbons. But now it was June and he left Paris at the head of his army to meet the enemy in Belgium. People still believed him capable of any triumph, and they waited confidently for news of victory.

But the news that came a few days later was of the Battle of Waterloo. Once more Paris was in confusion, the Bonapartists stupefied by the immensity of the disaster, the royalists openly gloating. Napoleon himself quickly returned to the capital, but he was there for only a day or two. He formally abdicated, and then retired to Malmaison, which he wished to see for the last time, knowing that he would have to leave France, and this time for ever.

Hortense was with him, Hortense who by the kindness of Alexander had been given the title of Duchesse de Saint-Leu. He remained at Malmaison for five days, his fate uncertain. It was not his first visit to the place since Joséphine's death, for he had gone there one day soon after his return from Elba, wandered sadly about the gardens and spent a long time alone in the bedroom where Joséphine had died. Now, in June, he spent many hours walking in the gardens with Hortense, talking of Joséphine with great affection. His doctor, Corvisart, had told him that grief had brought about her death, and that she should have lived for many years. He could not fail to see, looking back on the events of past years, how immediately and disastrously all had gone downhill for him when he repudiated the woman so devoted to him, who had had her faults but had been so true a friend.

The days were hot and sunny and the gardens were a dream of beauty. So it had been twelve years ago when they were all young and happy, so young that they played children's games on the lawns. What had gone wrong? What had changed them all, and himself most of all? How was it that, from his adoration of Joséphine when he married her, he had come to divorce her? And how had his early successes in organizing and improving France led imperceptibly to the country's ruin? It seemed to him that he had set off on his chosen course towards a splendid goal, and had never deviated from his good intentions; yet within a few short years he had somehow reversed his direction and was walking not towards but away from his desires, in love, in politics, in all. Had he, then, been driven by events all this time when he thought he was the master? With such sad thoughts Napoleon spent these last days near Paris, with Hortense weeping at his side, and often in tears himself. And then he changed into civilian clothes and left for Rochefort, hoping to sail to America.

At first Napoleon had wished to live as a private citizen in London. Though England had been his most implacable enemy, it had always been represented to him as a free and generous nation. 'There,' he said, 'I will taste the only consolation permitted to a man who once governed the world, that of associating with enlightened spirits.' But it was put to him that feelings ran too high in England for him to be able to count on the proverbial generosity, and he was urged to sail instead to the United States, then looked on as a quiet and uneventful corner of the world.

He resigned himself to this proposition with the words, 'Since I am refused the society of men, I will seek refuge in the heart of nature, and there I will live in that solitude so appropriate to my last thoughts.'

As he left Malmaison, after embracing his mother, Hortense, his brothers and his generals, everyone wept. Even the private soldiers on guard were weeping bitterly as he drove off, pale and sad, in his carriage. The whole scene is in the best vein of Romanticism, showing Napoleon as a true man of feeling, a man of polite eighteenth-century upbringing, and it is so disarming that one can hardly believe that this was the tyrant who had harassed Europe for so long. He was, indeed, a man of most intricate character, able to act many roles, each one impressive and convincing while it lasted. He could be Charlemagne, he could be Augustus; he could equally well be Werther when the right occasion presented itself, or Hamlet questioning the universe. He could be a sentimental lover, a warrior, a lawgiver or a criminal, the most detached and forgiving of men and the most susceptible and unforgiving. But of inward unity there was none. He presented a wonderful spectacle of human pesonality, with qualities the most brilliant, with virtues and faults and versatile powers of all kinds, not merged but alternately taking control with explosive results.

Now, anyway, he departed like another Werther, and, as we know, it was not to the United States but to exile in the remote island of St Helena that destiny now took him.

When the news reached Paris that the English were banishing Napoleon to St Helena, Georgina sent an offer to accompany him. He was taking a number of companions with him, including the wives and children of some of his officers. Georgina would have liked to join the small colony. In all her many love affairs, she had found no man who appealed to her in the way that

Napoleon did. She would be able to organize theatrical performances to help to pass the time, and to show her devotion in a thousand ways—and without rivals. Marie Louise had abandoned him; Marie Waleska had drifted away from him. He was alone.

But Napoleon, the Emperor, could hardly share his exile with an actress of the Comédie Française. He had his tragic role to play from now onwards, and it would not do to appear to be enjoying his banishment. And Georgina, who had made the offer more because she would like to make it than in any expectation that it would be accepted, was not surprised. Like Joséphine, and also like Marie Louise, she herself valued peaceful enjoyment above all things; but Napoleon, she knew, could not be expected to take so trite a view of life. She turned away from the alluring dream to cold reality, to the fact that once more the newspapers had changed hands and she had again become the Corsican Widow.

28

NOT only was she the Corsican Widow, she was hissed on the stage as a Bonapartist. Paris was in a state of chaos, and the general feeling of insecurity, national humiliation and fear found expression in the exchange of insults between the victorious and the defeated factions. Once more, Allied troops poured into the city, and on July the 8th Louis XVIII returned, smiling and complacent. At the Comédie Française excited and angry audiences forced Georgina and Mars to celebrate the King's return by shouting '*Vive le roi!*' To refuse would have been dangerous. The brave Marshal Ney and other soldiers were being executed for having served Napoleon after his return from Elba, and even a street beggar had recently been arrested for calling out '*Vive l'Empereur!*' and sentenced to banishment for five years.

Georgina took her revenge by appearing very seldom at the

theatre. On one pretext and another she stayed away, drawing her salary and doing little for it. She still had powerful friends, such as Talleyrand and Metternich, and was not afraid to defy the theatre. Even Alexander himself might be appealed to in case of need, although he had not communicated with her in Paris. There was plenty to interest her at this leisurely time. Again she watched Alexander riding about the streets, as handsome as ever and utterly fascinating to the women of all nations who were on holiday in the French capital. She could well believe that the courtesans of Paris society, of whom there were all too many, were scheming to lay hands on him; but she knew from all she heard about him that his mind was far from worldly pleasures and that he would elude them all. She knew he had at last left Mme de Narishkine and was inconsolable.

Alexander was concerned only with his plans for establishing peace and with religion. Once he had placed all his hopes in love; but lately he had had to face the fact that Mme de Narishkine did not feel as he did; his love was one thing, hers was another. The realization was a terrible blow to him, and he turned, not to other women, knowing it would always be the same, but to religion. Now, in Paris, he spent much of his time with Mme de Krudener, a middle-aged mystic who had joined the Moravian brotherhood and travelled about Europe as a revivalist preacher. The widow of a Russian diplomat, she was quite at home in royal circles and had made herself known to Alexander, bent on saving his soul. She practised Christian principles, as she understood them, sincerely enough, but with a certain loud emotionalism that many found distasteful. That Alexander should fall under her influence was displeasing both to the Orthodox clergy of Russia and to those diplomats who were working with him in Paris. The displeasure certainly had different causes; the Russian clergy saw heresy, and the diplomats saw a man making a fool of himself; but it was equally strong in both cases.

Regardless of criticism, however, Alexander and Mme de Krudener planned to improve the world and believed they could put a final end to war. Between them they concocted the Holy Alliance, which the majority of the delegates in Paris signed because of the respect due to the Czar and because there seemed to be no harm in doing so. It pledged them to behave like Christians, a reasonable thing enough, since Europe professed to be a Christian continent. But Metternich called it 'a piece of sublime mysticism and nonsense', and told Castlereagh that the Emperor of Austria and King of Prussia had signed with reluctance, being sure it was the composition of a lunatic. It was not easy to impose ideal conduct on the rulers and diplomats assembled in Paris.

Alexander left for Russia; the year ended, foreign troops gradually left, and the court of Louis XVIII set the social tone. The threads of pre-revolutionary days were picked up, and 1816 was marked by the delayed mourning for Louis XVI and Marie Antoinette, the erection of expiatory monuments and the restoring of former names to streets.

Now that the conferences and functions of the peace settlement were over, Georgina became depressed and asked for two months' leave from the theatre on the plea of illness. It was granted, but she remained absent for four months and was then furious because she received payment for the first two months only. In a fit of anger she handed in her resignation. But owing to the influence of friends, among them, no doubt, Talma, who had so often tried to save her from disaster, her resignation was not accepted.

She remained with the theatre, therefore, but not in any mood of gratitude or helpfulness. She had become a most difficult character to deal with, and after the years of adulation and luxury in St Petersburg could scarcely accommodate herself to normal life. Since the actors of the Comédie Française were now, as in the past, *les comédiens ordinaire du roi*, she delighted in being capricious and awkward, thus showing her contempt of the king. It was now that sly engravings appeared in the shops, purporting to show scenes from the days of her love-affair with Napoleon; and a farce was put on at one of the popular theatres in which the great love-affair was caricatured, Napoleon and herself being very thinly disguised. In this she appeared as an actress named Georgée, much to the amusement of the town. Everything seemed to be over; as an actress she was openly derided, and men of fashion had long since lost the urge to be seen about with her. It must have seemed to Georgina that there was nothing to hope for now apart from the pleasures of an obscure private life for which she had little taste. Yet the unexpected was to happen, and many brilliant and successful years lay before her.

Throughout the year she made herself insupportable, and a climax came early in 1817 when she flatly refused to learn the roles given to her in two new plays. At last the Duc de Duras, who had succeeded M. de Rémusat as director of the theatre's affairs, lost patience and a notice was given at the beginning of May stating that, 'from the date of the 8th of the present month, the demoiselle George Weymer will cease to form part of the Théâtre Français'.

She had become surpassingly exacting and tyrannical, yet she had never lost Talma's friendship, and he came to her rescue now, offering to take her with him to London, where he had been asked to give performances. She accepted the invitation gladly. They stayed at Brunet's Hotel in Leicester Square, and gave recitations together at the King's Theatre and the Covent Garden Opera House.

Londoners would perhaps have had more of a feast if Talma had brought Duchesnois with him; but they showed a great eagerness to see the two French stars and turned up in large numbers.

The Diary of H. Crabb Robinson, under the date of 26 June 1817, says of Mlle George's recitations at the Opera House:

Her acting I thought radically bad. Instead of copying nature in the expression of passion, according to which the master feeling predominates over all others, she merely minces the words. If in the same line the words *crainte* and *joie* occur, she apes fear and joy by outrageous pantomime; and in the suddenness of the transition forces applause from those who are glad to understand something, and gratefully applaud what has enabled them to understand. Her acting appeared to me utterly without feeling. She pleased me best in *Athalie*—the scene where she recounts the dream and first appearance of Joad. Her imprecations against Horace for slaying her lover were, I thought, violent without being sincere; and her performance of the sleep-walking scene in *Macbeth* was very poor.

The *Morning Herald* reported the same event as follows:

The Opera House presented last evening one of the most interesting theatrical novelties that has ever been produced upon our stage. The finest scenes in the *chef d'œuvres* of the French Tragic Drama, performed by one of the first actresses and emphatically the best actor in France.

The principal scene performed by Georges in *Phaedra* was the discovery of her passion to her confidante Oenone. It is finely wrought and may be considered a first-rate specimen of tragic eloquence. The disclosure of the object of her love towards the close of the scene is one of the triumphs of Mlle Duchesnois. It was given by Mlle Georges with the greatest effect.

This paper, describing George's appearance, says,

This lady is rather ample. Yet one could scarcely wish her otherwise, lest some grace or beauty should be lost in the diminution. Her countenance is finely formed of the Grecian cast, and capable of great expression. In her gestures and her attitudes there is occasionally something too vehement and too robust for our ideas of female acting. This, however, is not peculiar to Mlle Georges: it is the manner of the French stage.

The Times spoke appreciatively of the French performance at the King's Theatre:

The recitations of M. Talma and Mlle Georges, in the concert room of this theatre last night, drew a crowded and brilliant audience and excited the most extraordinary expectations. These expectations, high as they had been raised, were more than fulfilled. There was, we believe, but one sentiment of admiration raised in every person present, mingled with that species of interest and gratification which arises from witnessing an exhibition of excellency not more admirable than it is new. The face of Mlle Georges is handsome, and unites grandeur with softness. To great regularity of features she joins the most undulating flexibility of expression; and in this respect the transitions in her countenance, as well as in her action and her tones, instead of being influenced by the supposed monotony of the French stage, are more quick, more extreme and more unceasing than anything to which we are accustomed on our own. Indeed, once or twice the sudden change from masculine fierceness to a softness the most sensitive and feminine, jarred a little upon our habitual preoccupations of theatrical uniformity. Her person is large, and in some degree unwieldy, but not so as to interfere with the grace or dignity of her deportment in the more impassioned scenes. Of M. Talma's acting we can hardly speak highly enough.

The visit to London proved to be delightful and successful in every way. How quiet the audiences were! And how friendly London society was! Talma had many acquaintances, and they were widely received. The Duke of Devonshire gave Georgina the keys to his boxes at all the theatres, so that she and Talma were able to see Mr Kean and Mr Kemble acting in Shakespeare's plays, and *The Beggar's Opera* at the New Theatre Royal.

What was best of all was to be away from the violent anti-Bonapartist emotions of Paris. Here she and Talma were honoured in drawing-rooms as the favourite actors of Napoleon. There was no animosity towards the fallen Emperor. The English had cursed and lampooned Napoleon throughout the war, and now, grateful to him for having lost it, they were disposed to think well of him. In fact, Mlle Georges (the English always added an *s* to her name) was treated with extraordinary respect as the mistress of their former enemy and was an object of the greatest interest.

This was as it should be, and Georgina returned to Paris restored and soothed, having met King George III at a *soirée* given by the French ambassador, and having received a charming bracelet from the Duke of Devonshire as a parting gift.

The interlude had put her in a more reasonable and hopeful frame of mind. She accepted engagements in the provinces, and in 1818 she visited Brussels.

29

DUCHESNOIS, whose life became easy whenever Georgina was away from Paris, had now only one serious anxiety. Her lover was in political trouble and was exiled. This man, Jean Charles Harel, to whom reference has already been made, was born in 1790 and had entered the Civil Service. He always had his entrée behind the scenes at the Théâtre Français, since his father, Luce de Lancival, was a writer favoured by Napoleon; and he often went there, having a taste for theatres and all that went with them. There Georgina had without doubt seen him often enough, but without paying attention to him. Not only was he quite unimportant, he was plain and untidy. It was Duchesnois who responded to the overtures of the forward young man in search of adventure among theatrical stars; she was grateful to any man who was not indifferent to her, and she became his mistress and was now the mother of his child, a daughter named Rosa.

Towards the end of the Empire Harel had been made subprefect of Soissons, and at the siege of the town in 1814 he had distinguished himself by his bravery and had been given the Cross of the Legion of Honour. After the return from Elba, Napoleon had remembered the courageous Harel and appointed him governor of the department of Landes, a distinction that had nearly cost him his life. For after Waterloo he was arrested, like so many of those who had served Napoleon, and only the influence of the Bishop of Bayonne saved him from death. Instead, he was let off with banishment for ten years.

Penniless and without prospects, he left France for Brussels, and Duchesnois sent him money regularly. Without her he would have been in want for the barest necessities. In due course he found himself an occupation, though a precarious one. He was now editor of *Le Nain Jaune*, a violent little paper which

JOSEPHINE

HAREL

MLLE. GEORGE AS SEMIRAMIS
A Sketch by Alfred Chalon

fired insults at the restored monarchy in France from the safe retreat of the Belgian capital.

Georgina arrived for a season at one of the theatres, and he sought her out. Circumstances had changed, and she was ready now to pay a little attention to such as Harel. His anti-Bourbon sentiments and fidelity to Napoleon pleased her greatly, and they felt so attracted to one another that they lost no time in settling down together. No doubt the prevailing feeling was that they could be useful to each other. Georgina had no capacity for looking after her own affairs in a reasonable manner, and Harel persuaded her he could do this for her. He would be her business manager, her agent, her devoted slave in all things. And as for Harel, he saw in the beautiful and celebrated Georgina the means of making his own fortune. If she was in eclipse, he knew how to bring her out of it. And there now began a long and faithful collaboration between them which, although they did not marry, very well answered the French description of marriage as *egoisme à deux*.

Not a thought was given to the feelings of Duchesnois.

Harel is said to have resembled a waiter. He was clean-shaven, with bushy wide-whiskers, a heavy, awkward figure and quick, impatient movements. He was an odd companion for Georgina, who was usually to be seen with men of impeccable appearance. For if he resembled a waiter, it was not one of those who serve the rich in dignified surroundings; he was rather the harassed *garçon* of a large commercial café, attending to everyone at lightning speed and with never a moment to smarten up his own appearance. Harel was atrociously untidy and quite indifferent about cleanliness. Yet Georgina, fastidious though she was, was charmed by him. It is true that beneath an uncouth exterior there was much to interest her. Harel was a wit, and he was light-hearted, optimistic, daring and energetic. Georgina loved to laugh, and Harel could make her laugh as Napoleon had done in the days of the Consulate.

Since Harel could best restore her fortunes in Paris, Georgina appealed to one of her powerful friends for help. It was the Marquis de Lauriston who set in motion the process of approaching the Government for a pardon for the exile. The situation was complicated by the fact that Harel had employed his time abroad in producing seditious literature; but he was now represented as a reformed character and, the King being a tolerant man, he found himself set free at the end of 1819.

Returning to Paris, he and Georgina took a house in the rue Madame, and Bébelle went to live with them. During 1820, Harel arranged a series of provincial tours for his mistress; they took an entire company with them, including Bébelle, who now acted under the name of 'George *cadette*'. Harel arranged everything down to the smallest detail and did it very well. They travelled as luxuriously as was possible in those days of bad roads and uncertain inns, they were gay and the profits were excellent.

The year had been successful and, since political passions were dying down, it seemed safe for Georgina to venture once more on the Paris stage. Prompted by Harel, she applied for an engagement at the second national theatre, the Odéon, whose manager accepted her with alacrity. In May 1821, she signed a contract to play the parts of queens and princesses in tragedies both old and new. But her former associates at the Comédie Française were still smarting from her insolence, and they pounced upon her triumphantly with a regulation she knew nothing about, which forbade actors to pass from one national theatre to the other.

Ignoring this, Georgina took up her new work, and at the same time brought a lawsuit against the Comédie Française, claiming payment for the two months' extra leave she had helped herself to in 1816. She lost her case, but her friend the Marquis de Lauriston prevailed on the King to give her permission to act at the Odéon.

Grievous news came from St Helena at this time to add to the depression she felt over the loss of her suit. The great Napoleon was dead. He had died on May the 5th, seven years after Joséphine, and at the same age, fifty-one.

He had talked much to his associates at St Helena of the past, and he had often mentioned Georgina—*ma bonne Georgina*, he called her, having seen always the attractive side of her and never the arrogance from which the Comédie Française had had so much to endure. Often he had passed the long hours of exile by reciting from the tragedies he loved, and describing performances he had watched with Talma and Mlle George in the principal roles. So many who owed everything to him had turned against him in his misfortune that it consoled him to linger over his memories of Talma and George, whom he knew had liked him for himself and who had remained faithful in their friendship. His love-affair with Georgina marked the best time of his life, the time he most liked to look back to. 'When I knew Mlle George,' he said, 'I was young, I was happy. It was a time of expansion in my life. At the very height of the Empire, I often wished I had back the Consulate.'

He had endured a painful disease with patience and composure, and as death approached he had spoken much on religion and had asked that the Catholic rites should be observed at his funeral. When speaking of this imminent event, he had noticed a sarcastic smile on the face of a youthful doctor standing near. Turning towards him with a severe expression, he said:

'Young man, you are perhaps too clever to believe in God. I have not yet reached that state.'

He was Napoleonic to the end, unable to let an impertinence pass without rebuke.

But in a delirium preceding the moment of death he talked of the army. Outside the rain came down in torrents, the wind uprooted trees, and on his bed Napoleon dreamed of the Battle of Marengo.

30

THE Odéon Theatre was in constant difficulties; it was the only theatre on the left side of the river, and it was considered inaccessible. One director after another took it in hand, but no one succeeded in making it pay. Georgina's appearances there increased attendances for a time, but she sometimes had difficulty in obtaining the salary promised to her. She remained with the theatre for a number of years, but found it necessary to alternate her performances there with tours of the provinces and visits to foreign capitals.

Louis XVIII died and Charles X came to the throne. Georgina was now thirty-seven years old, and everything had changed about her. The effects of peace were beginning to show themselves, and prosperity was increasing. Imitation jewellery was on view in the shops; machines were coming into use, increasing production and lowering prices. Omnibuses were introduced, and fashions had changed.

There was a fashion in manners as well as in dress, and it was entirely different from that of the Consulate and Empire. The works of Sir Walter Scott, Byron and Goethe were beginning to influence the country. The era of Romanticism had arrived. Leroy and his fabulous clothes was forgotten; women now wore substantial, wide-skirted dresses with plenty of underwear. It was the fashion to be pale, thin and melancholy, with drooping ringlets, downcast eyes and an angelic expression. Smart young men assumed a Byronic gloom and made a habit of coughing. It looked well to be consumptive, to appear to be dying of some ill-fated passion. But Georgina, who had always been fond of eating, ate more heartily still and showed a fine contempt for the pale and slender beauties of twenty, playing on the fashionable harp. She was well satisfied with her opulent curves, which remained so well proportioned, and with her still young and unwrinkled face. She still followed the Roman tastes of the Empire and bathed daily, reclining for an hour in the water and receiving her friends, very often, as she did so. And before she stepped into this ceremonial bath, in which she was ready to display herself, she took a preliminary, private bath in which she washed thoroughly, so as to step into her second bath scrupulously clean.

Her love of cleanliness extended beyond herself to her possessions and household, where a perpetual spring-cleaning went on. She would not endure dust and disorder. 'George made everything clean about her,' says Dumas, 'apart from Harel.'

Harel, however, had his own private rooms where he did as he pleased. Georgina had said to him long ago: 'I am in love with your intelligence, but certainly not with your person. With *that* you can do exactly as you please.'

Their household, like that of many French artists of the time, was decidedly unconventional. Normal standards of morality were unrepentantly overlooked. Harel acquired a son during the reign of Louis XVIII, and another during the reign of Charles X. It was generally believed that these were the children not of Georgina but of the younger sister, Bébelle. To all intents and purposes, Harel was a man with two wives. Georgina herself appears to have led the life of a courtesan, while remaining devoted to Harel. She did not go out of her way to seek love-affairs, but accepted them at times when they were attractive. Her admirers now were mostly men of letters, and Harel, with his eye for business, was the last person to discourage them. He was charmed that the influential dramatic critic, Jules Janin, who occupied the top floor of their house, was attracted by his mistress.

The rising society of fashionable men and women had lost the taste for the classical tragedies so well loved in Napoleon's time, and the difficulties of the Odéon increased as time went on. At the Comédie Française, however, the public still went to see the brilliant Talma, though by now he was very ill and a dying man. With Duchesnois, herself something of an invalid, he was still giving inimitable performances. Mlle Mars, too, continued to attract large audiences with her appearances in Molière's plays.

In the autumn of 1826 Talma died, and Georgina attended his funeral with most of the actors and writers of Paris. He had been a great figure and his passing was a public event. In his youth, all his ardour had gone to the revolution and lack of religion had become a passion with him. Atheism was his last thought, and right at the end he murmured, 'Voltaire! Voltaire! Like Voltaire!' And he left orders that his body was not to be taken into any church.

Very different was the death of the Czar Alexander, which had taken place a few months previously at Taganrog. The circumstances had been so mysterious, and the Czar's recent years had been marked by such intensive religious exercises, that many believed his death was faked and that he had gone off in secrecy to lead the life of a hermit.

Since 1815 the reactionary party had grown stronger in Russia and despotism flourished. The Grand Duke Constantine, once in love with Georgina, had not been tempted to put on the oppressive purple mantle and had renounced his heritage to marry as he chose. The younger brother, Nicholas, now reigned.

The reign of Charles X was a happy time for the artists of Paris. Political arguments had subsided, hatred of the English, which had been so strong after 1815, had been forgotten in the general admiration for Sir Walter Scott and Byron. A company of English actors had come over in 1822 to perform in Shakespeare's plays, but angry audiences had driven them off the stage and they had had to go home again. In 1827 Georgina went again to London, where she performed successfully in *Semiramis* and *Merope*, and where she did her best to persuade her English colleagues to venture to Paris again, assuring them the whole atmosphere had changed. On returning home, she discussed the matter with the director of the Odéon, with the result that he invited the English company to visit his theatre.

They arrived in September, with Mr Kemble and Miss Smithson to play the leading parts; this time they received an enthusiastic welcome.

A wonderful generation of young writers, painters, musicians and actors was about to dominate Paris: Hugo, Dumas, Balzac, de Musset, Berlioz among them. Most of them found their way to the Odéon to watch the English players, and the unknown works of Shakespeare were a revelation to them. Night after night, very young men overflowing with talent and energy sat enthralled, gathering inspiration, and then rushed off to their attic rooms to write frenziedly throughout the early hours by the light of their candles. Victor Hugo, who had just completed his first play, *Cromwell*, was inspired by *Hamlet* to write a stirring preface on the Romantic movement; Dumas wrote his play

Christine; Berlioz fell in love with Ophelia and publicly paraded his despair before composing the music which emerged from his experience.

These young men, still unknown to Georgina and Harel, were soon to play a great part in their lives. Early in 1829 Dumas's tragedy *Henri III* was performed at the Théâtre Français with phenomenal success. It was a vivid, original and fascinating play which proved a landmark in the long and bitter struggle between classical and romantic drama. Napoleon's constant homilies on the sacred place of the classics in modern life had made their mark, and the majority of worthy citizens believed that the Comédie Française was bound to give incessant performances of the old masterpieces of the repertory, and to exclude all modern authors who did not closely imitate these earlier works. The classical writers upheld such virtues as self-discipline and the claims of ordered society; romanticism was in favour of self-fulfilment and self-expression. What particularly annoyed the critics of romanticism was that the inspiration came from abroad, from Shakespeare and Scott, from Goethe and Schiller. They were outraged by the appearance of *Henri III* at the Théâtre Français, and their wrath increased when it was followed by de Vigny's translation of *Othello*. The followers of the classical school shared Voltaire's disapproval of Shakespeare. However, *Le More de Venise* had the greatest success.

The actors themselves were divided in opinion, the younger ones being most readily attracted by the romantic school. Mars disliked the new fashion in plays; Duchesnois felt more strongly on the subject and raised her voice in protest against romanticism. Influenced, perhaps, by her plainness, she adhered to all that was intellectual, classical and inward in art, where the spirit shines forth and the outward appearance counts for little. She saw romanticism as a blow against herself and a descent towards popular conceptions. Dumas and Hugo, indeed, leaders of the new school, could not have envisaged a plain woman interpreting their principal roles. At this time Duchesnois was in failing health, and only appeared intermittently on the stage; the death of the supreme tragic actor Talma had virtually ended her own career, being an event that inaugurated the era of romanticism on the stage. Georgina, on the other hand, was an enthusiastic admirer of the romantics from the beginning.

The visit of the English players in 1827 had been the last success the Odéon was to enjoy for a long time. In the following summer, the actors were receiving only half their salaries, and by 1829 their situation was desperate and many of them were not being paid at all. A new director was sought and, despite the debts and difficulties of the theatre, there were many candidates. One of them was Harel, who had long wished to exercise his own talents and to offer his mistress a stage of her own.

It was to Harel that the appointment was eventually offered by the Baron de la Bouillerie, director of the King's household. How Harel contrived to be chosen, in view of his Bonapartist reputation and his unconventional mode of living, is not recorded; but no doubt it was largely due to the influence of Georgina's friends. The appointment was for two and a half years only, and with it went the large annual grant of 160,000 francs, with an additional allocation of 6,000 francs for the expenses of the committee of readers. There was much comment in the Press over this appointment and the favoured treatment Harel received. Previous directors had had nothing like so large a grant; they had, moreover, asked in vain to be allowed the rents of the shops in the galleries of the theatre, whereas Harel received this concession and in addition an interest in the café of the foyer. Ever since they met in Brussels, Harel and Georgina had dreamed of controlling a Paris theatre, and they were delighted by their achievement. The theatre was entirely redecorated; Harel engaged some of the best actors in Paris and set about seeking a play.

While the Odéon was being repainted, Victor Hugo was writing his play *Marion Delorme*. When it was finished he read it aloud to Alexandre Dumas, Alfred de Vigny and other friends, all of whom congratulated him on its excellence. News of the successful reading quickly reached the directors and producers of the theatres, most of whom were now eager to see any play written by the young men of the new school. Harel showed his mettle by hastening to Victor Hugo's house and making his way into the young man's study without ceremony. Hugo was out, but his manuscript was lying on a table. Beneath the title, Harel wrote firmly: 'Accepted by the Odéon Theatre, July 14th 1829.'

Unfortunately for Harel, Hugo preferred to offer his work to the Comédie Française, where it was accepted, though only to be banned later by the censor.

The Odéon opened in September with a historical drama by Arnoult. The new decorations and fine settings were much admired, but the play was only moderately successful. Harel, who thought in terms of the sensational, was disappointed. His next venture was *Christine à Fontainebleau*, by Frédéric Soulié, a friend of Alexandre Dumas. Georgina, who fancied playing the part of Queen Christine, ordered a superb costume in velvet and lace, and a broad hat trimmed with ostrich plumes. She felt she had never looked so well; yet, despite the striking outfit, the play fell flat. After the first night few came to see it.

By chance, no less than three playwrights had chosen the subject of Christine of Sweden simultaneously. Dumas had decided upon it after seeing the English actors and had invited Soulié to collaborate with him. Soulié had thanked him, but said he preferred to write a play on his own, and that Christine was the very subject he had in mind.

He added, since Dumas looked crestfallen, 'That doesn't prevent you writing about it also, of course, if you still want to.'

'The same subject as you?' said Dumas.

'There are two theatres in Paris, I suppose,' said Soulié, 'and there are ten different ways of treating a subject.'

'But which of us will offer his work to the Comédie Française?'

'The one who has finished first.'

Alexandre Dumas, by far the most energetic man in Paris, finished first and his play was accepted by the Comédie Française. Soulié offered his play to the Odéon, where Harel had found it, accepted and ready for use, on taking office. The third playwright who had taken up the subject had begun before either of the other two, but had finished last, though before the rehearsals of Dumas's work had begun.

This third writer, however, a M. Brault, was not without influence and reputation, not to mention self-assertion. He appealed to his friends and the mistresses of his friends, with the result that orders were given at the Comédie Française that M. Brault's *Christine* was to be performed before that of M. Dumas.

Dumas, very poor and quite unknown, had had to abandon hope of his *Christine*, and he had written *Henri III* with the courage of desperation, this time to be fully rewarded. And now M. Brault's *Christine* had been a failure at the Comédie Française, and Frédéric Soulié's *Christine* had been a failure at the Odéon. Mlle George looked regretfully at the costume to which she had given so much thought and which suited her so well.

She reminded Harel that Alexandre Dumas had also written a play on Christine. Why should they not put it on instead of Soulié's play?

That same day, Dumas received the following letter from Harel:

MY DEAR DUMAS,
What do you think of this idea of Mlle George's:
To perform immediately your *Christine* with the same setting and the same actors as the *Christine* of Soulié?
As for conditions, you have only to name them.
Do not be worried by the idea that you are strangling the work of a friend,—it is dead already.

Your very devoted
HAREL.

Dumas scribbled a few words on top of the letter:

MY DEAR FRÉDÉRIC,
Read this letter. What a brigand your friend Harel is!

Yours,
ALEX. DUMAS.

He sent the letter with his servant to Soulié, who returned it with his own comments added:

MY DEAR DUMAS,
Harel is not my friend, he is a director.
Harel is not a brigand, he's a speculator.

I myself would not do what he is doing, but I would recommend such a course to him.

Sweep up the fragments of my *Christine*, throw them into the basket of the first crossing-sweeper you meet, and get your own piece performed.

Yours always,
F. SOULIÉ.

After this cordial note, Dumas felt free to accept Harel's offer, and in due course he read his play aloud to the actors of the Odéon.

'The reading had a very great success,' says Dumas in his memoirs. 'But Harel seemed preoccupied by an idea to which he only gave expression the following day. The following day he came round to see me at the crack of dawn; he had come to suggest purely and simply that I should change *Christine* from verse to prose. It was thus, from the very beginning, that Harel revealed himself to me in all his glory. It goes without saying that I laughed in his face, and that after having laughed in his face I showed him the door. The day afterwards the first rehearsal took place as though this proposition had never been made. The piece was admirably cast and produced.'

Dumas now began what was to be a lifelong friendship with Harel and Georgina. Georgina was charmed by him. Though he was very much younger than herself, Dumas did not hesitate to make love to her with great exaggeration of expression. Even though the actress did not take his declarations very seriously, they added to the enjoyment of rehearsals; she was stimulated and amused and put real vigour into the acting of her role, which was no doubt the only response that Dumas really cared about.

The play began its run in March 1830, and was a success. On the first night, Frédéric Soulié turned up to applaud. He was in business, and he did not come alone but brought with him his fifty employees on the understanding that they were to clap heartily and otherwise show enthusiasm. Such was friendship among writers in those far-off times.

To Georgina, the play brought a remarkable renewal of celebrity. She was at her best in this role which she had studied well and enjoyed playing. The young followers of romanticism were filled with admiration, and she was acclaimed as the leading actress of the new school. She was once more in the fashion, and this new success was more fairly won than the first.

31

DURING the spring of 1830, Dumas not only dined frequently with Georgina and Harel but was one of those friends admitted to the actress's dressing-room while she took her bath. Bold though he was, the privilege was bound to be a little surprising to a man of his generation. Hairpins of gold, he says, kept her dark curls out of the water, and her beautiful form appeared to be carved in Parian marble. She remained, he records, so calmly unself-conscious that there was nothing suggestive of indecency in the rite. 'Those movements,' he says, 'which in another woman would have seemed provocative and lascivious, were perfectly simple and natural in George, and reminiscent of the gestures of a Grecian woman of the time of Homer.' No passions were aroused, indeed, and none were meant to be; Georgina had no thought but to indulge in two pleasures at a time, those of basking in warm water and of conversation; the guests were enlightened as if on a visit to the sculpture galleries of the Louvre.

At other times Georgina would receive her guests reclining in her salon. 'Apart from her theatrical activities,' Dumas says, 'for which she was always ready, George was incredibly lazy. Large, majestic, well aware of her beauty which had given her two Emperors as admirers, as well as two or three Kings, George liked to remain extended on a huge settee; in the winter she would be wrapped in velvet robes and furs, or Indian cashmeres, and in the summer in dressing-gowns of lawn or muslin. Reclining thus in a pose that was always graceful and easy, George received visitors, sometimes with the majesty of a Roman matron, sometimes with the smiles of a Grecian courtesan; and from the folds of her dress and shawls there would be seen the heads of two or three small pedigree hounds.'

Georgina liked to wear the splendid diamonds she possessed, among them the gifts of Napoleon and Alexander. She wore them not only at home, but on the stage, and Dumas often saw her in the fine ear-rings she had received at St Cloud.

These ear-rings were so heavy that very often, on returning home at night after her performances, she would take them off, complaining that they were lengthening her ears. One night we came in and sat down to supper. The meal over, we sat eating almonds. George ate a great many, and while she ate she complained of the weight of her ear-rings, took them off and put them down on the table.

Five minutes after, the servant came with a brush, swept the table, pushed the ear-rings into a basket with the nut shells and flung the lot out of the window into the street below.

George went to bed without giving a thought to her ear-rings and slept peacefully—a thing she would not have done, philosophical though she was, if she had known that her servant had thrown twenty-five thousand francs' worth of diamonds out of the window.

The next morning George *cadette* came into her sister's bedroom and woke her up.

'Well,' she said to her, 'you can congratulate yourself on your luck! Look what I've found!'

'What is it?'

'One of your ear-rings.'

'Where did you find it?'

'In the street.'

'In the street?'

'Just as I say, my dear . . . in the street, near the door. You must have dropped it coming in from the theatre.'

'I can't have done. I had them on when we were having supper.'

'Are you sure?'

'So much so that I know I took them off because they were hurting me and put them down beside me. What did I do with them afterwards? Where can I have put them?'

'Ah, my God!' cried George *cadette*. 'I remember. We were eating almonds, the table was swept with the brush——'

'Oh, my poor ear-rings!' cried George in her turn. 'Go down quickly, Bébelle. Go down!'

Bébelle was already at the foot of the stairs. Five minutes afterwards she came back with the second ear-ring. She had found it in the gutter.

'My dear,' she said to her sister, 'we are much too lucky! Have a mass said, otherwise some great disaster will fall on us.'

Georgina's domestic life was smooth and happy. Dumas describes her as being devoted to Harel and unable to dispense with his amusing conversation. Harel, light-hearted and full of zest for life, was always able to keep her in good spirits. Bébelle, who acted indifferently in minor roles, appears to have been a somewhat neutral character, pretty but without the abilities of her elder sister.

The two sons of Harel and the younger sister were now lively children of ten and six, named Tom and Paul. Both were actors, taking their place wherever they could be used to save the expense of an older actor. Tom always accompanied his aunt when she acted in the provinces; and Dumas records that for many years the placards outside the theatres announced him unchangingly as 'Young Tom, aged ten.' As it happened, Tom had an inborn antipathy to the theatre and all connected with it. He was never able to understand how anyone could want to sit down and watch a play being acted. It was, however, an affliction from which he had no possibility of escaping. He was born practically on the stage, as his mother and aunt had been, and no other life but that of an actor was open to him. He was often heard execrating the profession as he waited his turn to go on the stage.

'Horrible theatre!' he would murmur to himself. 'And to think it never burns down!'

'What's that you're saying, Tom?' Georgina would ask.

'Nothing, aunt. I'm just rehearsing my part.'

Paul, on the other hand, did not mind how long he was on the stage so long as he had something to eat or drink. Paul was a pretty child, called '*le petit Popol*'. His head was covered with chestnut curls, he had large, dark eyes and an expression of angelic innocence. He was remarkably intelligent and resembled his aunt George in many ways, particularly in his love of food. As she herself had done as a child, he found his way to the bakers' and confectioners' shops nearby and contrived to obtain supplies on credit. In fact, small though he was, he discovered how to open an account at a café in the rue de Vaugirard; and one day the bill came in, showing that little Popol had eaten cakes to the value of 300 francs, cakes bought in the name of his mother and his aunt and consumed in obscure corners.

It was the height of summer. Georgina and Harel gave elegant dinner-parties which Dumas and Jules Janin usually attended. Until one or two in the morning they sat round the table talking, Harel pouring out the finest wines, Georgina passing round superb fruit ordered from Chevet, the renowned supplier of the rich. In the realm of the arts there was much to talk about. In this year, 1830, Stendhal had published *Le Rouge et le Noir*, Balzac *La Peau de Chagrin*, Lamartine *Les Harmonies Poétiques et Religieux*, Alfred de Musset *Les Contes d'Espagne*. And Victor Hugo's play *Hernani* had been performed in February. This last event was very much talked of, for it had almost created public riots between those who supported the new art and those who detested it. In the theatre men had literally fought each other. Those who admired the play could not endure the presence of those who criticized it; an exalted enthusiasm had contended with violent disapproval; sticks were used and heavy blows struck. It was a phenomenon of the times, this capacity to fight over a work of art.

After sitting long round the dinner-table, Harel, Georgina and their guests would stroll over to the Gardens of the Luxembourg if the night was hot. To these nearby gardens Harel had a key, a privilege accorded to him because he had once been the secretary of Prince Cambacérès. These gardens were silent and splendid in the moonlight; the statues resembled phantoms and the fountains tossed up their water like cascades of diamonds. And Georgina, in her muslin dress, a cashmere shawl over her shoulders, and Napoleon's ear-rings gleaming beneath her dark hair, strolled arm-in-arm with Dumas or Jules Janin, listening to their compliments. Life seemed happy and secure.

32

YET violent changes were at hand. Revolution broke out towards the end of July 1830. Charles X lost control of the situation, and a provisional Government was set up under the Duc d'Orléans.

Dumas and Harel joined the National Guard, but only Dumas took any part in the skirmishing. Harel had lost his old interest in politics and thought only of his theatre, which he feared would be ruined. Not only had the alarmed public stopped going to the theatres, the grant which Harel had received for the Odéon from Charles X was now suspended. Knowing how little notice would be taken of requests normally made at such a time, Harel called on Casimir-Périer, member of the provisional Government, took a revolver out of his pocket and threatened to commit suicide then and there if 15,000 francs were not allocated to him for the immediate needs of his theatre. The ruse succeeded. Greatly alarmed at the prospect of a citizen's sudden death, the republican Government gave him the money forthwith. And now he was in search of a play, a really sensational play that would lure the public back to his empty theatre.

Between them, he and Georgina found the solution to this difficult problem. The time had come for a play on Napoleon.

Though Napoleon had been hated and vilified at the time of his downfall, and had then been gradually forgotten, he was now coming back to mind again, thanks to the younger generation of writers who found in him a subject of hero-worship. Victor Hugo had long been hypnotized by his victories, and wrote verses reminding the French of the so-called glory he had brought to the nation. Many poets sang his praises, and even the English had helped to create a romanticized legend about him. As in the great days Napoleon had loved to watch Talma playing the role of Caesar, Pompey or Agamemnon, so now he himself should be seen on the stage as a hero of tragedy.

One day early in August Harel managed to secure one of the few cabs still to be found in the streets and drove to Dumas's house. Paris was in confusion, and alarming rumours were flying about to the effect that King Charles X was at Rambouillet with 20,000 men, determined to fight his way back to power. Harel found Dumas in his dressing-room, putting on a hunting costume, watched by a friend who was similarly attired and carried a gun.

'Ah, good!' said Harel. 'I'm glad I've found you at home.'

'Good morning, Harel,' said Dumas. 'What brings you so early, my friend?'

'What brings me here,' said Harel, opening his snuff-box, taking a large pinch and scattering the surplus on Dumas's carpet, 'is that I have an idea for a play.'

'Well, my dear Harel, you will be able to impart it to me on my return.'

'Where are you going, then?'

'To Rambouillet.'

Dumas's valet now brought him his gun, and the two huntsmen prepared to depart, despite Harel's protests. Seeing Harel's cab at the door they promptly commandeered it, and the only concession he could get from them was a lift back to the Odéon, and that was only granted so that they could borrow the tricolour which he had bought for popular demonstrations on the stage.

Dumas was not long out of Paris, for Charles X did not remain to fight at Rambouillet, preferring to go into exile. The Duc d'Orléans was proclaimed King Louis-Philippe, and order was restored. Even now, however, Dumas would not listen to Harel's proposals; he had managed to obtain a diplomatic mission to La Vendée which amounted to a paid holiday, and he left Paris again for several weeks.

The Odéon had been nearly empty throughout the troubled times and Harel, in search of sensation, acquired a play by a man who had been serving a term of imprisonment for insulting Charles X. The fall of Charles X naturally set the author free; but before he had time to remove himself from his place of confinement Harel had made arrangements for Georgina to visit the prison cell and there hear him read his play aloud and make plans for the production. The event made a fine item of news for the papers and effectively drew the thoughts of the public back to the Odéon; but the play was without interest. Harel had soon to take it off and replace it by another, which was little better.

By now Dumas returned and Harel offered him a box one evening. Dumas accepted, and afterwards was taken home to one of the luxurious supper parties which Georgina knew how to make enjoyable. Apart from Dumas, the only guests were Jules Janin and the actor Lockroy. The party was gay; course followed course and fine wines were served, and they lingered long round the white table that shone with silver and glass in the light of wax candles.

When at last they rose and the guests prepared to leave, Georgina made some pretext to take Dumas off to her salon, and there she kept him in conversation for ten minutes or so. When they returned to the dining-room, Lockroy and Janin had left and Harel was alone. Dumas went towards the front door.

'Not that way,' said Harel. 'Everyone in the house is asleep.'

And Harel and Georgina led the unsuspecting playwright through the salon he had just left, through a bedroom and dressing-room and into a small room he had never seen before. A fire burned in the grate, wax candles lighted a table covered with books, pens and paper. In the shadows was a comfortable bed, whose purple eiderdown contrasted with the white linen sheets, and beside which was spread a fine bear-skin on which a pair of embroidered slippers had been placed. There were, too, a couple of armchairs, one upholstered in tapestry, the other in velvet. It was a most inviting room, and Dumas could not help exclaiming over it. In such a room, he said, one would be inspired to write a good book, and would be sure of sleeping well.

'Ah, *ma foi!*' said Harel. 'I'm really delighted to see it pleases you.'

'Why?' asked Dumas.

'Because it is your own.'

'What do you mean? Mine?'

'Yes. And as you are not leaving it until you have done my

Napoléon for me, it's essential you should like it and be in the right frame of mind for writing.'

'Harel,' cried Dumas. 'Come, now, my friend, no nonsense!'

'Exactly,' said Harel. 'No nonsense! It was the greatest nonsense your not setting to work the moment I gave you the idea. And it was nonsense on my part not to give the work to someone else. But I had spoken to you about it, and I'm a man of my word. I consider we've had enough nonsense, you and I, and that it's time we both came to our senses.'

'But I haven't an idea in my head for your *Napoléon*—I should need books . . . Bourienne, Norvins, *Victoires et Conquêtes*. . . .'

'You have *Victoires et Conquêtes* here in one corner, Bourienne in the other. Norvins is on the table.'

'But I should want *Memorial de Sainte-Hélène*. . . .'

'It is on the mantelpiece.'

'My son——'

'He is coming to dine with us tomorrow.'

'My mistress——'

'Oh,' said Georgina, 'you have managed to do without her these last six weeks, you can manage for another week or two.'

Dumas consented with a good grace. Taking Georgina's hands in his, he turned to Harel and said:

'My dear friend, you do things in such a way that it's impossible to refuse. Tomorrow I'll begin your *Napoléon*, and in a week you shall have it.'

'Surely you are in a great hurry to leave us?' said Georgina reproachfully.

'Good!' said Dumas. 'The play will be finished when it's finished. It is not I who am in a hurry, it is Harel.'

'Harel will wait,' said Georgina.

'I inclined my head,' Dumas writes. 'I had no more to say. Harel showed me my *cabinet de toilette* with all its fittings, and observed that there was no way out of my room except through that of George.'

With peace and silence throughout the days that followed, waited on attentively, and with excellent meals provided, Dumas worked in ideal conditions. It is hardly necessary to say that the play he produced was atrociously bad. He had written his first play in a poor garret in the teeth of many difficulties. By day he had had to work as a clerk, and at home he had had no privacy; yet in those circumstances he had written a good play, and now he wrote a bad one. *Napoléon* was an assemblage of disconnected, melodramatic scenes, long and formless. It was five times as long as *Iphigénie en Aulide*, and there were between eighty and ninety characters with words to speak, besides others who had only to appear.

But Harel and Georgina were satisfied. The play was read aloud in two long sittings, and they told Dumas they were prepared to spend 100,000 francs on the settings. The best actors were engaged, with Frédérick Lemaître to take the leading role, and rehearsals began at once. In celebration of the successful reading, a gay and lavish supper-party was given.

Many years later Dumas, who had reached the height of success and known the great and wealthy of his time, said that the supper-parties of Mlle George were among his happiest recollections. The guests were artists, poets, playwrights and actors, and the hostess was dazzling. 'It was impossible to be more beautiful, more like a queen, more disdainful, more caustic, more of a Grecian courtesan, more a Roman matron, more a niece of the Pope, than Mlle George.'

33

HAREL'S exasperation over Dumas's absence from Paris had not been without cause. Wonderful ideas, he felt, were not safe for long; one had to put them into immediate effect or someone else was sure to get wind of them. Such had been the case with his *Napoléon*. Even before Dumas's play was in rehearsal, Napoleons were appearing on other Paris stages. While he waited, Harel put on *La Nuit Vénitienne* by Alfred de Musset; but its reception confirmed his belief in his own ideas. De Musset's piece failed, and at the same time fortunes were being made at the Vaudeville and the Porte-Saint-Martin theatres. At the Vaudeville was *Bonaparte à Brienne*, and at the Porte-Saint-Martin *Napoléon à Schoenbrunn*. Harel closed the Odéon after taking off de Musset's play, and occupied himself with publicity for the *Napoléon Bonaparte* of Dumas. In a series of Press notices, he promised the public one of the most costly, spectacular and moving dramas ever produced.

Fortunately for Harel, the success of the rival Napoleons did no harm to the play put on at the Odéon. On the contrary, a great interest in Napoleon had been aroused and Parisians were very willing to see another play on the same subject.

Napoléon Bonaparte began its run on 11 January 1831 and enjoyed a considerable measure of success. It owed everything to the subject, the spectacular production arranged at such heavy cost, and to the acting of Frédérick Lemaître. Sensation rather than substance gave it its appeal; there was plenty of stirring music, and there were many passages that aroused political passions. It was a kaleidoscope of quickly changing, brilliant settings; the audience waited breathlessly for the rising of the curtains and applauded each change of scene with enthusiasm. All the successful episodes of Napolon's life were brought forth in turn, treated in their popular and legendary aspect. Napoleon was majestic, heroic and magnanimous, and in the last scene he died as a martyr. Louis XVIII, who, it was remembered in certain circles of society, had pardoned Harel in 1819, was openly derided.

If the genius of Talma has ever been equalled, it is probably in the person of Frédérick Lemaître, although in an entirely different way. Talma was the greatest of tragic actors, and Frédérick was a humble boulevard comedian who had begun his career as the lion in *Pyramus and Thisbe*. Though he had had to do no more than roar, he had roared very eloquently and had soon made himself beloved by the crowds of Paris. Now, at the age of thirty, his reputation was very great, and he was an actor with a real influence on the playwrights of France. Harel had shown his usual skill in engaging him for the Odéon, for he was not an easy man to get hold of.

As Napoleon, however, Frédérick had not much scope for his individual gifts. It was his sense of the absurd, his love of the unrehearsed and unpremeditated, that made his performances so entertaining. He liked to take the audience into his confidence, to give them a sly aside as to the merits of the play he was performing in, or perhaps hold up the proceedings while he paused to offer his snuff-box to the prompter. In the role of Napoleon he was forced by public opinion and the nature of the legend to take himself seriously for the whole evening. In addition to this, there was the drawback of his appearance, which in no way resembled that of the Emperor. He was so unlike Napoleon that he made no attempt to imitate his well-known postures and mannerisms, but acted throughout with a straightforward simplicity. The Napoleon of the Porte-Saint-Martin was preferred, for whom an actor strikingly resembling the original had been found. But Frédérick was impressive, none the less, and the death scene always caused the audience to weep.

Mlle George did not take part in the play, but preferred to be conspicuous as the one woman whose appearance would have been highly improper in all the circumstances.

After a few days, the play was reduced to more normal proportions, and some of the offending political allusions were removed. Violent emotions continued to mark the performances, however, and the actor who played the part of Sir Hudson Lowe, Governor of the Island of Saint-Helena, had to be escorted home every night by a guard. After the performances, a number of excited and enraged spectators were always waiting outside the Odéon to stone him. Decidedly the July revolution had brought Bonapartism into prominence.

The play was performed every night for two months, and after that was put on intermittently until May. It was a fairly good run for the times, but attendances had fallen off sooner than Harel expected, and the costly production had not made him a large profit.

King Louis-Philippe must have hoped that the public interest in Napoleon would now subside. In January, it had been proposed in the Chambre des Députés that no contemporary figures should be put on the stage without the permission of the Minister of the Interior. As Napoleon himself had said, the theatre had 'need of a little antiquity'. But the Bonapartist legend had taken a hold upon French society and before long Louis-Philippe himself was to be driven by public opinion into paying his homage to the fallen Emperor.

For the moment, however, Louis-Philippe was not a Bonapartist, and he did not feel inclined to renew the grant to the Odéon which had been on the civil list of his predecessor, Charles X. Harel was invited to dine at the Palace of the Tuileries one day with other members of the National Guard, and he broached the subject of a subsidy with his usual aplomb. But it was in vain. Louis-Philippe knew that Harel intended to encourage the new writers of the romantic school—these vain young men who upheld republicanism, Bonapartism, and anything but respectable monarchy. Why should he give Harel an annual grant to be squandered on lavish productions glorifying Napoleon? No, let Harel make the Odéon pay by his own efforts.

This was an unexpected and serious difficulty, and it was now that Harel and Georgina decided to make a change. Georgina did not really care for the Odéon, where the acoustics were bad and the stage had too great a slope, and she urged Harel to acquire the Porte-Saint-Martin, a delightful theatre of the boulevards, built for Marie-Antoinette fifty years or so previously. At this theatre, Alexandre Dumas had just achieved his most brilliant success with a new play, *Antony*; the Porte-Saint-Martin was much talked of at the moment.

Antony was an emotional drama, exciting, well constructed and very much to the taste of the youthful followers of romanticism. It had caused a great sensation, and at the end of the first night Dumas's coat had literally been torn to pieces by the excited admirers who surged round him, trying to seize his hands, cheering him, fighting each other to reach him and generally losing their heads. The play was the fashion of the hour; for the next decade young men were to stroll about the boulevards in the manner of Antony, their long hair in disorder, attired in cloaks, and uttering the picturesque curses of the desperate hero. From orderly citizens of old-fashioned views the play drew horrified protests; this new piece of romanticism was denounced as vicious and demoralizing. But such plays made the fortunes of the theatres, and Harel, while feeling his way towards the acquiring of the Porte-Saint-Martin, urged Dumas to set to work again on behalf of the Odéon, of which he could not rid himself immediately.

Towards the end of June, Harel produced *La Maréchale d'Ancre* at the Odéon, a play by Alfred de Vigny in which Mlle George took the leading part. De Vigny had written the play for Mme Dorval, a brilliant actress who was appearing in *Antony* and whom he loved. But being unable to have it performed at the Porte-Saint-Martin he had taken it to Harel. In fact, the leading role was more suited to the talents of Georgina than to those of Dorval, and she was outstandingly successful in it. Dorval was an actress of emotions; Georgina, as time went on, inclined more and more towards the traditional dignity of the theatrical queen. The heroine of de Vigny's play was described as being 'a woman of firm and masculine character; an affectionate mother and devoted friend; calculating and dissimulating like the Medicis of whom she is the pupil; of noble manner, though somewhat hypo-critical'. Mlle George excelled in just such parts. De Vigny him-self was greatly pleased by her performance, which was also praised by Sainte-Beuve.

Now forty-four years old, Georgina was still a most beautiful woman, and her acting found many admirers. She had become impressive, and most of the leading playwrights thought highly of her. But this wonderful renaissance she was experiencing did not at all please some of those contemporaries who had known her well during the Consulate and Empire and had heartily detested her as Napoleon's favourite. She had made herself many enemies, and at each success their smouldering resentment would flare up anew and find an outlet in gossip and scandal, and this was echoed in certain sections of the Press. Although Harel spared no pains to keep on good terms with critics and other journalists, and although most of the leading critics genuinely admired his mistress, there were a number of papers that were persistently hostile both to himself and to Mlle George and subjected them both to incessant attacks. It is true that there was often an element of truth in what was said. It was not without reason that Harel's blatant methods of publicity were held up to scorn, or that Mlle George was blamed for her great band of hired applauders. But much that was said came from personal feelings of antipathy towards Mlle George, and while her beauty was constantly in the news elsewhere, her enemies drew attention to her increasing weight.

Certainly the time had gone when her beauty was such that no one could fail to marvel at it, when people turned to look at her in silence as she passed. She remained beautiful, but only when seen in favourable circumstances. She was beautiful, but only if one admired the statuesque. Her profile was perfection still, and her eyes were expressive and keen; but her figure was slightly too well rounded; even those who admired so mature a form might complain that her upper arms (which she could not refrain from displaying) had lately grown exaggeratedly large. As it was the fashion at the time to be very thin, Mlle George could be assailed on this point, and, in fact, her size had for some years been the subject of jokes. Some months previously, one of the papers had written: 'The English horse which has recently run round the Champ de Mars in four minutes, took only five minutes yesterday to get round Mlle George.' And during the rehearsals of de Vigny's play, the same paper had remarked that more than a hundred yards of velvet had been seen arriving at the Odéon, which it was supposed was for repairs to the seats and ledges of the boxes. It had turned out, however, that the material was part of Mlle George's costume for the coming production.

De Vigny's play, which had thirty performances, was an artistic success, but did little to atone to Harel for his loss of the royal subsidy. He placed his hopes now in a new play written for him by Dumas, a tragedy in verse called *Charles VII chez ses Grands Vassaux*.

34

THE success of *Antony* had inspired Dumas with new ambitions and he had attempted to rise to Olympian heights. He wished to show the world that he could equal the masters, as well as delight the masses, and he had given himself up to the composition of *Charles VII chez ses Grands Vassaux* with a passionate interest. There were some who considered it a good play, his son among them in later years; Dumas himself was perfectly satisfied and assured Harel it was his best work. Harel was trusting, particularly as Georgina and the actors much admired the play when it was read aloud, and again he spent a fortune on the settings and costumes.

The first night arrived, 20 October 1831; the theatre was crowded; the confident author was present with his seven-year-old son. Yet, popular and admired though Dumas was, the audience saw nothing and felt nothing in the well-produced play. It was not the kind of thing they expected of Dumas, and they did not like it. Their interest was never once aroused. They did worse than hiss and deride, they yawned.

The play was a complete failure. Throughout his life Dumas's son, then a little boy of seven, remembered his father's silence as they walked home, remembered the cold moonlight, and their shadows falling on the ancient walls as they went up the narrow rue de Seine towards the river. It was a terrible moment. It was Dumas's first failure and the Odéon was ruined.

Neither Dumas nor Harel and Georgina wasted much time in vain regrets, however. Harel was on the point of acquiring the Porte-Saint-Martin, and Dumas was working on a striking melodrama with which the theatre was to open under its new director.

At the end of the year, Harel obtained the desired post. It cost him 250,000 francs. As he was still committed to directing the Odéon, he now ran both theatres; but he took his best actors to the Porte-Saint-Martin. In April 1832 his term of office at the Odéon expired. He left the theatre much as he had found it, in debt and without prospects for the future. In recent months he had been very much criticized for his methods, and particularly for his extravagance. One of his last productions at the Odéon was called *Dik-Rajah* and included an elephant. It was all that was needed to damn him finally in the eyes of respectable citizens who took pride in the national theatres.

To return to December, Harel began his career at the Porte-Saint-Martin with Dumas's play *Richard Darlington*. Less certain of himself after his astonishing failure at the Odéon, Dumas had worked with collaborators, a couple of men who had had long experience in the fabrication of boulevard successes. Between them they produced a really sensational piece of work, cold and violent. With Frédérick Lemaître in the leading role it was immensely successful, though it did not add to Dumas's good name. But it made money and enabled Harel to begin his new venture in suitable style.

In this play the young Popol took part, although he had no more to do than ring a bell and rap on a desk. Standing on a concealed stool at the back of the stage, he was arranged to appear as a fully-grown actor. He represented a judge in a court scene. Before him was a glass, filled at each performance with a pleasant, sweet drink with which he was permitted to regale himself at suitable moments. It was his payment for his services. Unhappily this was to be little Popol's last part: his promising career was to be cut short.

Political disorders and the troubles brought in their train had been surmounted; but 1832 brought its own crop of disasters, though it opened quietly. In January the theatrical world talked about Mlle Duchesnois, who gave a farewell performance at the Théâtre Français. She was now fifty-seven years old; her health had always been poor, and since it was deteriorating she had to retire. Little is known about her, and one can only imagine what her feelings may have been as she gave up the stage while her old rival, so happy in her domestic life with the man she herself had loved, flourished in full vigour. Of Duchesnois's inner disposition nothing is known, so quietly and discreetly did she pass through life. One would like to know more, for by many who saw them both she was said to surpass Rachel, while those who saw Rachel only could never believe that she had even been equalled.

Winter and spring were followed by an exceedingly fine and radiant summer, and with it cholera arrived from Asia, spreading havoc in Paris. The sun shone gloriously out of a sky perpetually cloudless and vividly blue; the air was hot and motionless and Paris had never looked more enchanting; yet people fell by hundreds, and then by thousands. The hospitals were crowded out, drums rolled all day long, warning pedestrians to keep out of the way as stretchers were carried along the streets. Funeral processions followed each other with scarcely a gap to the cemeteries, and the terrified populace avoided all assemblies. The theatres were effectively emptied.

Harel, always without scruple, persuaded his journalistic friends to insert paragraphs in their newspapers saying that the theatres were the only safe places in Paris, and that no one had ever been known to catch the disease while watching a play; but the public paid no attention.

Little Popol caught the malady. It had been a source of much amusement to Harel, who was a materialist, that Popol could never be made to say his prayers. During the epidemic, however, it had been noticed that Popol prayed fervently night and morning; and as his family were certain he had never learnt a Christian prayer they were curious to know what he said. One of them therefore hid behind a curtain and listened. It was the following petition that went up:

'Oh, Lord God, take my Aunt George, take my Uncle Harel, take my brother Tom, take Mama Bébelle, take my friend Prévost, but please leave little Popol and the cook!'

But poor Popol, with his zest for sensual pleasures, was swept away none the less, the fifteen hundredth to die of cholera on the day which was his last.

35

UNDER Harel's direction the Porte-Saint-Martin theatre enjoyed a dazzling success for some years. Some of the most notable works of the rising dramatists were performed there, and it became the most fashionable theatre in Paris. Victor Hugo followed Dumas, and other writers, equally well known in their hour though now forgotten, saw Mlle George applauded in their best works.

Night after night Georgina looked across at brilliant audiences. Elderly men and women who had once shone at Napoleon's court were faithful patrons; all fashionable modern society came, and with them the artists of Paris: Alfred de Vigny, George Sand, Liszt, Berlioz, Scribe, Béranger and a hundred others.

After *Richard Darlington*, another play by Dumas was put on. This was *La Tour de Nesle*, a melodrama of the most sensational type. A young and unknown author had brought the play to Harel in the first place; it was useless for the stage as it stood, but it contained a lurid and extraordinary story. Harel hurried with the manuscript to Dumas, who was in bed with cholera. Immune himself, he stood over the author until he had agreed to rewrite the play. In this way Dumas employed his convalescence, preserving little of the original work but the theme. It was to be the source of much trouble to him as, owing to certain small deceptions on the part of Harel, the original author took offence and was disposed to quarrel. But the play was a highlight of romanticism and one of the outstanding successes of the century.

Georgina played the part of the heroine, Marguerite de Bourgogne, a French queen of the Middle Ages who made a habit of enticing young men into her abode, spending a night of passionate indulgence with them and then rounding off the episode by having them murdered before her eyes. With her opulent figure, richly clad and bejewelled, the actress was well qualified to play a role in which, with no attempt at reticence, sex was the substance of the entertainment offered. In the words of Jules Janin, she 'threw herself into the ardent fray whole-heartedly'.

La Tour de Nesle proved to be an irresistible attraction to Parisians, and they went in their thousands, filled with eager curiosity to see the obscene and lustful heroine in the midst of her orgies. Yet the play contained more than mere horror; it was splendidly acted by a notable company of players, and it had a power of fascination that appealed to the educated as well as to the boulevard crowds in search of sensation. Mlle George was said to be superb, and to strike terror with a capacity reminiscent of Talma himself. The respectable royal family went to one of the performances, and Victor Hugo was filled with admiration.

Hugo's enthusiasm, indeed, was such that he wrote two plays for Mlle George, *Lucrèce Borgia* and *Marie Tudor*, preferring the Porte-Saint-Martin to the Théâtre Français. Such plays were among the great literary events of the day and gave prestige to the theatre. They were interspersed with other notable successes, dramas in which it was usual for Mlle George to appear as a royal person of supernormal passions. Hugo considered her the perfect interpreter of his leading feminine roles. As Lucrèce he found her 'as sublime as Hecuba and as touching as Desdemona'. And of her acting in *Marie Tudor* he says: 'As for Mlle George, there is only one word to be said: sublime. . . . She creates within the very creation of the poet something which astonishes and enthralls even the author himself. She caresses, terrifies and moves, and it is one of the miracles of talent that the same woman who horrifies us can so easily move us to tears.'

Another writer describes her as dazzling in *Marie Tudor*: 'Reclining on a couch, in a robe of scarlet velvet, and crowned with diamonds, her beauty was indeed royal.'

That her acting now had great vigour is shown by a passage from the *Revue de Paris*, quoted by Maurice Descottes in *Le Drame Romantique*. The writer quoted is criticizing a performance of Mlle Mars in Hugo's *Angelo*.[1] 'In her place,' he says, 'Mlle George would have made the house tremble. She would

[1] Performed at the Théâtre Français in 1835.

have come on the scene, furious, terrible, clamorous, overwhelming with her rage and her insults, and terrifying a thousand times more with the tones of her voice than with the hatred in her heart.'

Georgina was at her best at the Porte-Saint-Martin in her rather overbearing way. She had always dominated Harel, and now she had her own theatre, which she ruled as an autocrat. Not since she was a child with the theatre of Amiens as her nursery had she felt so free and at home on a stage; she was absorbed by every production and worked with zeal. She took the plays of the new school with great seriousness, as all society did at the time, and worked indefatigably as their interpreter. Although these plays called for no refinement of understanding, they were not at all easy to act in. Plays have dwindled miserably since those times, the great days of the theatre; they were then very long and called for five hours or so of strenuous effort from the actor and actress taking the leading parts. The historic dramas in fashion demanded great emotional display, and an exacting public went to them expecting to be alarmed, excited and moved to tears throughout the evening. They also expected a fine spectacle. The poorer citizens of Paris, in particular, went to gaze at Georgina's renowned diamonds, worn with flowing, embroidered dresses—sleeveless and low-cut when possible—and velvet cloaks.

In 1835 Duchesnois died. Since her retirement the Comédie Française had been neglected by the public and its theatre was always half empty. Romanticism had won the day, and the classical tragedies so greatly in fashion during the Consulate and Empire were now regarded as tedious and completely out of date.

Around Georgina the new art grew and flourished and prevailed. And regardless of the fact that her illustrious lover, Napoleon, would have detested romanticism and deplored her departure from the Comédie Française, and would have been shocked beyond expression by the commercial use to which his former love for her was now being put, she was in her glory as the divinity of the hour and leading devotee of Bonapartism.

Her reign at the Porte-Saint-Martin coincided with the rapid expansion of the Bonaparte legend in France. The King of Rome, his name modified after 1814 to the Duc de Reichstadt, had died in 1832, and this had added to the prevailing sympathy for Napoleon; during the following summer, Louis-Philippe allowed the erection of a new statue of Napoleon on the column of the Place Vendôme, the first of many respectful tributes to the Bonapartes. Harel made full use of his mistress's former association with Napoleon. 'Mlle George will be wearing the magnificent diamonds given to her by Napoleon,' the public was often told on the eve of some new production. No one was allowed to forget for long that the great George had been loved by the Emperor.

All this time her beauty continued to call forth eloquent praise except in those journals that were hostile to her. Happiness, perhaps, and the satisfactions of her career, gave a perpetual sparkle to her eye and kept her free from wrinkles. Yet by now she was becoming massive.

Even in the far-off days of her first visit to London *The Times* had remarked that she was unwieldy, and she had never ceased to indulge in sensual pleasures, eating among them. But her devotees made a virtue of her ever-increasing size; it may be that the accentuations of her natural form enhanced her power to excite emotion, for they spoke of the intoxicating effects of her seductive appearance and of her imperial grace. She was a muse, a goddess, the spirit of Melpomene, but never a middle-aged woman.

But while she could charm her personal admirers, she had become an alarming character to work with, and many of the actors at the Porte-Saint-Martin detested her. She was as tyrannical as Napoleon had been at his worst. She considered no one's feelings, but gave her orders arrogantly and would endure no criticism from others. Frédérick Lemaître was among the men whom she failed to attract. Called upon to make love to her on the stage in some of the most passionate dramas of the time, he disliked her intensely and he disliked Harel also. He disapproved of their commercialism, their incessant advertising of Mlle George's association with Napoleon, and he was repelled by close contact with the great actress.

Her personality had become formidable, and can be divined from a description of her given by Théophile Gautier in 1839, at which time she was fifty-one years old: 'She exactly resembles the image from a medallion of Syracuse . . . the arch of her eyebrows, traced with an incomparable purity of line, extends over two dark eyes full of fire and tragic passion; the nose is fine and straight . . . joining the forehead with a line of magnificent simplicity. Her mouth is powerful, arched at the corners and superbly disdainful, like that of an avenging Nemesis. . . . That mouth, however, is capable of the most charming smile that lights up her face with a grace altogether imperial. . . . The chin is full of strength and resolution, and its firm contour completes majestically a profile more that of a goddess than a woman. Like all beautiful women of the pagan age, Mlle George has a broad but rather low brow, full and rounded at the temples, a brow at once self-willed, voluptuous and powerful, and as appropriate to Clytemnestra as to Messalina.'

In her pride she insisted on keeping up ridiculous and old-fashioned ceremonies. Every night, according to a contemporary, when she left her dressing-room, the stage-manager walked slowly ahead of her, knocking the floor with his baton at each step. It was a signal that she was approaching and that all were to step aside. But the malicious had it that the stage-manager was testing the soundness of the floor to make sure it would withstand her weight.

36

HAREL's feats in advertising his theatre and his mistress, in obtaining the plays and actors he wanted, and in dealing with crises of all kinds, made his name proverbial and he was often called 'the Napoleon of the theatre'. He revelled in publicity and his imagination was fertile in presenting to him new and ever varied means of drawing attention to himself as well as to Mlle George. He was artful and specious, and he was never happy with a straightforward situation, but had to complicate it with peculiar schemes and intrigues. He knew everyone from the King downwards, and he used his keen wit and genial manner as a screen which hid his lack of conscience.

Being clever was Harel's hobby, and he loved to swindle people for the benefit of his theatre, or out of a misguided sense of humour and love of sensation. It was this cleverness that proved his undoing in the end. Harel could never let well alone, and many stories are told of the tortuous little conspiracies he always had in hand. One of these concerns Victor Hugo's play, *Lucrèce Borgia*. Hugo was exacting. He was a successful man and could get what he wanted; he insisted upon a most costly production. Harel conceived an idea for inducing a very rich man, the Russian Prince Demidoff, to subsidize the play. There were only two female roles, the second being quite insignificant, an affair of twenty lines in the third act. All that was required was a beautiful girl who knew how to wear her clothes with effect. Prince Demidoff had a mistress who was trying to make her way on the stage, although entirely devoid of talent. Harel suggested to her that she might like the minor role, and then persuaded her opulent lover that it was well worth while patronizing the production with his gold for the pleasure at seeing Mlle Juliette in a fine play. Everyone was pleased with the arrangement, Harel most of all.

Yet the ruse was to lead to a host of troubles. The play was splendidly successful, and night after night long queues formed at the doors of the theatre. Then, suddenly and unexpectedly, it was removed. Mlle Juliette had fallen in love with the author. Hugo, to the astonishment of his friends, was unable to resist her and they were now living together. Prince Demidoff's friendly patronage of Harel and his theatre was transformed into a lively hostility. The atmosphere became explosive, and it was impossible to continue the run of the play.

Worse followed, for in his next play, *Marie Tudor*, Hugo wrote a special and important part for his mistress, that of Lady Jane Grey. Georgina took the part of Queen Mary, but both she and Harel were too tactful to demur over the casting of Lady Jane. They assumed that the rehearsals would show Hugo how incapable Mlle Juliette was of playing the part. But Mlle Juliette's vanity and Hugo's infatuation were proof against all reality; rehearsals followed one another, with Mlle Juliette showing herself hopelessly incompetent, but quite self-satisfied. Harel dropped a discreet hint and Hugo was mortally offended, assuming that Georgina was envious of his mistress's youth and beauty. Bocage, the celebrated interpreter of Dumas's *Antony*, was playing the role of Lady Jane's husband, and both he and Georgina began to lose patience with Mlle Juliette and to treat her with a marked contempt. She complained to Hugo, and he withdrew Bocage's role from him and gave it to another actor. This high-handed action caused a sensation in theatrical circles, for Bocage was one of the leading actors of the day.

Mme Dorval, who had remained at the Porte-Saint-Martin under Harel for some time, had now left, and her place had not yet been filled; Hugo was determined that his mistress should take her place, an enviable one in such a theatre. With Georgina becoming daily more infuriated by Mlle Juliette, who took the life out of every scene in which she appeared, and with Harel equally enraged with Hugo, who did not mind offending his best actors, the atmosphere was more than stormy. To make things worse, Alexandre Dumas also had a mistress who was a young actress thirsting for fame. This was Mlle Ida, whom he was eventually to marry. Dumas had made up his mind no less firmly than Hugo that his mistress should be given the desirable vacancy at the Porte-Saint-Martin. Mlle Ida, however, was an actress of reasonable though not outstanding talent; anticipating the worst, Harel was pleased to let her learn the part of Lady Jane. He felt it was impossible that *Marie Tudor* should survive, and he was openly discussing another play with Dumas, *Angèle*, which had been written specially for Mlle Ida. Jealousy between the rival actresses was intense, and Hugo angrily accused Harel of wishing for the failure of *Marie Tudor*.

On the eve of the first performance, Harel, in extreme agitation, said to Hugo:

'M. Hugo, have you really decided not to change your cast?'

'It would be a little late, since we begin tomorrow night.'

'I have an understudy for every part. Would you like to avail yourself of this?'

'No.'

'Very well. Your play will collapse.'

'Which means that you will make it collapse!'

'Which means anything you like!'

'Very well, M. Harel! Ruin my play for me, and I will ruin your theatre.'

The play began its run with everyone concerned in the highest state of exasperation. Harel, after promising Hugo two hundred and fifty free tickets for the first night, thought better of it and sent him only fifty. Hugo returned them all indignantly. The weather was atrocious, cold and wet. Mlle George was not politely visited in her dressing-room by the author, and took additional offence over the omission.

The curtain rose, and the play went reasonably well while Georgina dominated the stage; but as it rose to its climax, written for Mlle Juliette as Lady Jane, everything went disastrously wrong. It was seen that Mlle Juliette could not act at all, and the audience just laughed at her. Mlle George alone won an ovation at the end of the evening. Even Hugo could not now insist on keeping his mistress in the play; she retired on the plea of illness, and the following night the triumphant Mlle Ida played the role. But Hugo projected the disaster on to Harel and did not forgive him.

Dumas's *Angèle* brought success after *Marie Tudor*, which did not run for long; and after this he wrote *Catherine Howard* for his friend Harel, a strange travesty of English history in which Mlle Ida, now comfortably established at the Porte-Saint-Martin, again played the part of the heroine. It was not a good play, but it followed a formula that was sure to please a certain public; the acting was good and the production, as usual, was effective. For Dumas and the Porte-Saint-Martin there was always an appreciative audience.

Yet in the later half of the 1830s there was a marked decline in the standards of the theatre. Dumas produced *Don Juan de Marana* in 1836, but it was only moderately successful. Frédérick performed in some of his early successes, and Georgina appeared in such melodramas as *La Nonne Sanglante*. But there were no more plays on the level of *Antony*, *La Tour de Nesle* or *Lucrèce Borgia*. Dumas had taken to travelling abroad for long periods, and he was beginning to interest himself in the writing of books rather than plays; Hugo was offended; it was difficult to find authors to replace these two men. Harel had several failures and was beginning to fall into debt. Georgina at times created difficulties; there were quarrels with Frédérick and other actors. And then—there was no denying it—she was steadily increasing in size and had acquired an elderly air, at least by daylight.

But the spell of Harel's fortunes at the Porte-Saint-Martin was really destroyed by the appearance of a genius at the Comédie Française. This was Rachel, who made her début at the national theatre in 1838. Her gifts were of the highest order, and she won immediate fame. There was a revival of interest in the classical masterpieces in which she acted most splendidly. The whole situation was changed. Rachel was the latest fashion, the Théâtre Français was crowded out each night, and the Porte-Saint-Martin was deserted.

Harel's last successful play, put on in February 1839, did not greatly help the situation, for he was by now in great financial straits. It was *Le Manoir de Montlouvier*, in which Georgina was much admired. 'After the curtain fell,' Théophile Gautier said in his review, 'Mlle George was called for. She was most beautiful, and most richly attired, with her fine taste and her usual royal furs.'

Théophile Gautier said elsewhere in 1839 that the face of Mlle George was like pure marble which the years passed by, powerless to change the fine profile of a Grecian Melpomene. None the less, literary eloquence apart, the celebrated George was still putting on weight at an alarming rate, and a realistic view of her showed that she had a double chin.

1840 arrived. All Harel's hopes were now centred in Balzac. Balzac had written him a play, an excellent play, called *Vautrin*.

Balzac had a very great reputation at this time, particularly among the artists of Paris, who understood the originality and power of his work. But he was notoriously unlucky, and his fame brought him no material rewards. All his literary ventures went wrong and he was perpetually in debt. He was not the ideal character to lean on when shipwreck was imminent. Yet Harel and Georgina were confident. Balzac himself was always specious and had talked them into the belief that his play had all the elements of a popular success; Frédérick Lemaître was to play the leading role, and all Paris was interested in the coming event.

Yet once again Harel was over-ingenious. An idea occurred to him on the eve of the first performance. What a sensation it would create if he put Frédérick in a wig that was unmistakably a copy of the King's very peculiar and distinctive wig! Harel disliked Louis-Philippe, and so, on the whole, did the artists and critics and other intellectual persons whose pronouncements could decide the fate of a play. It was the fashion to be a Bonapartist or a republican; and Bonapartism and republicanism were great, seething movements, always creating unrest and seeking opportunities to embarrass the now unpopular King and his Ministers. The wig, worn by the unscrupulous central character, would give the play terrible political and anti-royalist implications, and the consequent scandal would place the Porte-Saint-Martin at the centre of everyone's thoughts.

Gleefully Harel took the *perruquier* on one side and gave him his instructions, and when the first night arrived the unsuspecting Frédérick sat down as usual to be made up, preoccupied with his role, and the grotesque wig was placed on his head.

It was 14 March 1840. Balzac had written to a friend: 'You may imagine what my anguish will be on the first night of *Vautrin*. Five hours will decide whether or not my debts will be paid.' Harel's anguish was equally great, for his actors had been unpaid for some weeks now and were all in difficulties.

The theatre was full, a brilliant audience was present, including King Louis-Philippe's heir, the Duc d'Orléans. The performance went smoothly and in a most satisfactory manner until Frédérick appeared in his unmistakable pear-shaped wig. Though Balzac, a royalist, had had no political intention in mind, the whole meaning of his play had been transformed by Harel's trick. The theatre was suddenly in an uproar as political passions were let loose. People stood up to shout, protest, whistle, hiss and applaud, and Harel watched from the wings, rubbing his hands together with satisfaction.

But the Duc d'Orléans stepped quietly out of his box and hurried home to the Palace of the Tuileries, where he roused his father, who was already asleep.

'Father,' he said, 'they are openly joking at your expense at the Porte-Saint-Martin. Surely you won't put up with it?'

The next day the Government issued an order forbidding any further performances of *Vautrin*. Balzac had had his usual luck, and the Porte-Saint-Martin stood mournfully closed.

Harel made light of the situation and prepared to replace the banned play. But his actors were hungry and were seeking work elsewhere, and his creditors were after him. With his usual bravado, he boasted to his friends that he spent all his time at the theatre standing on the stage trap-door, so that he could vanish whenever an unwelcome visitor arrived. But he was bankrupt and was given no time for new ventures. The theatre was seized and its contents sold forthwith.

37

MADAME,

At the risk of appearing indiscreet, I address myself to you with entire confidence in your long friendship.

You will know about the disaster of the Porte-Saint-Martin, which has swallowed everything we had. I must now go back again to being a travelling actress, and for a very long time. As I take my own company with me, I am obliged to spend considerably in advance. . . . It is to you, great artist and true friend, that I turn, hoping that you will lend me for a few months a thousand franc note.

I am arranging to leave at the end of the month.

This sad note, which survives in the archives of the Comédie Française, was written by Mlle George on 21 June 1840, and shows the extent of Harel's ruin. One can assume that Georgina had gradually sold her jewellery in recent years, or most of it, for her note shows that she had no time to lose in trying to earn a living for herself and her family.

No doubt Harel himself hoped to find a new post in due course; but at present no theatre in Paris had an opening for him. Bébelle had only very mediocre talents and was without initiative; young Tom was devoted and willing, but was no actor, having been forced on to the stage against his will. Yet he had been debarred from all other careers by the demands of his family, and so was now unable to help them.

Georgina, always unbearable at the height of good fortune, rose to the occasion with her usual courage and resolution. Once more her best qualities shone forth and she settled down uncomplainingly to the hardships of travelling about the provinces as an ageing actress.

It was a very hard life. Accustomed to living easily, she now travelled as economically as possible. Praised for her cleverness and beauty from her earliest years, she had had no experience of being treated as an ordinary and insignificant person; but now that she was deprived of beauty and position, men looked at her with indifference, without a smile. It was as though the world had suddenly grown ill-mannered. Flanders, Poitou, Auvergne, Berry: she went from place to place with her small company of third-rate actors and the faithful Tom. Harel remained in Paris, organizing her tours, seeing people, writing to her, and always awaiting the moment when he could find an opening for her in the capital.

It was not difficult to find provincial engagements, for everyone in France had heard of the celebrated George; people came to see her, indeed, in great numbers. But they had been told of her fabulous beauty, and they were amazed and disappointed to see an immensely fat and elderly woman.

'Mlle George has been beautiful for a very long time,' Théophile Gautier had said recently. In recent years no serious critic in Paris—certainly none of her friends—had wished to hurt her feelings by failing to praise her beauty. Mlle George and beauty had really been one and indivisible from the beginning; in no other actress had beauty meant so much, for in no other had it been so superb and classically correct. Now that it was gone, now that she had become grotesquely oversized, polite criticism was at a loss. What was to be said? Usually, out of sympathy and loyalty, beauty was imagined though no longer seen; it was kindly remembered and spoken of as ever present. But provincial audiences who went from reading these reports to their theatres to see the actress for the first time were stupefied; gazing at her with literal eyes they sat in silence.

Even in her own city of Amiens she was no longer admired. After she had performed there as Esther a local journalist wrote facetiously about the 'great actress of yesterday who has become the huge actress of today'.

After touring France she went abroad, to Italy and Austria and then to Russia. Once more she drove into St Petersburg, the scene of such pleasures and triumphs in the past. It was here that she realized to the full that everything had gone from her. Here she had once been worshipped and adored; here she had had lovers who swore eternal fidelity, and here fashionable audiences had cheered her nightly at the theatre.

This was the same beautiful northern city, with its marble palaces, its blue canals, its dazzling snow, the city where Alexander had ruled. St Petersburg had not changed in any way, and she had not changed either. She was the very same person, back again. Only now no one loved her, no one applauded her, no one cared whether she came or stayed away, whether she ate or starved.

Alexander had jumped from his sleigh at her approach to smile and bow as she passed by. The Imperial family had watched her perform at the theatre and said they had never seen so wonderful an actress. But the Czar Nicholas remained indifferently in his Winter Palace and did not ask to see her. A handful of spectators watched her at the theatre and barely applauded her. Yet when she looked about the radiant city, shining and silent under the autumn sun, she saw it was exactly as it always had been, just as she, too, was as she always had been. Whom, then, had Alexander saluted so respectfully? Who had been applauded and admired? Who is loved by men? Is the answer no one? Yes, that must be the answer. One responds with one's self, thinking the self is loved. But the self remains from one end of life to the other, only to realize that it has never been seen or loved. And that which is loved cannot even feel, for it is not even real. And perhaps the love poured forth so effusively does not mean anything, either. One is loved by men in the hours of good fortune; but if one is in want one turns to a friend of one's own sex and asks if she can spare one a few francs. In one's need one has to turn towards the real.

The visit to St Petersburg cast a chill upon Georgina, and she was thankful to leave, thankful to return to France. In all, she travelled from place to place with her company for three years. And then, in 1843, Harel persuaded the director of the Odéon to engage her for a season. It was with great thankfulness that she settled down in Paris with her family. Harel, though still without employment, had written an essay on Voltaire, and he received an award for it from the French Academy. Life had become a little easier.

For two years she remained in Paris. At the Odéon she appeared in the plays of Dumas and Hugo and in classical tragedies, and at times she performed at other Paris theatres, including the Porte-Saint-Martin. At this last theatre she played successfully once more in *La Tour de Nesle*, and acting with her was her old adversary, Frédérick Lemaître. P. A. Cheramy, the editor of her memoirs, records an incident of this time that throws light on her disposition. Frédérick, brilliant and temperamental, sometimes fell into a flat, lifeless condition of mind in which all drive to act would leave him. On these occasions he would resort to champagne, taking it in excessive quantities. Thus primed, his powers of acting would be fully revived and he would often surpass himself. But Frédérick drunk, though impeccable on the stage, was more than difficult elsewhere. In such a state he turned up at the Porte-Saint-Martin one night, truculent to the last degree. He announced that he was not going to act that night until a certain sum of money was advanced to him by the director. The director refused to give it to him, Frédérick grew more obstinate. The moment arrived for the curtain to rise, and Frédérick would not move; though everyone protested, he demanded his money then and there. Then Georgina, wearing some of her few remaining pieces of jewellery, sent them with a messenger to a nearby pawnbroker and settled the altercation by giving Frédérick the desired sum. The play then began.

In Paris her audiences were usually sympathetic; old men and women who had seen her début came to applaud her at the Odéon, and friendly critics still gave her a kind word in the press. Even young Parisians admired her acting at times. Victorien Sardou saw her in *Rodogune* and Hugo's *Lucrèce Borgia* during this season. 'Her obesity,' he writes, 'had reached the point of the ridiculous. After falling at the feet of Genaro, she was unable to get up again without his assistance. I remember her hands, like those of a child, attached to colossal arms, and her head—the head of an ageing Juno—placed on massive shoulders. And yet she was so practised in tragedy, in good carriage, gesture and delivery, and the tone of her voice was so beautiful, that her performance that evening is always present in my memory. I can still see Lucrèce, masked and clad in white—a costume that did not help to diminish her size—moving about the stage with the younger Monrose, who played Gubetta. . . . The settings were atrocious, particularly the first: an old, worn back-cloth with no visible trace of design or colour left, and which was used indiscriminately to represent a London fog and the Grand Canal in Venice. The costumes were absurd, the direction was childish. . . . But George triumphed over everything.'

But while Parisians were ready to look past her infirmities to the memory of what she had been, strangers gazed with a merciless eye. Charles Dickens went with Macready to the Odéon one night at the end of 1844 and saw her in Dumas's *Christine*. 'Once Napoleon's mistress,' he writes, 'she is now of an immense size, from dropsy, I suppose; and with little, weak legs which she can't stand upon. Her age, withal, somewhere about eighty or ninety. I never in my life beheld such a sight. Every stage-conventionality she ever picked up (and she has them all) has got the dropsy too, and is swollen and bloated hideously. The other actors never looked at one another, but delivered all their dialogues to the pit, in a manner so egregiously unnatural and preposterous that I couldn't make up my mind whether to take it as a joke or an outrage.'

38

HAREL had followed up his success with the essay on Voltaire by writing a play; but this turned out to be a failure. Georgina's contract with the Odéon came to an end and it was not renewed. Nor did she find other work in Paris. Once more she resigned herself to travelling, and Harel arranged new provincial tours for her. The following letter was written to Jules Janin in the summer of 1845, soon after she left:

MY DEAR FRIEND,

Mlle Mélingue is playing *Mérope* today. If you are reviewing the performance, will you be good enough to introduce a word or two recalling the success Mlle George has so often had in this work? There is nothing to prevent full justice to Mlle Mélingue being combined with the useful little souvenir you can very kindly give here to Mlle George who is touring at the moment and may well be doing so for some time to come. A bravo of recognition on the occasion of the performance of *Mérope* will appear only natural, and it will be most favourable to the commercial ends of Mlle George's travels.

I repeat, two words only. *Multa paucis.*

You have no need to be reminded of my constant friendship,

HAREL.

So Harel importuned his friends in Paris, and Georgina was punctilious in thanking anyone who gave her a little space in the Press. To Théophile Gautier she wrote:

MONSIEUR,

You invariably show me a most generous and helpful kindness.

Your article of last Monday, which was brought to my notice yesterday, is a new and most obliging proof of that interest which you have shown in me for so long, and which I value most sincerely.

Please accept, Monsieur, the heartfelt gratitude and devotion of your very humble servant,

GEORGE.

The following letter to Harel has survived, written, presumably, in 1846. Harel had been taken ill, and Georgina had just heard the news.

Cher bon chéri,

I send you my news, for I know how much you like to have it. I believe, my adored love, that our little affairs are beginning to go better. This evening I play *Mérope*, tomorrow *Semiramis*, and no doubt on Wednesday I shall play at Louviers which is only 6 leagues off. On Thursday, here again, perhaps. It depends on the takings. They say that Bernay and Elbeuf are better. We will follow your itinerary carefully. Your indisposition won't be serious, my dear; but you must give yourself every care you need. A little patience, and all will be well. I must leave you, my adored one, they have come to rehearse *Semiramis*. Good-bye for a little while, my dear, whom I love with all the force of my soul.

Always yours, yours all my life. I'll write tomorrow,

GEORGE.

Give my sister a kiss for me.

Harel, however, was really ill, and the following letter was to be the last he ever wrote to George:

Just a line to you, my dearest. My heart always beats for you.

Alas, we have to be separated for the time being, but your image is always in front of me.

Bébelle overwhelms me with attentions.

You have our dear Tom with you. He will be more useful to you than anyone else in your efforts. Your sister will always give me

news of you. And you yourself know that my affection for you is
eternal. Your letters do me a great deal of good.

Embrace my son for me.

To you both, as always,

HAREL.

Tired and worried, and blaming himself, perhaps, for the
ordeal which Georgina now had to face in the struggle to earn
a living, Harel had long been distracted. And now, without
warning, his reason gave way. His own life vanished utterly from
his consciousness, and he believed he was Bossuet.

In this demented state he did not linger very long. His last
letter to Georgina was dated 1 June 1846; he died in August of
the same year in a mental home at Chatillon.

His death was a heavy trial to Georgina, for she had grown
deeply attached to him during the years they had spent together,
and she had depended on him in all things. The loss of wealth
and position had been endurable, but this was very different and
she was overcome with sorrow and depression. Despite her
strength of character, she liked to be guided by others in her
domestic life, and she had never had to manage her own affairs.
Now she was responsible for her helpless sister, for Tom and
herself.

She continued her provincial performances wherever anyone
would engage her; but hope, optimism and confidence had gone.
She was a tired and grief-stricken woman of fifty-nine, flogging
herself on through necessity.

One day early in the following summer, Jules Janin received
a long letter from a stranger who happened to be in the provinces
where she was acting. It ran as follows:

MONSIEUR,

She who used to be one of the greatest of French actresses, the
most beautiful and one of the most brilliant women of the century
. . . is now reduced to dragging out a wretched existence in village
halls where the most obscure actors of Paris would blush to be seen.

Not long ago we were at Saumur. She was there, giving performances with a few poor devils she had collected round her. They
were giving *Mérope*, and the bills said that if there were not more

people than at the last performance, money would be returned. This aroused our curiosity, we went to the theatre and counted forty people in the audience. Mlle George apparently found the number sufficient, for the performance took place.

We were then witnesses of a most distressing spectacle. The actress appeared, still almost beautiful; but the theatre was only half the size of the Palais-Royal, and illusion was impossible. The wrinkles, the white hair, the monstrous figure, the unsteady movements, the broken voice and hiccuping of the poor actress struck the spectators with such stupefaction that a unanimous feeling of pity and disgust took possession of them and drove them to flee in horror, so that the play was finished in solitude.

From Saumur the unfortunate actress went to Chinon and Azay, towns of four or five thousand souls, where she played before peasants who kept on their hats before her.

I will not dwell any further on the picture.

Would it not be possible, Monsieur, to rescue this unhappy Hecuba of dramatic art from such an unheard-of position, forced upon her by complete ruin? Could help not be organized for her in one way or another, perhaps by means of a special performance at the Opera, in aid of her retirement? In this case, the most celebrated artists of Paris would be only too pleased to lend their support, and if the price of seats were doubled and the profits were 20,000 francs, this would provide her with a pension of 2,000 francs.

There seems no reason why this should not be done promptly, for the great actress has so many friends and colleagues whose zeal and charity would be equal to the occasion, and who are in a position to help her. Mlle George, I believe, would willingly consent to such a plan, and the regrettable performances we have witnessed, and which have already been going on far too long, and will continue if no steps are taken to prevent it, will be brought to an end.

I hope, Monsieur, that you will forgive the liberty I have taken in addressing myself to you in this matter. But I and my friends feel that you, in your eminent position as a dramatic critic, would be better able than most people to realize such a project as I have suggested.

We feel that, even if Mlle George were not in want, and continued to appear in tragedy for her own pleasure, we should ask you to write to her with the aim of opening her eyes to the fact that she is doing herself the greatest possible harm in thus continuing to act, and bringing contempt on to the name she has made so great in the past.

But, alas, such a supposition is not credible, and we believe that necessity alone forces a woman turned sixty to appear on the vilest boards of France.

If you can organize assistance for her, Monsieur, you will be doing a really good deed.

Your humble servant,

A. MOREAU.

Jules Janin responded to the appeal and rallied the actress's friends. It was agreed that a benefit performance should be held for her as soon as arrangements could be made.

In the autumn Georgina was back in Paris. Victor Hugo, in *Choses Vues*, records a visit she paid him in which she admitted the difficulties of her situation. 'I have done my best in the provinces for over a year,' she said, 'but it's all impossible to me without Harel. I am incapable of dealing with actors. What is one expected to make of such an unreliable crowd? I was supposed to finish on the 24th, but I paid them all on the 20th and came away. I have come back to Paris to visit Harel's tomb. It is frightful, a tomb! All the same, I couldn't cry. I just felt cold and dry. What a thing this life of ours is! To think that a man who was such a wit should die an idiot!'

Sad in her mourning clothes she left him, to return on foot to the modest rooms she had taken for her sister, Tom and herself in some dismal street where rents were low.

39

BEFORE arrangements could be made for her benefit performance, political events threw social life into chaos: the revolution of 1848 broke out. Almost everyone was in difficulties and many were ruined. Dumas, a very rich man until recently, had to sell the house he had built himself; shops dismissed their employees in thousands and the theatres were empty. Louis-Philippe had fled into exile and a republic was proclaimed. Prince Louis Napoleon Bonaparte, however, had hastened across the Channel from London where he had been living for some time. He was now staying at a hotel in the Place Vendôme, preparing his candidature for the presidency.

Prince Louis Napoleon was the third son of Louis Bonaparte, one time King of Holland, and Hortense, Joséphine's daughter. The two older sons of Louis and Hortense had died, and Louis Napoleon was Napoleon's heir and pretender to the French throne. He had twice attempted to rally the French to his cause since 1830 and had spent some time in prison as a consequence of this. Now his hour had come, or was about to come. The Bonaparte legend had prepared the way for him; France was weary of Louis-Philippe's quiet and unambitious reign and thirsted for the heroics of the Empire.

Since 1815, members of the Bonaparte family had been obliged to live outside France, and Georgina had seen nothing of them. In the midst of her tragic difficulties, it was no doubt a source of pleasure to her to see them coming back again. Confident of her status as a friend of the family, she did not wait long before calling on Prince Louis Napoleon, whom she had never met. He received her graciously. However, there was something about him that rubbed her up the wrong way altogether. Prince Louis did not in the least resemble his famous uncle, and Georgina took an immediate dislike to him. She felt outraged that this man, with his dull eyes, large nose and huge bushy moustache, his rather shuffling walk and hesitant speech, should be allowed the name of Bonaparte.

He talked at length to his visitor about his hopes for France, and at one moment he led her to the window and pointed to the statue of his uncle on top of the column, saying that there was his model.

'It stands very high,' said Georgina, rather sharply. And she called afterwards on Victor Hugo, who liked to hear items of gossip when they concerned the power-seekers about him.

At the end of the year, Louis Napoleon was elected President of France by a great majority, and he moved from the Place Vendôme to the Elysée. There he lived in style, as befitted a man who was aware of his great destiny. King Louis-Philippe had strolled about the boulevards like an ordinary citizen, carrying an immense umbrella if rain threatened. But this would not do for a man who proposed to take France by storm as the embodiment of the great legend. Who could imagine a Napoleon carrying an umbrella? Prince Louis galloped about the streets on spirited horses and carried a sword. Louis Napoleon was surrounded now by place-seekers of all kinds; he gave splendid balls and receptions and, since he was a single man, his cousin Princess Mathilde Demidoff, acted as hostess. He was making the Republic dance, his adversaries said, preparatory to blowing it up.

Gradually the country settled down; the theatres re-opened, trade slowly revived. The arrangements for Georgina's benefit performance were now resumed. 1848 had been exceedingly difficult for her; she had acted here and there when there was the possibility of doing so. Many friends had helped her, among them Dumas, who for some time had possessed his own theatre, the Théâtre-Historique. Dumas, however, was almost bankrupt. In May he had put on another of Balzac's plays, *La Marâtre*, in which Bébelle had played a minor part; but though it won praise the theatre had remained empty and it had soon been taken off. He offered his old friend Georgina a part here and there as often as he could, for he was magnanimous enough to assist his friends against his own interests. In August she appeared once more in Hugo's *Marie Tudor*, acting with Marie Dorval, who took the part of Lady Jane Gray. Even Dorval, so brilliantly successful ten years ago, was in great difficulties and had fallen into poverty. No one had eyes now for anyone but the highly fashionable Rachel.

One thing alone was needed in these difficult times to ensure that a theatre would be crowded, and that was the presence of Rachel. Georgina's benefit performance was arranged for the end of May, and her friends were influential enough to bring pressure to bear on the reigning favourite so that she would participate.

Rachel was a genius, but her character was tyrannical. Like Duchesnois, she came from the lowest levels of society; her parents had been wandering pedlars, and as a small child she had been taught to sing and beg in streets and cafés. Duchesnois had been too close to the pre-revolutionary world to arouse sympathies because of her humble birth; she had been looked down on as a former servant and had certainly not traded upon her origin. Rachel was fortunate in appearing at a time when romanticism had worked upon people's minds so that they were disposed to marvel over a little street-singer who had won fame. Wonderful it certainly was that such a girl could so eloquently interpret the works of the great French dramatists; but in private life she had instincts other than those that ruled her acting. Her smiles were reserved for people of wealth and importance and for attractive young men, and she had no courtesy to spare for her inferiors. She was exasperated by the suggestion that she should act with the ageing Mlle George and, although the friends of the retiring actress included some of the leading writers and artists and she would not risk offending them by a refusal, she could not help showing her displeasure to Mlle George herself. When Mlle George called on her to make the request herself in person Rachel, instead of receiving her, sent a message with her servant asking her to write if she had anything to say. The slight was intentional and obvious.

Victor Hugo, in his *Souvenirs Personnels*, records a visit Mlle George paid him at this time. Almost in despair, indiscreet as usual and forceful in expression, she touched in life itself, instead of on the stage, one of those hours of high tragedy that her former Corsican lover had so greatly admired. She had just been to see Napoleon's youngest brother, the ex-King Jérome, who had known her in the old days. Jérome, three years older than herself, was still at this time living in uncertainty, with very little money.

I am at the point of death [she said]. I have been to see Jérome. He is ready to receive me, anyway. He said to me: 'What do you want, Georgina?' I said: 'I want nothing. I believe I'm still better off than you are, although I haven't a sou. But walk about for me. Stand up. It seems to me I am seeing a little of the Emperor once again.

That's all I want.' He began to laugh and replied: 'You are quite right. I'm more of a beggar than you are. You haven't a sou, but at least you can eat potatoes. I haven't a sou, and I'm expected to provide people with truffles. . . . I am told I ought to appeal for help. I say that I have been in the habit of commanding but not of demanding.' M. Hugo, that is how things are with Jérome. As for the President, he's a fool. I detest him. In the first place, he is extremely ugly. He rides well, and he makes a good coachman, but that's all one can say. I called on him, and he sent a message that he was unable to receive me. When he was nothing but the poor devil of a Prince Louis he received me by the two hours together. That was in the Place Vendôme where he made me look at the column, the stupid fellow. He has an English mistress, a very pretty blonde who deceives him at every turn. I don't know if he knows it, but everyone else knows it. He goes about the Champs Elysées in a little Russian carriage that he drives himself. He'll be thrown out one of these days, either by his horses or by the people! I said to Jérome: 'I detest your so-called nephew.' [1] He put his hand over my mouth, saying: 'Be quiet, mad woman!' But I said: 'He speculates on the *Bourse*. Achille Fould goes to see him every day at noon and receives the news before anyone else; then he goes off to arrange a rise or a fall. That's an absolute certainty as far as the recent affairs at Piedmont go. I know it.' 'You mustn't say things like that,' Jérome said to me. 'It's talk of that kind that brought down Louis-Philippe.'

M. Hugo, what on earth does Louis-Philippe matter to me? He never did a thing for Harel. That's the truth, and here I am, in want. I took my courage in both hands and called on Rachel, on Mlle Rachel, to ask her to play *Rodogune* with me at my benefit. She did not receive me and told me to write. *Ah! par exemple, non!* I am not yet reduced to that! I am a queen of the theatre as much as she is, and one day she will be a poor old woman like me. I am not going to write to her, to ask for help. I won't dance attendance on this baggage! So she doesn't remember she was once a beggar! She doesn't imagine she'll return to it! A beggar in the cafés, M. Hugo! That's all she was. She used to sing, and people threw coins to her. Everything seems fine to her at the moment. She plays cards at

---

[1] A reference, no doubt, to the rumours of the time that suggested Louis Napoleon was an illegitimate son of Hortense.

Dr Véron's for louis stakes and wins or loses ten thousand francs in an evening. But in thirty years she won't possess a brass farthing and she'll walk in the mud in worn-out shoes. In thirty years she perhaps won't call herself Rachel as surely as I call myself George. Some other tart will have come along who will be young and have talent in her turn and will simply trample her underfoot, and she'll sleep on the bare ground, mark my words! No, I will not go. I will not write to her. It is true I have nothing to eat. Tom earns nothing. He has a post under the President, who does not pay him. I have my sister to look after—Bébelle, you know. Hostein would not engage her for the *Historique* at fifteen hundred francs. I have been to Boulay, to the President, to Rachel; I find no one at home except you. I owe my porter ten francs. I have been forced to sell two diamonds that I had from the Emperor. I act at the *Théâtre Saint-Marcel*, I act at the *Batignolles*; I act in the suburbs, and I haven't twenty-five sous to pay for a cab. But I will not write to Rachel. I will rather drown myself!

But having uttered this tirade, which Hugo, with typical energy, hastened to put on record, the unhappy Georgina soon forgot her pride. She wrote to the powerful Rachel, endured her slights, and obtained from her a grudging consent. The play chosen was *Iphigénie en Aulide*, with Rachel as Eriphyle and Georgina as Clytemnestra. Rachel also agreed to appear afterwards in a one-act play, *Le Moineau de Lesbie*.

Now the great night arrived, and George and Rachel appeared side by side on the stage of the Théâtre-Italien. All fashionable society had come to see Rachel, and the old had come to applaud for the last time the reigning beauty of their youth, the incomparable Venus of Paris. There were a few present who could remember George's début and still saw something of her phenomenal youth as she moved about the boards, though to most she was but an elderly woman of monstrous size.

Yet little by little her acting improved under the stimulus of a fine production and a large and sympathetic audience. An illusion was created round about her, and she was able to create a certain illusion herself. This was the role of Clytemnestra which she had played that very night, so long ago, when Napoleon, watching with his clear and penetrating eyes from the Consular box, resolved to send his valet Constant to her with a message of love. Now, as though she was still the fair Helen whose place was on the centre of the stage, she turned to the audience with her old confidence while Rachel, who expected all to revolve about herself, was unable to create her usual effects and felt herself thrown out of scale. 'While Mlle George,' wrote Auguste Vacquerie, 'escorted by the general sympathy, expanded more and more in the amplitude of her beauty and talent, Mlle Rachel, left behind, irritated, alone, seemed to shrink and disappear.'

The play ended, the curtain was falling, and bouquets lay at Georgina's feet. Cries of enthusiasm filled the theatre.

The audience called for both the actresses, but Rachel refused to appear. Instead, she ordered her carriage and drove home, pale and furious. There was an interval, and then the manager appeared on the stage.

'Ladies and gentlemen,' he said, 'Mlle Rachel begs you to accept her apologies. She is unfortunately too tired to appear in *Le Moineau de Lesbie*. Mme Pauline Viardot-Garcia has very kindly offered to sing in Mlle Rachel's absence.'

Rachel's insult spoilt an evening which had otherwise been happy and successful. It was, perhaps, a slight such as Georgina herself in the pride of youth and success might have offered Duchesnois; but she could not be expected to console herself with such reflections. She remembered, rather, her own invariable courtesy towards Raucourt and the great actresses in retirement and thought how all had changed for the worse since the beginning of the century.

Fortunately the evening had been profitable. With the proceeds Georgina decided to open a school of acting. Yet, having money at her disposal, she began to spend too freely. Economy was impossible to her, and the proceeds of the benefit performance dwindled away at an alarming rate.

The school she opened soon had to close, for she was unable to make any profit from it. The pupils did not always pay their bills; if they were hard up she was too kind to press them, and it may be that she gave them all the impression that she did not mind whether they paid her or not.

Alexandre Dumas put on *La Tour de Nesle* for her, and once more she was seen in the famous melodrama, although Parisians had believed they were taking leave of her at the benefit performance. But Dumas was not able to help her for long, for his own difficulties were increasing, and at the end of 1850 he had to close his theatre. Georgina moved to the outskirts of Paris, to a poor street in Passy where the rents were very low; friends helped her to find work, and she was glad to have any small role. But it was becoming increasingly difficult to find work for her. And the day came when all the money made at the benefit performance was spent and her embarrassed friends were faced with the problem of arranging another one for her, unless, indeed, Prince Louis Napoleon would give her a pension. But Louis Napoleon, whose own mistresses caused him very great expense, did not show any inclination to interest himself in the welfare of his uncle's elderly mistress.

40

GREAT political events had been taking place which Georgina watched with scant pleasure. Prince Louis Napoleon, after being proclaimed President, had first staged a *coup d'état* and seized dictatorial powers, and he now took the title of Emperor. Once more there was an Emperor Napoleon on the throne, Napoleon III.

But Georgina, who had been the favourite of all the Bonapartes in 1802, was forgotten. For the revived Empire she was without interest. Only a few weeks after he was proclaimed Emperor Napoleon III married the beautiful Spaniard, Mlle de Montijo, and a brilliant new era opened. The relations and friends of the Bonapartes were back in full force, all of them enriched. Count Walewski, the son of Napoleon and Marie Walewska, was much in evidence, as were the Murat princes. There was a cult of all the First Empire had admired, but not of Mlle George. The

Empress Eugénie was never seen in the evening without a bouquet of violets, and violet perfume was the latest fashion. Violets were in evidence everywhere, and the scent of violets was wafted from end to end of Paris. But no one remembered that Georgina and Mlle Mars had made these flowers the Imperial emblem.

However, the Emperor was at last prevailed upon to give Georgina a small pension. An impressive document, dated July 20th 1853, was sent to her announcing that she would receive 2,000 francs annually. At this time Napoleon III was committed to paying immense sums to Miss Howard, the English mistress whom he had abandoned in order to marry and who was not to be kept quiet cheaply. He did not feel he had much to spare for Mlle George.

The cost of living was so low at that time that it was possible to live comfortably on 2,000 francs a year if one were careful; moreover, since 1852, Tom had been employed in the Ministry of the Interior. But Georgina was not qualified to live reasonably, and the pension seemed a mere pittance to her. She had, too, been without means for some time and had consequently fallen into debt. She was in very great difficulties, and in these circumstances worried her friends for minor roles in their plays and sent unavailing appeals to the Emperor for an increase in her pension.

Theatrical friends could not easily help her now, for it was really too great a sacrifice of their interests to put her on the stage. Though she had few illnesses in her long life, something was physically wrong with her and the process of putting on weight could not be arrested. In Passy, where she lived, the local children referred to her as 'the whale'. The few performances she gave caused much adverse criticism.

She haunted the Tuileries, shabbily dressed, a strange contrast with the young actress whom Constant had introduced at nights when the master of all was impatient to receive her.

'M. Ludovic Halévy,' P. A. Cheramy writes, 'has told us that one day at the Tuileries, where he was employed in the administration of the Emperor's household, he received a visit from George who came to solicit help. It was the time of the changing of the guard, and the drums were beating. The Emperor

Napoleon III appeared on the steps of the Tuileries to take the salute. George had gone over to the window to watch the spectacle, and she turned round deeply moved, with tears in her eyes. "I have so often watched that in the past," she said, "under the other." '

She would write to anyone she knew who could approach the court officials: 'My dear Sir, I am writing to ask you to plead my cause with M. Mocquard. . . . I have written to the Emperor and sent a copy to good M. Mocquard. I know he is not able to deliver the letter, but I have asked him to advise me how to ensure its being read. If you are able to help me I shall be deeply grateful!. . . .'

The Emperor saw no reason to do more for her, but his half-brother, the Duc de Morny, came to her aid. De Morny was the illegitimate son of Hortense and the Comte de Flahaut, and was a man of immense popularity in high society. He gave his patronage to a new benefit performance for her. It took place at the Théâtre Français on 17 December 1853. The play she chose was *Rodogune*, and this time there was no need to call on Rachel to support her. De Morny was powerful and court society was very rich; the theatre was full, and she appeared with all the youth of the Comédie Française about her, honoured and fêted.

The event was given much publicity, and the papers referred to it as a 'solemnity'. In view of the actress's age and weight, the word 'entertainment' was perhaps out of keeping. The evening was memorable and successful. 'She was still a moving actress,' says a contemporary, 'but she had difficulty in getting about and could not stand. During the long monologue, she was obliged to lean on the back of an armchair.' Flowers, compliments and applause were lavishly given, and the actress and her family had a welcome addition to the Imperial pension.

Perhaps the money from the new benefit performance was foolishly spent, or perhaps Georgina had needed it all to pay her debts. However it may be, she was soon in need again. Even now she appeared from time to time on the stage, a grotesque and embarrassing spectacle. Few in those thoughtless, pleasure-seeking audiences can have dreamed that once the great Napoleon and his brother Lucien had argued as to whether she was the most beautiful woman of Europe or merely one of the most beautiful.

Paris had become a dazzling and wonderful city of pleasures; but Georgina did not care for it at all. Napoleon III was having it ruthlessly pulled down and rebuilt, with broad, straight avenues and great modern shops and houses. It was hardly recognizable. Railways now extended from the city and industrial developments of all kinds were to be seen. There was a war in progress, the Crimean War, and the new Napoleon instead of going forth in person to win his victories, sent orders to the scene of action by telegraph while he remained comfortably at home. All was strangely changed.

A great international exhibition of industry was shortly to be opened in the Champs Elysées; the new Empire had brought prosperity; the innumerable beggars of the day of Louis-Philippe had disappeared. There was work for everyone, so much work, in fact, that even Georgina might find something she could do. Her old arrogance had faded away with the circumstances that had brought it into being; she was willing to do anything that would help her to keep her modest home going. She had heard that women were needed to organize the various cloakrooms of the exhibition, and she applied to be put in charge of the left umbrella sections. For this she was too late, but she was given the ladies' cloakrooms to organize.

The exhibition was very successful and brilliant, and Paris was full of foreigners. On warm days Georgina liked to sit in the gardens of the Tuileries for an hour or two, watching the well-dressed crowds stroll by, and the children skipping and playing with their hoops and balls. There Sarah Bernhardt, still a child and unaware of her own future on the stage, saw her one day and screamed in excitement. She had never seen such a fat woman before.

'Look, look!' cried the little Sarah. 'She's so big she's sitting on two chairs.'

'Be quiet,' she was told in a whisper. 'That is Mlle George, the great actress.'

It was a successful season for the theatres. Mme Adélaïde Ristori was the favourite of Paris. Scribe, Emile Augier and the younger Dumas were the playwrights in fashion, and a small new theatre had opened, the Bouffes-Parisiens, where Offenbach was charming all society with his lively music. The Opera House and the theatres were crowded every night. And Mlle George, the memory of her former status growing dim, kept her eye on the exhibition cloakrooms. Having her measure of philosophy she did not complain but was glad to make a little money and to enjoy such small pleasures as came her way.

41

GEORGINA'S weight made her increasingly infirm; time passed, and she came less and less often into the centre of Paris. With her sister and Tom, she had now adapted herself to a modest position and had grown accustomed to frugal dishes and *vin ordinaire*; acting was now out of the question, and she lived in obscurity, keeping careful accounts of all she spent, forgetful of her prodigal past. Paris, under the best days of the Second Empire, was a scene of perpetual festivals and show, prosperity and fashion; but the brighter and noisier it grew the quieter her own life was.

It was 1857, and Europe was peaceful and untroubled. Universal peace and an ever-increasing well-being for the human race seemed a feasible proposition, and it was popularly believed that this was what lay ahead. Napoleon III liked to pose as the man who had made this happy state of affairs possible. But with an air of modesty, though he spoke of himself as a man of destiny, he would point to the real founder of human wellbeing, his uncle, the great Napoleon. He himself had merely revived the Napoleonic régime and let loose its full torrent of benevolent ideas on the parched soil of mortal needs. Napoleon was the true subject of everyone's worship. This, indeed, was good enough for

Napoleon III, who now had an heir who in the course of time would be Napoleon IV. The country was willing to revel in such pleasing illusions since the third Napoleon appeared to be astonishingly successful in his foreign policy, and had restored French prestige in Europe. A rapid industrialization of the country, too, was enriching all classes and the most ordinary man could make a fortune if he had a little enterprise. There was a widespread feeling of confidence and optimism. The crinoline was in fashion and was growing steadily wider from month to month; the shining top hats of fashionable men grew correspondingly taller. In supreme confidence, men and women made much of themselves as they walked the earth.

The newspapers were filled with social news about the Bonapartes, stories about the small heir to the throne, and anecdotes about the great Napoleon. The veterans of the Grand Army were always in the news. And lithographs were on sale in which the Emperor and Empress, with their recently born son, were seated side by side while Napoleon I floated just above them on a cloud, apparently looking down from Heaven.

Never, indeed, had the first Napoleon been so greatly loved and admired as he was now. Georgina's friends suggested that she should write her memoirs. Often she would talk of the past, and she remembered her youth with a clarity that made her reminiscences unusually interesting. So many who had known the Emperor had written about him—even Constant; and not all these books had been very reliable, either. But she who had known the Bonapartes so well in the great days, and whose loyalty was proverbial, could give an account which everyone would be eager to read.

At first she believed the task would be impossible, for she was not used to writing and could not spell at all. But she was urged to set down in a plain and straightforward way all she had done and seen, without troubling about style. M. and Mme Desbordes-Valmore, both well known in the world of letters, offered to take the work in hand. She was to take it to them as she wrote it, and they would put it into good French for her. Mme Desbordes-Valmore, who was a poetess, would add eloquence and style, and her husband would see that the whole was grammatical and put into correct literary form.

Georgina, therefore, set to work, not only hoping to earn a little money, but pleased to have an occupation for the long days. In due course she sent her friends the opening pages of her book: her story was rather disconnected and contained mistakes of spelling and grammar, but it was full of life and contained many fascinating passages from a forgotten world. On this M. Desbordes-Valmore worked conscientiously; but he could not catch the spirit of the narrative and succeeded only in flattening it out. His work, in the words of P. A. Cheramy, is 'very lifeless and very boring in the monotony of its conventional would-be elegance. Mlle George felt this. In the margin of this sixth-form exercise she has written her reflections: *rather long*; *to be developed*; *it is necessary to speak of this, of that, etc.*'

This well-meant help must have been altogether discouraging. Fortunately Georgina did not try to imitate the style of M. Desbordes-Valmore; she disregarded the corrected manuscript and continued to write in her own way, although her confidence had been undermined and she was never to complete the book. Mme Desbordes-Valmore died in the summer of 1859, and this finally removed Georgina's hopes of earning money as a writer. She wrote now only for her own pleasure and the work went very slowly.

It was in 1859 that she at last succeeded in obtaining a good position for Tom. Tom, almost forty years of age, probably resembled his mother. He certainly did not take after his father and his Aunt George. He is described as being a man of gentle and kindly nature, rather shy and content to dedicate himself to his mother and his aunt. Nothing in his character would have taken him near the world of the theatre had not destiny made him a close relative of the great George. But it was to a theatre and away from the Civil Service that Aunt George now triumphantly led the diffident Tom. She had acquired the directorship of the Folies Dramatiques for him. Curiously enough, he made a very good director. Quiet, sensible and reliable, he got on well with everyone and avoided the mistakes of more self-assertive men.

Once more Georgina had the satisfaction and pleasure of having the freedom of a theatre. Victorien Sardou saw her one night in 1860 at the Folies Dramatiques and was much astonished by the large pinches of snuff she was taking. The public use of snuff had long gone out of fashion; but it had been one of Napoleon's most typical habits, and Mlle George was not the one to deny herself an indulgence with such happy associations, however the modern generation might stare.

It must have been a great sorrow to her when the old Boulevard St Martin was sacrificed to Louis Napoleon's modernization of Paris. It had been known as the *Boulevard du Crime*, a compliment to the exciting nature of the entertainments to be seen there. Almost every building was a theatre. There Frédérick Lemaître had played as the lion in *Pyramus and Thisbe*, there the greatest of all clowns, Dubureau, won fame at the Funambules. This was the street of pantomimes, tragedies, comedies, dramas and melodramas; and the actors had lived where they worked, mingling with the crowds by day and well loved by them. News came in 1865 that, with many other old theatres and the pavements raised on steps above the road, the Folies Dramatiques was to be demolished. Tom had made a great success of it, but the Government ignored all protests in its work of transforming Paris.

Tom opened a theatre elsewhere under the same name; but the venture swallowed every penny he had made. The new theatre did not do well, and Tom was obliged to give it up after a year or two, a ruined man. Fortunately he was able to remain in possession until shortly after his aunt's death.

Distressed by the disastrous change Tom was obliged to make, Georgina was nevertheless accustomed by now to troubles and was patiently composed. Paris saw her no more. There was no money now for a cab, nor could it give her pleasure to see the city so drastically altered and, in her eyes, altered much for the worse.

On fine days she would emerge slowly from her home, 31 rue de Ranelagh, and hobble along drab streets to the green spaces where children played and her neighbours took their knitting. The world had forgotten her; she was just an old woman of the people, remarkable only for her size. She would sit down on a public bench and gossip easily with other old women who treated her as one of themselves. She was amiable and kind and everyone liked her. Long ago she had forgiven her enemies, and she never spoke a sharp or disagreeable word.

In the evening she would sit in her shabby room and perhaps write by the light of a paraffin lamp. Her dingy surroundings faded, and she would live again with Napoleon and his family, with Talma, Raucourt and Talleyrand. 'My memories are very dear to me,' she wrote, 'and it is a great consolation to me never to have varied in my affections. I am poor; but after all, what does it matter? I am enriched by many inward things.'

She died a few weeks before her eightieth birthday. One day at the beginning of January 1867 she went out for a walk and caught cold. She went to bed with a high temperature, and her doctor was sent for. She did not recover, but died on January the 11th.

The expenses of her funeral were paid by Napoleon III, and the Comédie Française turned out dutifully to pay her their last respects. But the event created little stir. Her last thoughts had been of the stage, her last words a request to be buried in the cloak she had worn in *Rodogune*.

Overwhelmed by the passing of his aunt, Tom left Paris for the provinces and obtained some modest post with one of the railway companies. His mother died a few years later, and he himself lived quietly and uneventfully to the age of eighty-two, pious guardian of the letters of famous men, manuscripts of plays, Press-cuttings, portraits, costumes, theatrical crowns, faded flowers, and all the thousand and one relics of the long and wonderful career of Mlle George.

BIBLIOGRAPHY

THE following are the books mainly used:

MADEMOISELLE GEORGE

AUBRY, Octave, *Napoléon et son Temps* (1936)

AUGUSTIN-THIERRY, A., *Mademoiselle George, Maîtresse d'Empereurs* (1936)

BONAPARTE, Lucien, *Mémoires* (1882)

CABANÈS, Docteur, *Dans l'Intimité de l'Empereur* (1924)

DESCOTTES, Maurice, *Le Drama Romantique et ses Grands Créateurs* (*1827–1839*) (1955)

DUMAS, Alexandre, *Mes Mémoires* (1863)

FLEISCHMANN, Hector, *Une Maîtresse de Napoléon* (1908)

GEORGE, Mlle, *Mémoires Inédits de Mademoiselle George, publiés par P. A. Cheramy* (1908)

HAHN, Reynaldo, *La Grande Sarah* (1930)

HUGO, Victor, *Choses Vues*

HUGO, Victor, *Souvenirs Personnels 1848–1851* (1952)

MASSON, Frederic, *Napoléon et les Femmes* (1894)

RÉMUSAT, Mme de, *Mémoires* (1880)

NAPOLEON

BOURIENNE, *Mémoires* (1829)

CHAPTAL, Comte, *Mes Souvenirs sur Napoléon* (1893)

CONSTANT, *Mémoires* (1830)

LECOMTE, L. Henry, *Napoléon et le Monde Dramatique* (1912)

MASSON, Frederic, *Le Sacre et le Couronnement de Napoléon* (1908)

RÉMUSAT, Mme de, *Mémoires* (1880)

THIERS, M. A., *Histoire du Consulat* (1865)

THIERS, M. A., *Histoire de l'Empire* (4 vols., 1865–7)

THOMPSON, J. M., *Napoleon Bonaparte: His Rise and Fall* (1952)

JOSÉPHINE

MASSON, Frédéric, *Madame Bonaparte* (1927)

MASSON, Frédéric, *La Journée de l'Impératrice Joséphine* (1933)

Rémusat, Mme de, *Mémoires* (1880)
Saint-Amand, Imbert de, *La Femme du Premier Consul* (1893)
Saint-Amand, Imbert de, *La Cour de l'Impératrice Joséphine* (1892)
Saint-Amand, Imbert de, *Dernières Années de l'Impératrice Joséphine* (1889)

OTHER CHARACTERS AND THE TIMES OF MLLE GEORGE

Cain, Georges, *Anciens Théâtres de Paris* (1906)
Caulaincourt, A. A. L. de, *Mémoires* (3 vols., 1933)
Choiseul-Gouffier, Comtesse de, *Reminiscences sur l'Empereur Alexandre I* (1862)
Fleury, *Mémoires de Fleury de la Comédie Française, 1757 à 1820*
Fusil, Louise, *L'Incendie de Moscou* (1817)
Gribble, Francis, *Emperor and Mystic* (1931)
Kotzebue, A. F. F. von, *Travels from Berlin to Paris in the year 1804* (3 vols., 1804)
Lyonnet, Henry, *Dictionnaire des Comédiens Français* (1914)
Manne, E. D. de, *La Troupe de Talma* (1866)
Manne, E. D. de, and Menetrier, Charles, *Galerie Historique de la Comédie Française* (2 vols., 1870)
Pugin, Arthur, *Dictionnaire de Théâtre* (1885)
Regnault-Warin, *Mémoires sur Talma* (1904)
Ricord, Alexandre, *Les Fastes de la Comédie Française* (1821)
Stenger, Gilbert, *La Société Française pendant le Consulat* (6 vols., 1903–8)
Taigny, Edmond, *D. B. Isabey* (1859)
W(eston) S., *The Praise of Paris* (1803)

INDEX

241

246